A WIDER VIEW OF VATICAN II

A WIDER VIEW
of
VATICAN II

MEMORIES AND ANALYSIS OF
A COUNCIL CONSULTOR

ARCHIMANDRITE
BONIFACE LUYKX

Edited by Julie Rogers
Foreword by Dom Alcuin Reid
Preface by Father Joseph Homick, COSJ

Angelico Press

First published in the USA
by Angelico Press 2025
Copyright © Julie Rogers 2025
Copyright © Angelico Press 2025

For information, address:
Angelico Press, Ltd.
169 Monitor St.
Brooklyn, NY 11222
www.angelicopress.com

ppr   979-8-89280-119-5
cloth 979-8-89280-120-1
ebook 979-8-89280-121-8

Book and cover design
by Michael Schrauzer

Come, children, and hear me
that I may teach you the fear of the LORD.
(Psalm 33/34:12)

CONTENTS

FOREWORD

FOR A GROWING NUMBER OF CATHOLICS, THE Second Vatican Council and all its works and all its unfulfilled promises is an increasingly irrelevant historical event. The much-vaunted "New Springtime of the Church" it was supposed to usher in has failed to appear, as any serious statistical study of key Catholic indicators has made plain for some time now. In its place the frenetic pursuit of further reform (in fact the deification of dialogue and process in the place of actually doing the hard work of formation in liturgy, doctrine, and pastoral care) serve to mask the severe ecclesiastical winter the Western Catholic Church is currently enduring.

Accordingly, many Catholics, particularly young adults who have studied the question, discard the Council. "It simply didn't work," some opine politely. Others may use more "direct" language, particularly in respect of the liturgical reform that bears the Council's name.

For a certain generation of ecclesiastics (and their acolytes) whose entire careers have been spent propping up "all things Vatican II," this is utter heresy: one simply cannot reject the Second Vatican Council! Its fruits are unimpeachable, they shout, and no means shall be spared (as we have seen in respect of the Sacred Liturgy in recent years) to ensure that we all eat of them and enjoy them — regardless of their age, condition, or taste.

Even those scholars who respectfully underline that the Council was by its own definition *pastoral* and not *doctrinal*, and that it bound no one to hold anything it itself decreed as revealed truth, but rather proposed and even ordered the adoption of pastoral policies it judged apposite at the time (such as the increased use of the vernacular for readings at Mass) have been included amongst the Council-denying heretics to be burnt in the public forum. Whilst the opinion that vernacular readings are either a good or a bad thing does not fall under the oath required of a convert to "believe and profess all that the holy Catholic Church believes, teaches, and proclaims to be revealed by God," it seems that the children of God are nevertheless currently subject to super-dogmas in respect of the Second Vatican Council and all that bears its name. Rejection or critical appraisal of the Council is simply not tolerable.

The present writer, who has much sympathy for his afore-mentioned younger brethren, but who nonetheless hesitates to dismiss a valid Ecumenical Council of the Church by a simple curt remark, is one who has sought, at least in respect of recent liturgical history, to make the appropriate and highly necessary distinctions between the Council itself and the official and local implementation of reforms in its name. This, it seems, is essential if we are to discover what good the Second Vatican Council sought and where and how that good was ignored, buried, or derailed. For what was good then remains good now, even if it has been grotesquely distorted since.

In this task (which is in no sense out of date — and our frustrated young friends would do well to study recent history thoroughly) Archimandrite Boniface Luykx's manuscript, finally published here, is an important new source, though naturally it must be carefully studied together with other primary sources.

There is no question that Luykx believed in the probity of the Council and of its Constitution on the Sacred Liturgy, *Sacrosanctum Concilium* (CSL) solemnly promulgated on December 4, 1963. One will look in vain here for critiques of that document or of its preparation, or indeed of the liturgical reforms under Pius XII or John XXIII. It is perhaps instructive that for men of his generation these earlier reforms presented no problem and were readily accepted as advances, whatever legitimate critiques may in fact be made of them.

For Luykx, the devil made his hay in the postconciliar sunshine, distorting the Constitution and producing reforms that had little, if anything, to do with the Council. You will find herein many anecdotes bearing witness to the details of this debacle, and scholars will benefit thereby from the account of the reform that the author provides "from the inside," as it were.

For many, "the devil" is personified by Father (later Archbishop) Annibale Bugnini, CM — certainly a key player in liturgical reform following the Council. I say "following the Council" because whilst he was "on the scene" as it were from 1948 onward, his real moment of opportunity came only after the Constitution was promulgated and he was rehabilitated by Paul VI. Luykx certainly credits his involvement in the liturgical reforms of Pius XII, including the reform of Holy Week and the new Code of Rubrics, but thankfully, unlike many who know nothing of the realities involved, he does not overstate Bugnini's role. Bugnini was a junior official in the presence of other, more senior, reformers who were calling the shots, as has been made perfectly clear elsewhere.[1]

Yet Luykx's memoirs do serve to enhance the portrait we have of this crucial figure. Indeed, they highlight one aspect of his approach that perhaps, up until now, has not been seen as clearly as Luykx portrays.

Bugnini was "a very capable man and an adroit politician with a special charism for bringing people together and bridging oppositions," Luykx tells us. Bugnini "exerted a strong (and often problematic) influence in the liturgical developments during and after the Council." [pp. 45–46] "During" the Council may be a slight overstatement—as Luykx notes, Bugnini was in exile during the Council's consideration of the Schema on the Sacred Liturgy. But the influence of his preparatory work during the Council itself cannot be entirely excluded.

Luykx relates one incident from the period of the Preparatory Commission for the Council:

> At one point, Secretary Bugnini called into his office some Members and Consultors, including me, to give us a friendly yet serious "warning" about our activity in the Liturgical Movement. What he said was quite erroneous. When he had finished, I told him so and got up to leave, saying, "I did not ask for this appointment to the Council; I am ready to leave right now." He was surprised, and said in a conciliatory manner, "I did not mean to lecture you. You are very precious to us, and we are very glad you are willing to work with us." [p. 48]

So, too, he relates the exile of Bugnini and his co-workers during the Council:

> Our whole Preparatory Commission for Liturgy—Members, Consultors, and Secretary Bugnini—was deposed and officially reproached on the Council floor. Before this coup, and indeed before the Council began, our Commission's president, Cardinal Cicognani, had died, in February 1962. He was succeeded by Cardinal Arcadio Larraona of the Congregation for Religious, a man filled

---

[1] See Yves Chiron, *Annibale Bugnini: Reformer of the Liturgy* (New York: Angelico Press, 2018).

xiv

with goodwill but unskilled in matters liturgical. During
this upheaval, we greatly missed the gentle Cicognani,
who certainly would have been our great defender.

Because of the press of my duties in Africa, I was not
in Rome when this coup occurred. On my next trip, I
visited the ignominiously-deposed Secretary Bugnini to
comfort him. He was still so affected by the events that
he wept on my shoulder! As a token of appreciation for
my concern, he gave me a bottle of excellent liqueur his
brother had just brewed, to feed our friendship. [p. 61]

This friendship was not, however, to be long-lived. Amidst the
potent mix of strong-willed scholars charged with implementing
CSL in the postconciliar Consilium, Luykx describes Bugnini as "a
horizontal 'overview scholar,'" who "often gently overcame these
experts' tyrannical misgrowth and brought them to agreement
beyond their specialty." Despite this, Luykx continues, "personal
differences quickly came to claim the status of absolute values
which the more aggressive experts imposed upon others." [p. 85]

But this volatile play of personalities was not all. According to
Luykx, a fundamental change took place in Bugnini:

The trend away from adherence to CSL spread even to
the top, to Secretary Annibale Bugnini. Throughout the
Liturgical Movement, the Preparatory Commission for
Liturgy, and Pope John's Consilium, Father Bugnini had
been faithful to Tradition and the Magisterium. But after
the Council he changed. Based on my personal friendship with him, I believe that this change arose not from
purposeful malice, but rather from weakness. He seemed
to me very impressionable: if someone pushed him one
way, he went that way; if someone pushed him the other
way, he went there instead. [p. 86]

There are those who would disagree with Luykx's rather benign
diagnosis of the earlier Bugnini, suspecting a good deal of "malice aforethought" in Bugnini's activities. But Luykx continues:

Bugnini was also a politician, and one who wanted power.
In order to gain power he had to appear successful, so
he went along with those who were the most vocal and
apparently powerful. He was heavily influenced by the
modernists who broke from fidelity to CSL, the most

outspoken being Johannes Wagner from the Trier Institut in Germany. Before long, Bugnini stopped inviting to the meetings those "reactionary" members who dared to adhere to the text of CSL or to sound principles of religious anthropology. I know this as fact, because Bishop Malula[2] and I were among those who fell out of his favor. [p. 86]

In passing, it is worth underlining the value of the contribution to liturgical history of Cardinal Malula himself that this book makes available — a young, zealous, and faithful African bishop. But let the reader discover that for himself herein.

Luykx does relate the incident that caused Malula to cut ties with Bugnini, which reveals a crucial anthropological stance on Bugnini's part. Luykx relates: "The revolutionary boutique of scholars made [Malula] feel useless; they treated him as an ignoramus and even insulted him. In addition, the subcommissions' entire work was going counter to CSL and was useless for the mission countries, especially those of Africa." [pp. 86–87] Malula protested to Bugnini only to receive the following response:

> Bugnini: If you cannot agree, set up your own commission in Africa.
>
> Malula: Where will our Church, poor as a beggar, get the funds to do such a thing, while you here avail of the money of the whole rich West?
>
> Bugnini: *N'importe.* We here work from the assumption that the modern Western man is *the* man *tout court*, the model of all true humanity, for all countries and cultures, and for all ages to come. [p. 87]

For Malula that "was the straw that broke the camel's back." Luykx's own ostracization for insistence on fidelity to the Constitution was soon to follow.

But let us return to what Luykx calls "Bugnini's revealing response":

> It became apparent that his opinion about the supremacy and normative value of modern Western man was part

---

[2] Bishop Malula was Auxiliary to Archbishop Félix Scalais of Léopoldville (later Kinshasa) beginning in 1959; Luykx was his *peritus* throughout the Council. Malula was elevated to archbishop in 1964 and cardinal in 1969.

of his agenda — and consequently part of the agenda
of the Consilium's subcommissions he oversaw. [p. 87]

Luykx continues:

> At this point, one might ask the obvious and serious
> question: from whence does one man, or group, get the
> right to impose his way of praying or celebrating upon the
> whole Western Church? This question goes to the heart
> of the dubious validity, or at least the liceity, of much of
> the work of the Consilium's subcommissions, for they
> often worked in defiance of CSL, the only authoritative
> norm given by the Council. [p. 87]

This question has echoed down the decades ever since — though
few have been prepared to consider its implications, let alone
address them. Yet — and if this is the only contribution this work
makes, it will have been an important one — Luykx makes it
clear that "Bugnini and the proponents of change believed that
the first and real foundation of 'good worship' was its horizontal
(i.e., man-oriented) dimension; that its vertical (God-oriented)
dimension was secondary, following from the other." [p. 135]
Luykx's reflection on this is not without its own importance:

> When Father Annibale Bugnini humiliated the great
> African Bishop Malula, he was proclaiming Western tech-
> nological civilization as the norm for all culture, and even
> for the adaptation of the liturgy. On the contrary, Father
> Romano Guardini, a wise modern Church father, in his
> book *Letters from Lake Como: Explorations in Technology and
> the Human Race*,[3] shows that the goal of technology, by
> its very inner principles and logic, is precisely to destroy
> culture: to replace the childlike, loving, spiritual man
> of the Gospels (Mt 18:4; Mk 10:15) with the impersonal,
> money-making, power-driven machine-man, subjected
> to technology and production. [p. 166]

We are in Luykx's debt for highlighting this seemingly fundamental aspect of Bugnini's outlook and its influence on the postconciliar liturgical reform so clearly, just as we are for his many
other historical reminiscences. Students of the Council and of

---

[3] Grand Rapids: Eerdmans, 1994 (originally published in 1940).

its liturgical reform cannot afford to ignore this work.

The Second Vatican Council is not an irrelevant historical event. Indeed, it is a very important one. But the dismissive impatience of younger brethren does make a valid point: the endless and vain propping up of all that marches under the banner of the Council, or of its so-called "spirit," is now more than tiresome. Quite frankly, to any serious scholar, it is simply embarrassing.

It is time to be good historians, good liturgists, and good pastors. It is time to evaluate the Council and all its works for what they were and are. If some of its pastoral policies have failed, let us have the courage to admit this. If its liturgical reform has not brought forth the fruit with which it was marketed, "sold," and imposed, let us stop propping it up with authoritative, if not draconian, measures and consider honestly what urgently needs to be done for the eternal good of souls.

History, such as we read herein, is vitally important. Being willing to learn from history's lessons is essential if we are to avoid the cold rigidity of those inexorably stuck in the past of the 1960s and 1970s and are to move forward like the scribe trained for the kingdom of heaven, who knows when to bring forth from his treasure what is new and what is old (see Mt 13:52).

Dom Alcuin Reid
Monastère Saint-Benoît
Brignoles, France
20 January 2025

EDITOR'S FOREWORD

THE BOOK IN YOUR HANDS, DEAR READER, was written by one of the unsung heroes of the Catholic Church in the twentieth century. Archimandrite Boniface Luykx (1915–2004) was a Norbertine monk, Liturgical Movement pioneer, priest in Belgium's Resistance, professor of theology, missionary in Africa, founder of monasteries, and composer of liturgical music—in addition to his work for the Second Vatican Council. He served the Western (Latin) Church for decades but was attracted to the Eastern Christian Churches and later embraced their ancient tradition while remaining in union with Rome. The honorary title Archimandrite, which in the Eastern Churches signifies the spiritual father of one or more monasteries, was bestowed upon Abbot Boniface in 1988, fifteen years after he founded Holy Transfiguration (Mount Tabor) Monastery in northern California.

Volumes could be written about Archimandrite Boniface's life, full of struggles, hardships, near-death experiences—and victories for the kingdom. (Appendix A, About the Author, contains a brief summary.) Most important is this: he was a warm and loving man of deep prayer who seemed to live in the heart of the Blessed Trinity. He was a spiritual father, teacher, and inspiration to countless people throughout his life.[1]

* * *

This book is primarily about Archimandrite Boniface's liturgical work for Vatican II, from his appointment to the Preparatory Commission for Liturgy in 1959 to his postconciliar work in Pope Paul VI's Consilium and the Sacred Congregation for Divine Worship, ending in 1975. He notes in Chapter 2 that his work for the Council was twofold: "I had my own scholarly work as an appointed Consultor. In addition, as [African Bishop Joseph Malula's] secretary (*peritus*), I prepared all his reports, answers to questionnaires, and other papers for the Preparatory Commission and for the entire four years of the Council." He and Bishop Malula were the authors

---

[1] Some notes for the reader's sake: a) In this book I will also refer to Archimandrite Boniface as "Abbot Boniface," "Father Boniface," or "the author," depending on the circumstances; b) Archimandrite is pronounced Ahr-kuh-MAN-dright; Luykx is pronounced Loyks; c) See Appendix C for an explanation of the Eastern Christian Churches.

of Articles 37–40 of the Constitution on the Sacred Liturgy (*Sacro-sanctum Concilium*), which treats their field of expertise: adaptation of worship to the genius of peoples and cultures.

Archimandrite Boniface describes in this book how the renewal movements in the Church *before* the Council prepared the way for Vatican II. He also recounts, from his own experience, how, *after* the Council, many of the Consilium's liturgical experts became infected with a prideful spirit rather than the Holy Spirit, and began to abandon objective Revelation in favor of their own subjective ideas. From his Introduction:

> The problem lies not in the Council itself or its primary documents ... but in what the postconciliar commissions made out of it and what the dissenters have prevented it from being. ...
>
> The principal prayer of the Church is the liturgy. ... The dissenters recognize the ultimate primacy and neces-sity of the liturgy; this is why they use the liturgy as their battlefield.

He notes with great sadness that the common postconciliar appeal to the "spirit of Vatican II" is "an appeal that is in essence invoked not in favor of the Council and its documents but rather against them."

Abbot Boniface especially grieves the loss of reverence and holiness in the Mass and in Catholic life as a whole, and he explains the negative theological, anthropological, and even societal implications of "horizontalizing" the worship of the Triune God. His carefully-reasoned conclusion is that "the entire postconciliar liturgical 'renewal' must be overhauled." He writes in Chapter 4:

> As liturgy is the first victim of the crisis, *working to restore true worship must be one of the first tasks in any effort to over-come the crisis* and restore true culture — and such work will produce the first benefits. If one understands this fact, he will understand the importance of my in-depth coverage of the postconciliar liturgical crisis in this book.

*   *   *

Because this is a posthumous publication, some background and clarifications may be helpful.

THE MANUSCRIPT AND ITS REDISCOVERY

As a nun attached to Mount Tabor Monastery, I was privileged to type and edit three of Abbot Boniface's manuscripts. The most complex was the book at hand, composed in installments between 1995 and 1997 and written in tiny European-style cursive on the backs of envelopes and correspondence. Because Abbot Boniface was fluent in many languages, his English word usages and sentence structures were sometimes unusual. I came to know him so well—which was a tremendous blessing—that I usually understood his meaning, but when I made mistakes, he kindly but firmly made corrections.

In 1997, after all the chapters were written but much editing was still needed, Abbot Boniface told me he wished to reconfigure the manuscript; he did not specify how. As my further assistance was not requested at the time, I returned to him all handwritten texts, typed drafts, floppy disks, and related materials—at least I thought I did—and heard nothing more about the project. In early 2000 Abbot Boniface retired from the monastery and moved back to his home abbey in Belgium, taking with him all his manuscripts and source materials. That autumn, in his last letter to me, he noted with sadness that he had not secured a publisher for this manuscript.

On Easter Sunday in 2004, Archimandrite Boniface went to his reward in the bosom of the Blessed Trinity. I was glad for the end of his sufferings, but I also feared that this manuscript might be lost forever; I heard nothing further about it.

Years passed. Then in 2022, while sorting old personal papers, I found a small envelope marked "Vatican II." In it were a few mementos Abbot Boniface had loaned to me, including two official Vatican booklets listing all the participants of the Preparatory Commission for Liturgy and Pope Paul VI's Consilium—and a three-and-a-half-inch computer disk containing the entire 1997 fourth revision of this manuscript!

Thanks be to God, I was able to access and convert the old files. The manuscript needed extensive work, and dozens of questions for clarification I had posed to the author were left unanswered. With months of research, the assistance and prayer support of several friends, and guidance from the Holy Spirit, I have attempted to finish the manuscript in the way Abbot Boniface would have wished.

This book reflects the author's remembrances, thinking, reading, and analysis in the mid-1990s, during the papacy of John Paul II. I have made no attempts to update the text, except that in passages where clarifications or details were lacking, I have sometimes inserted explanatory text and added editor's footnotes. My overall goal in editing was to make the text as accessible and helpful as possible for a wide variety of readers, including college or seminary students, laypersons, clergy, and academics. Readers seeking historical details not contained in this memoir will find an abundance in Yves Chiron's *Annibale Bugnini: Reformer of the Liturgy* (cited above), which makes an excellent companion to this book.

Abbot Boniface states in his Introduction: "This book is not intended as an exhaustive work of research, nor is it purely scholarly in its approach. I write as a firsthand witness of, and participant in, the Council." Being a scholar, however, Abbot Boniface did include many citations. Some of these are in languages unfamiliar to me, and in older books or periodicals I could not access to check them. I have kept all these citations, as originally handwritten and typed, for those wishing and able to dig deeper. The reference works he recommended are listed in Appendix B, Further Reading.

I beg the reader's forgiveness for the mistakes in this book that inevitably resulted from my work. I am not a theologian, liturgist, historian, or professional editor, just an Eastern Catholic who wishes to honor Archimandrite Boniface and share his unique experiences and wisdom with the Church. The verses of Psalm 33/34 at the beginning of each chapter are my additions in his memory: he chose this Psalm for the holy card commemorating the fiftieth anniversary of his ordination in 1990.[2]

FURTHER CLARIFICATIONS

The reader will note, as the chapters progress, that Abbot Boniface often repeats his points and covers material a second or third time, though in a different way or in a different context. This is a method he used during five decades of teaching at the graduate level. Hermit-Monk Seraphim of Mount Tabor Monastery kindly provided this description:

---

[2] These verses are from *The Psalms: Singing Version* (New York: Paulist Press, 1966), which we used in the monastery. The dual numbering indicates differences between Septuagint and Hebrew: most Eastern Churches use Septuagint numbering, generally one less than the Hebrew.

Abbot Boniface tended to organize things in the form of
outlines, often deep outlines with many levels. Sometimes
he first presented only the main points; then he went over
them all again, treating each one in greater detail. This was
his way of keeping the main outline in his students' minds
and giving them a structure to which to attach the details.

In this book I have added some subheadings and numbering to
help the reader keep track of the outlines; however, these are far
from perfect, due in part to late (1997) additions to the manuscript
whose intended locations are not now clear. The chapter and
article titles, and most of the main article subdivisions, remain
those of the author.

The reader will note that Abbot Boniface uses the word "man"
throughout this book to denote both men and women, as was
standard usage in the past. In his Chapter 5 discussion of inclusive
language he states: "God has created all males and females equal
in personal dignity, rendered by the term 'man'." This usage does
not mean he did not value women—quite the contrary! He urged
great respect for women as a reflection of the great respect due
to the Mother of God.

Descriptions of friendships with colleagues abound in this
book. Many of Abbot Boniface's close friends from the Liturgical
Movement and Council years remained always faithful to the
Church and the true intent of the Council. But he shared with
me, in deep sorrow, that some of them (including a few mentioned in this book) became part of the postconciliar "rebellion."
He said that men such as these, to varying degrees, gradually
abandoned their foundation of deep prayer, spiritual discipline,
and humble devotion to the Mother of God. As a spirit of pride
took hold, they started considering action more important than
prayer—and valuing their own opinions over Holy Tradition and
the Council's primary documents they were tasked with implementing. In Chapter 5 he succinctly evaluates the most severe
results from a Gospel perspective: "*The rebels' hateful, disobedient,
faithless, and worldly actions betray them—for the hallmarks of true
followers of Christ are brotherly love, obedience, faith, and holiness.*"

*   *   *

Overall, in this book Archimandrite Boniface provides a "wider
view" of Vatican II: the good intentions of most participants

and the great value of its primary documents, as well as personal accounts of sabotage by an aggressive minority of experts who often overpowered the bishops after the Council. He acknowledges the good fruits of the Council and strongly criticizes the bad.

He also stresses that the Church must "breathe with her two lungs," the East and the West. He invites the West to learn from the Eastern Christian Churches, "for they have preserved intact and vibrantly alive the heritage of the Apostolic Church, the Mother of East and West." And he cautions in Chapter 6: "Are we not guilty of disobedience ourselves if we ignore or reject the pope's urgent and solemn teaching that we must learn from the East if we are to solve the Western Church's problems?"

Near the end of Chapter 4, Abbot Boniface summarizes the entire situation of the Western Church:

> We are witnessing, above all, a crisis of grace. We are in dire need of a renewed outpouring of the Holy Spirit, which Pope John XXIII meant the Council to be.... We need a renewed return to the gospel, especially to the whole Sermon on the Mount, so ignored in the present culture. We need a renewed return to Holy Tradition, as was called for by the preconciliar movement. We need a return to the Council itself. This does not mean turning the clock back, but returning to the Wellspring of all truth and life in the Blessed Trinity and Revelation.

Hermit-Monk Seraphim of Holy Transfiguration (Mount Tabor) Monastery and Father Joseph Homick of the Contemplatives of Saint Joseph have encouraged and assisted in this work since the manuscript was discovered in 2022. Drs. Joseph Dyer, Tanguy Hubert, Peter Kwasniewski, Anthony Lilles, and Paweł Milcarek; Father Martin Nagy; Matthew Brown-Pazmino, John Mesarch, Marilyn Thomas, Robert Way, Esq., and several faithful personal friends, plus others whose names I may have unintentionally omitted here, have assisted at various times in various ways, and I am most grateful to them all.

May Church leaders and laity alike learn from the wisdom in this book. Archimandrite Boniface, pray for us!

Julie Rogers
Feast of the Presentation of Our Lord
February 2, 2025

PREFACE

"LEARN FROM HIM." I RECEIVED THOSE WORDS interiorly but clearly. It was, I think, around 1998, before Abbot Boniface returned to the monastery of his profession in Belgium. He was in his early eighties then, slowing down a little, but still full of wisdom, ever-ancient and ever-new.

At that point I did not know he would be returning to Belgium in two years, nor did I know how much time he had left on earth. Still less could I have imagined that soon I would become his successor, the second abbot of Mount Tabor Monastery. But it became clear to me that the clock was ticking for him, and so I should not miss opportunities to learn whatever I could from his vast and deep knowledge, experience, spirituality, and practical wisdom.

I had entered Mount Tabor Monastery in 1982, at the tender age of twenty-four. In need of guidance from someone who "knew the ropes" of the monastic adventure, I was grateful to become a spiritual son of the diminutive yet robust, white-bearded man of God.

His encyclopedic knowledge of many subjects was formidable, but he didn't speak much about his degrees or accomplishments, only numerous experiences from which he could draw lessons to share with us.

We lived in a beautiful natural setting, in the forested Northern California hills, with a palpable silence and a night sky that never ceased to take my breath away. Yet Abbot Boniface was given mostly "city boys" as his spiritual sons, so he had to teach us a lot of practical things as well. He let us carry pocket knives for various uses, for "every boy should have his knife." He also helped us learn things by simply applying ourselves to unfamiliar situations.

At one time, the lockset on my cabin door broke, so I sought permission to get a new one. Having obtained the lockset, I then asked him if someone could install it for me. He told me to do it myself. This city boy said, "But I don't know how to do it." The wise Abba replied: "Just do it, and then you'll know how to do it." Taking these paradoxical words with me back to my cabin, I just did it, and then I knew how to do it! That was his famous "just do it" principle.

Perhaps such little anecdotes seem not to be a fitting introduction to a work of this magnitude, depth, and import. But along with Father Boniface the theologian, liturgist, and historian, there is Father Boniface the man, who still retained something of a joyful and childlike spirit, even after many long years of suffering. He retained the twinkle in his eyes. His stocky build and long white beard reminded children of Santa Claus, or even God the Father. Once I was with him on an errand in town, and a small boy came up to him, wide-eyed, asking: "Are you...? Are you...?" Father Boniface gave him a Santa-like smile and said, "No, but I know him very well!"

So as you read these incisive and sometimes fiery pages, remember the spiritual father, founder of monasteries, and contemplative soul. Remember also that he was something like a new Moses, who was allowed to view the Promised Land from afar but didn't live to see what he had so ardently hoped and prayed for. And then learn from him.

Father Joseph Homick, COSJ
Contemplatives of Saint Joseph
(Abbot Emeritus of Mount Tabor Monastery)

INTRODUCTION

THE END OF A CENTURY ALWAYS INVITES RET-
rospection. This twentieth century, remarkable perhaps beyond
any other since the time of Christ, has abounded with momentous
events. While writing these memoirs, I have of necessity reflected
much on these events, from the vantage point of one born near
their beginning. Like a blind pianist going over the keys of his
instrument, trying to call forth the beloved (and sometimes painful) melodies that keep singing in his heart, I have searched my
memory primarily for those recollections that beg to be recorded
for the good of the Church. Here I set them forth in the hope
that others may find them beneficial.

THE IMPORTANCE AND CONTEXT OF THE COUNCIL

Among all the events of the twentieth century, three stand out
as most decisive for mankind: World War I, World War II, and the
Second Vatican Council. All three events have had an immense
impact upon millions of lives (including my own)—and they are
all interrelated. The first war left a terrible swath of destruction,
redesigned the map of central Europe, and witnessed the birth
of communism. The second—the inevitable result of the first,
like the second act of a cosmic drama—shook the whole world
and sacrificed millions of people to the communist "Moloch."

The third event, Vatican II, was an inevitable result of these
two wars and the changes that accompanied them. By the 1950s,
the image and needs of the Church had changed profoundly
under the pressure of new political and cultural configurations.
It became necessary for her to rethink the divine heritage she had
received from her Lord, in light of the new shape of the world in
which this everlasting heritage had to be incarnated, especially
due to the new ways of "free-thinking," the hidden powers of
international atheism, and the move of Christianity from the
old West to the New World.

Perceiving this need, and under the inspiration of the Holy
Spirit, on January 25, 1959, hardly three months after his election,
the elderly but spiritually youthful Pope John XXIII announced
his intention to convoke a general Council. The Council's purpose
would be to cope with the Church's new situation by restoring

the vital power and ever-modern heritage of her divine Founder and her apostolic beginnings.

This Council, Vatican II, was held in four sessions: October 11 to December 8, 1962; September 29 to December 4, 1963; September 14 to November 21, 1964; and September 14 to December 8, 1965. Pope John died during the Council, on June 3, 1963, and Pope Paul VI promulgated its reopening that same month, on June 27, 1963.

In this book I will often refer to three periods pertaining to the Council: the years before, during, and after Vatican II. These periods may be defined either strictly, encompassing only the work of the Council itself, or broadly, including wider influences before and after the Council. In the strict sense, the time frames are the *pre*conciliar period (1959–62), during which the ten Preparatory Commissions began their work; the Council itself (1962–65); and the *post*conciliar period (1965–81), during which commissions charged with implementing the Council issued their documents. In the broad sense, which I will use in this book, the preconciliar period includes the renewal movements of the 1940s and 1950s; and the postconciliar period truly extends to our present troubled times.

I propose that Vatican II is the single most important event of this nearly-completed century. My reasons for this strong statement are worked out in these memoirs. But here, early in our discussion, I will give a three-part chronological preview, because I am convinced that we cannot begin to understand and appreciate the Second Vatican Council's full value unless the Council is placed in its broader context.

In reference to the *past* (the time before the Council), Vatican II was the climax of several centuries' development in Western history, most especially since the "enlightenment" of the French Revolution. That revolution brought no enlightenment but rather brazenly confronted the everlasting wisdom of divine Revelation that the Church carries through the ages, in both Scripture and Holy Tradition, as the heritage of Christ.

The Council was also the expression of Christian thought and problems following World War II. There was then a growing awareness among many forward-looking theologians, myself included, that the Constantinian era was hastening to an end and that the actuality of the Christian message needed to be rethought from its roots. For this a general Council was needed, a Council in which the whole Church could participate and contribute.

In reference to the *present* (the time during the Council), awareness of the Constantinian era's end caused many to feel that the precise moment in which they lived might prove decisive not only for the immediate future but also for decades and even centuries to come. The Council Fathers perceived this and thus felt obliged to treat all the Church's major issues of the time, from Revelation to worship, to ecumenism, to "the Christian in the world." This last subject especially drew much attention because of the existence at that time of an often-naïve optimistic expectation of a forthcoming world movement of general conversion, set against an even stronger, organized world movement of hostility toward the Church and Christianity at large.

In reference to the *future* (the time after the Council) — and this is perhaps the Council's most important dimension — patterns were set in place after Vatican II for a fermentation that is still growing and will probably continue to affect Christianity for centuries. This situation exists primarily because, as I said above, Vatican II was not an isolated event. It was the expression of a long preparation that was one of many agents in a deep, universal whirlpool of evolution.

SPIRITUAL WARFARE

Since the Council, the Church has become gradually overwhelmed by the very forces she intended to convert to the gospel: for example, the old secularism, the new sexual licentiousness, pagan feminism, and hedonism, with all their consequences. This process of weakening the Church has been masterminded by the "prince of this world" (Jn 12:31). It is as Pope Paul VI said, in a speech given at Lombard College in Rome on December 7, 1968:

> It was believed that after the Council a sunny day in the Church's history would dawn, but instead there came a day of clouds, storms, and darkness.... From somewhere or other, the smoke of Satan has entered the temple of God.

Significantly, when Pope Paul was later questioned about this reference to the smoke of Satan, he did not remember saying it.

Assured by others that he had, Pope Paul acknowledged it to be a prophetic utterance, given through the Holy Spirit.

Here we come to a crucial element in this century's events: that of spiritual warfare. This cannot be underestimated. Together with many clear-sighted leaders, grace-filled mystics, and especially the Mother of God in her many authentic interventions—why pretend they do not exist?—I am convinced that we are now assisting at a cosmic warfare between the powers of darkness and the Holy Spirit, who is pouring himself out anew. And both sides are looking for an ally in every human heart.

Vatican II must be viewed in the context of this cosmic spiritual warfare for our culture's allegiance. Either the Council was a powerless plaything in the hands of the powers of darkness, or it was the irresistible tool of the Spirit of God. We must also use the same spiritual criteria when evaluating the treason of weak bishops and dissenting theologians, whose actions threatened to abort or sterilize the entire Council. By our time, all the destructive, secularistic movements in Western culture have strongly penetrated the Western Church, so that the Church has become part of the crisis. Consequently, the whole work and impact of Vatican II is jeopardized. The sacraments are being desecrated and man's need for the holy and for reverence is being violated under the pressure of secularism, sanctioned by the dissenters' "new liturgy."

Something very anthropologically significant is happening here: the little and defenseless are robbed of their soul. Among the many victims are the children, who are deprived of their innocence (their inalienable privilege), and the teenagers, whose awakening sexuality is being unduly aroused. This is an assault on the poor and defenseless that calls to heaven for revenge. The ultimate result of this betrayal and rebellion is the growing apostasy of Christians, which I firmly believe will be soon followed by a growing persecution of the truly faithful.

The basic remedy for these problems is the sincere conversion of all those involved in this deep crisis, from top to bottom. We are witnessing a crisis of grace. The solution is a renewed return to deep personal prayer, the gospel (especially the Sermon on the Mount), and Holy Tradition. Let us pray in our time for a new outpouring of the Holy Spirit, which Pope John XXIII meant the Council to be.

PROBLEMS OF INTERPRETATION

Because of the present lack of leadership within much of the Church's hierarchy, it is becoming increasingly more difficult for Christians to see clearly what Vatican II really means for the Church and for themselves. As we living participants in the Council become more rare — we are not immortal! — this situation is becoming even more critical. Therefore I hope that my witness will shed some light on the situation.

A growing tendency toward two erroneous attitudes about the Council has arisen of late: a tendency either (1) to put the Council aside as a grandiose but failed endeavor to update the Church from top to bottom, or (2) to misinterpret the Council in accordance with current theological fads. Significantly and ironically, those who seek to undermine the Council in these ways reject the work and teaching of Pope John Paul II precisely *because* he believes in Vatican II and is striving to make the Church accept its actual, true teachings and make them work.

Some dissenters in the Church assert that the values at stake after Vatican II are more important than documents, even the documents of this most important Council. This concept may be correct in itself; however, the reality is that the most efficient antidote to the ailments the dissenters seek to cure is *simply to put into practice the directives of the Council's sixteen primary documents!* Other dissenters, citing the late Paul Ricœur's basic work, *De l'Interprétation*,[1] say that the whole situation is merely a question of interpretation. This may be true, but such dissenters seem conveniently to forget that Ricœur insisted that interpretation be based on correct principles.

My own unhappy experience, during many years of work in the postconciliar subcommissions appointed to implement the Council's documents, was that *from the very beginning, some commission members in high positions never intended to abide by the scope or spirit of the Council decrees*; they intended rather to promote their own ideas. Their spurious interpretation was largely foreign to the Council decrees and was rather that demanded by current fads and by liturgists and theologians of certain schools. In the

---

[1] This was abridged and translated into English under the title *Interpretation Theory: Discourse and the Surplus of Meaning* (Fort Worth: Texas Christian University Press, 1976); it is one of the most significant studies on this crucial topic.

pages to come, I will give clear but painful witness to the existence of this frequent, purposefully misleading interpretation of the Council documents.

We must approach a final problem of interpretation before we can tackle the contents of the Council's sixteen primary documents. Looking at these documents from hindsight, we discover that they can be taken as belonging to the past or to the future. Seen from the past, they are the end of an evolution that has solved all the problems of that period; thus we must adhere to the documents as they are. Seen from the future, it is their deeper spirit that matters; thus the documents, especially those on the liturgy and the Church, may be seen as blueprints of a new evolution that has become more and more necessary. Both vistas, past and future, are correct; they must implement each other, as John Paul II says again and again. This is crucial. These documents do give the blueprint of a new evolution, *but only if one approaches and accepts them as the Council Fathers meant them.*

Hence, the guiding attitude of commentators on the Council, and of all Christian people, must be this: we must truly and objectively penetrate into both the letter *and* the true spirit of Vatican II. In doing so we must treat the Council not as a hunting ground for dark politics, but as the Holy Spirit at work in his bride, the Church, in his usual mysterious ways that only incarnational faith, eschatological hope, and evangelical love can understand.

Why is Pope John Paul II's attitude regarding both past and future the correct one, and why have I adopted it? Because it is based upon two deeper foundations of Vatican II and all Councils. First, all Church Councils, in continuity with one another, have been supported by Holy Tradition, overarching and all-surpassing, from the time of the apostles until our day. Thus Vatican II is at the service of Holy Tradition and carries it on.

Second, the active element of Holy Tradition is the Holy Spirit, who has at his service various organs in the Church to express and adapt Holy Tradition without altering it: for example, Councils, the Petrine Ministry, the Magisterium of the bishops in union with Peter, and the Spirit-filled life of the faithful. It follows that the basic authority of all Councils from age to age, including Vatican II, comes from Holy Tradition, which teaches the Church in the Holy Spirit through these organs.

Hence the arising of "new problems" is not cause for alarm. Many dissenters posit that the Church today faces new problems, unlike those of old. They object to many post-Vatican II papal interventions, saying that the popes are not being sensitive to the needs of today. But the popes' statements are not their own inventions; they are rather calling upon Holy Tradition, which it is their duty to preserve and teach. As the popes continue to remind their flock, no one, not even a pope, can change Holy Tradition, which has been constant from the apostles until our day.

This awareness of the ruling, normative value of Holy Tradition wherein all the Councils' authority is rooted has practically disappeared in the modern Western Church, under the pressure of rebellious theologians, some of whom have totally rejected Holy Tradition and are essentially in a state of heresy. In *this* entire book, on the contrary, the reader will find a strong awareness of the role of Holy Tradition in the life of the Church and in the Council.

STYLE AND OVERVIEW OF THIS BOOK

This book is not intended as an exhaustive work of research, nor is it purely scholarly in its approach. I write as a firsthand witness of, and participant in, the Council. My main resources are my personal notes, documents, and remembrances, the last of which I acknowledge are subject to gaps in my memory. I am aware that many books have been written about the Council, but I use them very little as sources, enabling the reader to receive a fresh, *inédit* presentation. Further, because I lived in Africa during the entire Council, and travelled to and from Rome for my Council work, I had a great advantage from which the reader will benefit: I remained relatively free from the politicking between sessions and was able to keep a more objective perspective of the Church's real needs that the Council was required to address.

In order to evoke both a general impression of the Council's historical atmosphere and an awareness of its enormous importance, in this book I will mix personal details with anthropological and theological principles; thus the tone and value of this book will be a bit unequal. But this style is required in order that each area — the anecdotal and the theological — might fertilize each other. It should also bring interest and variation to the account.

This book will focus largely on events and insights pertaining to the liturgy, which has long been a field of my research and practice.

Because the majority of my work for the Council pertained to the Constitution on the Sacred Liturgy (*Sacrosanctum Concilium*), my experiences with that document in all its phases — preparation, approval, and reception — will naturally permeate my witness.

The Second Vatican Council was neither a *deus ex machina* (an artificially called-for solution) nor a *generatio spontanea*, nor even a sudden inspiration from Above. I am deeply convinced that Pope John XXIII's inspiration to hold the Council at that moment did indeed come from the Holy Spirit. But the Council did not happen "suddenly." It had been prepared throughout the Western Church for over two decades by a well-developed, orthodox renewal movement in the Church.

In Chapter 1 we will explore this exciting preconciliar renewal movement and clear up some misunderstandings surrounding Pope John's announcement of, and intentions for, the Council. Almost all the main areas of reform taken up by the Council's commissions had already been embraced by this movement, and the Council worked in organic continuity with its efforts. To understand the Council aright, it is absolutely necessary to keep in mind this continuity and the resulting optimism at the opening of the Council.

My personal memories of the Preparatory Commissions and the Council itself are recorded in Chapter 2. We will follow the development of the Constitution on the Sacred Liturgy (CSL) from the beginning of the Preparatory Commission for Liturgy until CSL's approval on the Council floor in late 1963. We will meet some key figures, including the influential Father Annibale Bugnini and the remarkable Cardinal Joseph Malula of Kinshasa (Zaire), who was my bishop at that time. We will also delve into CSL's theological content and give an inside view of the true meaning and intent of its authors, of which I was one.

In Chapter 3 we will begin to explore the decisive period of the Consilium — established by Pope Paul VI to implement the directives of CSL — from its creation in January 1964 until the new Roman Missal was released in 1970. Because I was highly active in two of the Consilium's subcommissions and assisted in others, this may be my most valuable witness. I am convinced that the Consilium's subcommissions misunderstood their true task and hence, wittingly or unwittingly, betrayed the Constitution on the Sacred Liturgy. This chapter will recount several revealing incidents within these subcommissions, and give an initial summary of the repercussions caused by the promulgation of CSL without proper preparation for the clergy and faithful.

Chapter 3, and truly this whole book, will elucidate the following statement, which I cannot emphasize enough: *the problem lies not in the Council itself or its primary documents (including CSL), but in what the postconciliar commissions made out of it and what the dissenters have prevented it from being.* I witnessed this personally during more than two decades of work and struggle.

In Chapters 4 and 5 we will follow the postconciliar passage from Church crisis to world crisis, from occasional disagreement to organized dissent, from differences of opinion to open rebellion, from legitimate adaptation to neo-paganism, and from God-centered verticalism to man-centered horizontalism. In these chapters I will present both theological and anthropological analyses of the postconciliar decay, showing, among other things, how the deterioration of the liturgy has led to deterioration in many aspects of life in the Western Church, and thus even in Western civilization.

Yet healing must come, and it will, but only by a return to true holiness. As a Byzantine Catholic monk, with long, intense experience in the service of both the Western and Eastern Churches, I am convinced that the road to *ressourcement* (return to the Church's sources) and *rapprochement* must pass through the Eastern Christian Churches, which have preserved intact the heritage of the apostolic Church, the Mother of both East and West. Thus, in Chapter 6, I will demonstrate why the Western Church must "look to the East" and learn to "breathe with her two lungs" — as Pope John Paul II wrote in his encyclical *Ut Unum Sint* (That they may be one) — the Eastern as well as the Western. This was the true way of Vatican II, which appropriated much from the Eastern Churches, including essential values the West had lost down the centuries. (A brief description of the Eastern Churches is given in Appendix C.)

THE CALL TO WRITE

Writing this book has been very costly for me. The greatest difficulty has not been remembering and recording the details, but the knowledge that many of my former, beloved colleagues will misunderstand or reject my words, for many of them have

abandoned the true intent of the Council and the liturgical reform
it prescribed. Thus for quite some time I resisted writing, not
wishing to open old wounds.

But many friends in recent years have repeatedly insisted that
I record my experiences and insights, precisely because so many
critically important facts about the Council, such as the purposeful misinterpretation mentioned above, are so little known. They
urged me to include details of the events at which I assisted and
my relationships with persons who played decisive roles.

The U. S. Bishops' 1994 pastoral letter entitled "Confront-
ing a Culture of Violence: A Catholic Framework for Action"
finally convinced me to write. Therein the bishops denounce all
forms of violence that destroy the lives of millions, including the
unborn—violence that paralyzes and polarizes our communities
and yet is glorified by the media, secular music, and video games
that poison the hearts of our children. It is good and necessary
to speak out against such violence. Yet, one heinous form of violence is constantly overlooked, including in the bishops' letter:
that committed by Church superiors who allow theologians to
spread lies and false teachings from their pulpits and in schools
and seminaries. By their lack of proper leadership, these superiors collaborate, at the very least by neglect, with a culture of
falsehood in which the little ones—the youth and most of the
faithful—are thrown to the lions and left to perish.

Faced with this situation of spiritual violence and injustice—
more subtle, perhaps, than the saber-rattling of the Middle Ages
or the evils denounced in the pastoral letter, but nevertheless fatal
to many souls—I finally found the courage to write these pages.

A major portion of this book was completed in 1995, but unfore-
seen circumstances delayed its reaching the publisher.[2] Looking
back, I see this delay as a blessing. In the beginning, the book
was to be only, as my friends had urged, a humble "distillation"
of my experiences and participation in the Council's work, and
my witness of its further dispatch during the postconciliar years.
I soon realized, however, that it was impossible to separate my
personal memories from the enormously broad and deep intent
and impact of Vatican II. The book would have to far exceed my

---

[2] The author added this paragraph in 1997, in his last revision. As the
Editor's Foreword indicates, thereafter this manuscript was lost until its
discovery in 2022.—Ed.

personal part in it and even the very events of the Council itself. And so it does.

There was—and still is—nothing less at stake than the very survival of the Church and of Christian civilization. This threat to her survival comes not from a "spontaneous evolution" resulting from practices becoming worn out or meaningless, but rather from an organized and concerted agenda of actions that aim, by all available means, to tear down the Church and destroy Christianity. While many leaders of the Church and Christianity are sleeping, the wolves are decimating the unsuspecting flock.

From whence then do I get the courage to try to wake up these leaders and denounce the conspiracy? I am humbly convinced that the times have become too serious and decisive to waste time even asking this question. Besides, the great Pope Leo XIII answered it in 1890, at the moment when the enemies of the Church began their agenda that has reached its climax in our days. I urge the reader to ponder his wisdom:

> To recoil before an enemy, or to keep silence when from all sides such clamors are raised against truth, is the part of a man either devoid of character or who entertains doubt as to the truth of what he professes to believe. In both cases such mode of behaving is base and is insulting to God, and both are incompatible with the salvation of mankind.[3]

It was in a cultural milieu of moral and societal evils that Vatican II was set up as the true remedy. This gigantic task is now deeply jeopardized by the postconciliar dissenters. In this context I recall an oft-repeated saying of a modern Church Father, Father Werenfried van Straaten: "We're all together in the same boat, in the raging storm of modern crisis. The boat is leaking; all hands on deck! There is no time for useless discussion and life-threatening dissent." The deeper purpose of Vatican II was and is to endow the Church with the resources necessary both to survive this all-comprising crisis and to renew the bride of Christ for the return of her Bridegroom.

By my writing I certainly do not wish to put salt in the wounds inflicted by Vatican II upon many of my friends, nor do I wish

---

[3] Leo XIII, *Sapientiae Christianae* [Encyclical Letter On Christians as Citizens], The Holy See, January 10, 1890, sec. 14.

to increase the confusion that followed the Council. Therefore I apologize in advance for any hurt feelings that may arise from what I have written. May my friends and readers understand that I dared to take this odium upon myself out of love for both the Church, who is in need, and the many truly poor of the gospel who know not where to turn because they feel betrayed and abandoned. If in bearing this stigma I wish to side with the leadership of the Church—the pope, with the Magisterium—it is because I fully share with Cardinal Ratzinger the belief that *"the Magisterium has the task of defending the faith of simple souls against the elitist presumptions of intellectuals."*[4]

More and more I see this whole crisis as a matter of the need to return to God and his revealed religion. Turning to God means conversion, and conversion is a question of grace. Grace is conditional, a fruit of sacrificial prayer. The same Spirit of God who inspired the Council must now be fervently and sacrificially invoked to change hearts and minds. Only through deeply-converted persons can a new God-centered culture be generated as the organic milieu wherein true religion can breathe and live.

The principal prayer of the Church is the liturgy. Therefore this book focuses primarily on the liturgy and its central and vital role in the work and plan of salvation and, hence, in the real life of the Church. The clear teaching of the Council about the centrality of the liturgy must be taken as the primary norm for evaluating all of Vatican II:

> [T]he liturgy is the summit toward which the activity of the Church is directed; it is also the fount from which all her power flows. (CSL 10)

This leads us to a fact crucial to understanding the aftermath of Vatican II: *the dissenters recognize the ultimate primacy and necessity of the liturgy; this is why they use the liturgy as their battlefield.*

Therefore I put my work in this book into a threefold context. First is the faithful's growing weariness of unending tinkering with the Mass and constant criticisms by the dissenters. This tinkering and criticism continues even though, as far back as April 1980, the Vatican put an end to further experimentation, because "in these cases [of wild experimentation and abuse] we are face to

---

[4] Statement made December 12, 1979, quoted in *30 Days*, March 1991, pp. 68–71.

face with a real falsification of the Catholic liturgy."[5] This first context calls attention to the all-pervading neglect of, and assault on, the poor and defenseless in Western civilization — all of whom are hungry for God, for ritual, and for the truth.

The second context of this book is the growing awakening of the Catholic laity to the problems created by the postconciliar rebellion against Church authority, especially in the liturgy — an awakening visible and promising in many new groups of outstanding laborers in the Lord's vineyard.[6] This book will constantly apply the Aristotelian principle of cause and effect, showing how particular acts *must* elicit irresistible particular effects in this whole postconciliar drama.

This book's third context, closely following from the previous two, is the growing discussion about the need for a *reform of the reform* — a question asked more and more since Cardinal Ratzinger conceded the "failure of the liturgical reform" in 1996.[7] By now the necessity of such a reform is generally accepted among orthodox churchmen. Why? Because the reform intended by Vatican II has generally turned instead into a *de*formation operated by two agents: the initial betrayal by the postconciliar commissions, and the secularism of the dissenters. My conclusions about Cardinal Ratzinger's extremely important and carefully-reasoned stand in 1996 will be worked out in these pages.

May this book be a bridge to bring all sides together, for we all serve the same Church and, sooner or later, we will all be called to account for our stewardship.

---

[5] John Paul II, *Inaestimabile Donum* [Instruction Concerning Worship of the Eucharistic Mystery], prepared by the Sacred Congregation for the Sacraments and Divine Worship, April 17, 1980.
[6] In various contexts the author has praised, among others, Adoremus, the Society for Catholic Liturgy, and the Fellowship of Catholic Scholars. — Ed.
[7] See article in *The Latin Mass*, Winter 1996, pp. 6, 51ff., explaining the exact intent of the Cardinal: i.e., not to reject Vatican II, but rather the opposite, to make an honest *return to the Council.* The same position is taken by Cardinal Ortas, Prefect of the Congregation for Divine Worship and the Discipline of the Sacraments, in *30 Days*, November 1995, pp. 16ff.

CHAPTER 1

Before the Council:
Optimism and Expectancy

I will bless the LORD at all times,
his praise always on my lips;
in the LORD my soul shall make its boast,
the humble shall hear and be glad.
—Psalm 33/34:2–3

ARTICLE 1: WHO, ME?

At our Abbey of Postel in Belgium, usually Father Prior distributed the mail, unopened, before noon Office and lunch. But one day in the summer of 1959, a letter from Rome arrived for me. The abbot opened it, then called me to his office. "Congratulations!" he said. "This is your letter of appointment to the Council!" My heart pounded. For us, in that far-away abbey in the woods, the forthcoming Council was *the* great event, the object of intense prayer and expectation. And I had been appointed to it!

My appointment was quite a surprise, for at that time I was preparing to spend the rest of my life in Africa, specifically the Belgian Congo, later called Zaire. I had been asked to join a group of Scheut missionaries as advisor to the bishops, and to become Professor of Liturgy at the University of Lovanium in Kinshasa, the capital.[1]

So I read and reread the letter from Rome. It was quite clear: I was appointed as a Consultor of the Preparatory Commission for Liturgy. Soon afterward, my appointment was confirmed by the arrival of a large bundle of material, complete with an invitation to the first plenary session of the Preparatory Commission on November 11, 1960. And so the work began, full speed ahead!

Often I have asked myself, "Why was I appointed, and who was instrumental in it?" I will never know for sure, but the primary reason was probably my active role in a Spirit-led theological and Liturgical Movement sweeping the Church in Europe and

---

[1] This city was called Léopoldville until 1966, but for consistency in this book I will refer to it as Kinshasa.

America at that time. This movement of renewal was inspired and carried on by a large group of capable theologians and pastors who met regularly to exchange their ideas, plans, and publications. We were all obedient sons of the Church, whom we loved and wanted to serve and defend, even at the price of our health or careers. As part of the creative *avant-garde* of this movement, I had published many studies, articles, and books in its fields, and was a faithful participant in the national and international meetings that nourished and spread the renewal.

Soon I learned that numerous members of the movement had been appointed to the Council. From this I joyfully concluded that the Council would truly be what Pope John XXIII had announced: the vehicle for a "new Pentecost." We members of the renewal had been for years officially sidetracked by a certain small, inbred element in the Church. But something must have changed. Now apparently the Church was acknowledging our service and requesting our contribution. Now we were being officially consulted as laborers for the future life of the Church!

Two more factors may have played a part in my appointment. First, I was actively involved in not only the Western (Roman) Church but also the Eastern Christian Churches. As the Council valued highly the spiritual riches of the Christian East, my knowledge of them proved exceedingly valuable. Another factor — although at first I thought it a hindrance — could have been my imminent move to the Belgian Congo, which had one of the most advanced Churches of Africa. As an adviser to her bishops, I would be able to represent the missionary Church as well; indeed I did much work for the Council's Commission for the Missions.

Whatever the reasons for my appointment, there I was, parachuted into the midst of that wonderful elite of scholars and pastors from all over the world, appointed by the Church's highest authority to work for this century's greatest event. It humbled me and gave me a holy expectancy of the power of the Holy Spirit called down upon us by Pope John.

ARTICLE 2: THE PRECONCILIAR RENEWAL MOVEMENT

If one is truly to understand Vatican II, he must first of all understand the general situation and spiritual climate in the Church before the Council. This article will focus heavily on the renewal movement mentioned above, for it laid the foundations for the Council throughout the Western Church, and most of the Council's areas of reform were taken over from its work. But for a complete picture we will look also at the opposition to the movement, and at some liturgical practices that were truly in need of reform. Further, we must consider Pope John XXIII's goals for the Council, and delve into the true meanings of the oft-misused word *aggiornamento* and the term "active participation."

A note about terminology is in order here. The renewal movement consisted of three interlocking branches: the Biblical Movement, Liturgical Movement, and Theological Movement. When I do not specify a certain branch, but refer merely to "the movement," "the renewal movement," or "the preconciliar movement," the reference is to the movement as a whole.

LEADERS OF THE PRECONCILIAR MOVEMENT

The preconciliar movement was born immediately after the First World War, in 1919, at the Catholic Congress of Mechelen, in Belgium. It began to spread throughout Europe and somewhat in America during the next two decades, but came to full fruition after World War II. Its purpose was broad yet clear: *the renewal of the Church, on all levels, by a return to her sources*: the Gospel (Biblical Movement), the liturgy (Liturgical Movement), and the Fathers (Theological Movement). It sought to build up in the Church both a genuine life of prayer and a celebrating community, and thus to blaze the trail to heaven.

The participants came from all walks of life and all levels of the Church in Europe and America; its leaders were primarily orthodox yet forward-looking theologians, liturgists, and pastors. Some were young and aggressive; others were older and widely respected. They were "progressives" as well as "conservatives" — but such terms had no political connotations then, for we were all friends.

The movement was supported by outstanding Bible scholars, philosophers, and patrologists of highly-respected schools — such as the Catholic University of Louvain (Leuven), and Le Saulchoir of the French Dominicans — and nearly all the seminaries and religious schools in the "old countries." It was nourished by the spiritual fervor, piety, and love for the Church of contemplatives in numerous monasteries. And it was upheld by the fidelity, commitment, and labors of churchmen and women in parishes throughout the Western world. Because of its enthusiasm, truthfulness, and competence, the movement was irresistible and truly spoke to all ranks of the Church.

Due to the polarization that exists in the Church today between so-called liberals and conservatives, or radicals and reactionaries, another clarification may be helpful. As I said, the movement's main emphasis was renewal via a return to the Church's sources. This did not mean that its leaders were reactionaries, clinging only to the past: they embraced the wisdom of both the great medieval saints and sages and the leading thinkers in the Church in their own time. Nor were they radicals, rejecting the past: for instance, they considered Gregorian chant the greatest cultural creation of the Western Church and desired to retain it. These leaders and thinkers were orthodox in their theology and fervent in their spiritual lives — and yet at the same time highly creative and progressive in their efforts on behalf of the Church.

Let us be clear: the leaders of the preconciliar renewal movement had absolutely nothing in common with present-day dissenters. They were totally obedient to the Magisterium, even in the face of opposition from some members of the hierarchy who were entrenched in certain sclerotic practices or institutions. Positive in their approach, the renewers did not criticize but rather sought to build upon the good already existing in the Church.

These men were not the usual crew of happy followers; rather, they formed the leading wing of the Church both before and during the Council. They were men of indisputable authority, both human and spiritual, who commanded the respect of the highest Church authorities because their work was supported by excellent scholarship and experience. (Later I will cite an instance in which my own scholarly work was personally approved by Pope Pius XII.) Their work was disseminated by a multitude of scholarly publications in Europe and the New World.

The renewers' influence was enhanced by regular international meetings — the great Congresses of Assisi (1953) and Munich (1955) being the most outstanding — which drew spiritual leaders from all areas, backgrounds, and responsibilities in the Church's life. There the fire of enthusiasm for the movement's work was communicated to the thousands who attended. In between meetings the flames were fanned by small scholarly groups in which the in-depth work was done, and by magazines and literature for all areas of the Church's needs.

CHARACTERISTICS OF THE MOVEMENT

Braving the reproach of being considered a *laudator temporis acti* (a praiser of the past), I must state that the preconciliar period was one of the great periods in the history of the Church. Some will dispute this as an exaggeration, but many spiritual leaders have shared my assessment. Here are four reasons for this period's greatness.

1. First, *the preconciliar movement was a "holy pilgrimage," a return to the sources*: to Scripture, the Early Church, the Fathers, and the great saints. This gave the movement its objective and ecclesial solidity and authenticity. Almost all the movement's outstanding scholars — their work fertilized by much prayer and self-discipline — strove diligently toward the restoration of these sources as norms for the Church's life.

2. The movement's return to the sources was enhanced by its second characteristic, a corollary to the first: *its loving and respectful submission to the hierarchy and the Magisterium.* The renewers knew very well to make a distinction between the real Rome, namely the pope as the Petrine Ministry with his immediate collaborators, and the "secondary Rome" of unsavory ambitions and inbreeding, including a reactionary element of the Curia, which often jeopardized the real Rome. The movement's leaders often suffered from this secondary Rome. But they did not indulge an ambition for recognition that puts oneself above the teaching of the Church, so their sufferings did not in the least diminish their respect for Rome or their obedience to the hierarchy.

In fact, the leaders knew well, and were grateful, that the highest members of the real Rome — namely Popes Pius X, Pius XI, and Pius XII — were the true fathers of the movement. These popes repeatedly expressed in their writings the movement's own concerns: (a) the spiritual starvation of the faithful even as they gathered around the richly-laden table of the liturgy, (b) the need to return to the sources of the true Christian spirit through active participation in the liturgy, and (c) the need for a return to the sources in the study of the Bible and theology.

Let us look especially at the role of Pope Pius XII (1939–58). Vatican II would have been impossible without the long and fruitful preparation this holy pope provided. For example, the Constitution on the Church, *Lumen Gentium,* is a fruit of Pius XII's encyclical *Mystici Corporis* (1943); the Constitution on Divine

Revelation, *Dei Verbum*, owes much to his encyclical *Divino Afflante Spiritu* (1943); and the Constitution on the Sacred Liturgy, *Sacrosanctum Concilium*, relies heavily on the preparation provided by his famous encyclical *Mediator Dei* (1947), appreciatively called the "Magna Carta of the Liturgical Movement."

As a side note, I would add that the *moral* teaching of Vatican II as well, in large part, is the moral teaching of Pius XII. His successors, John XXIII, Paul VI, and John Paul II, continued faithfully in his footsteps, assuring an organic continuity; and this teaching was embodied in the 1992 *Catechism of the Catholic Church*. (The reader should bear in mind that John Paul II assisted at all the Council's sessions — as Bishop and then Archbishop Karol Wojtyła — and has always remained its faithful promoter and interpreter.) Thus we may say that Vatican II represents a significant portion of the everlasting teaching of the Church.

3. A third vital characteristic of the preconciliar renewal was this: *its theology, liturgy, catechetics, and Church life were all the fruit of prayer — deep personal prayer*. It was primarily and ultimately a movement of piety, of contact with God. The renewers wanted to make all of life an homage to God; they were great men of prayer who desired to help others grow in prayer. Thus, for instance, the renewal leaders made especially great efforts to propagate the Divine Office (now called Liturgy of the Hours) among not only the clergy but also the laity, in order to help every Christian share in the prayer of the Church.

These leaders knew that the real reason for active participation in Church life is not to exert a "right" but to build up the Body of Christ in the Spirit. As Pope Pius X wrote in 1903 in his motu proprio *Tra le sollecitudini*, the purpose of active participation is to draw life from the main source of the true Christian spirit, by means of personal and communal prayer. (Further on we will delve into the true meaning of "active participation.") I can attest from my friendships with both scholars and simple believers that their personal prayer lives were very similar in fervor and intimacy with their Lord.

4. Following from the above is this: *the preconciliar movement touched all levels of the Christian community*. Here I will discuss only the social layer most involved in the renewal: the Catholic youth movements in Europe. These youth movements wrote a beautiful page of preconciliar history that deserves special attention: they

were like a kaleidoscope of the whole movement and gave it its optimistic and dynamic ardor. Anyone who ever participated in the huge eucharistic youth gatherings on the forecourt of Tongerlo Abbey will know precisely what I mean by "optimistic dynamism."

The mother of the Catholic youth movements was Quickborn, founded in Berlin during World War I by Father Romano Guardini, Professor Johannes Pinsk, and Edith Gurian, my friend and student from Notre Dame. The Young Christian Workers movement, founded by Father Josef Cardijn in Brussels in 1912, also soon spread throughout the world. The Catholic Boy Scouts and Girl Scouts in practically all the Western European countries joined the renewal, as did the national youth movements.[2] All these profited from the renewal movement, especially in the Catholic formation of their leaders and members. In return, they contributed much of the enthusiasm, idealism, and courage that characterized the movement from beginning to end.

Many of the movement's pacesetters in theology, philosophy, and liturgy, and most abbeys and Catholic colleges, were active with both youth and parishes, including as priest-chaplains. For example, I was one of three head chaplains for the Flemish Rover Scouts: at ages sixteen to early twenties, these Scouts already played active roles in Church life. My work with the youth provided some of my best memories of the renewal.

GEOGRAPHICAL OVERVIEW

Now let us look at the development and progress of the preconciliar renewal, following a geographical scheme. Full histories of this period are already available; here I want only to *colligere fragmenta ne pereant*, to "gather some general memories that should not be forgotten" from my personal experience, and to provide a background for understanding the Council. I will give special attention to the liturgical renewal, as I am convinced that it formed the movement's most creative, active core.

This overview of countries and their active agents is necessary, not only for understanding Vatican II but also for an appreciation

---

[2] Deserving of special mention is Ernest van der Hallen, a spiritual giant and father of the national youth movement in Flanders. See my book, *Ernest van der Hallen* (Mol, Belgium: Abdij Postel, 1955). [This was also published as *Ernest van der Hallen: Begenadigde en Leider* (Zele, Belgium: Ganzenheove, 1955).—Ed.]

of modern Church history. Unlike the postconciliar movement, the preconciliar movement had strong national or local features and contributions. I have tried to enliven the enumeration of places and persons by my personal experiences and remembrances, as an eyewitness and fellow participant in this great drama.

1. Belgium

Our overview begins with Belgium, because there the preconciliar movement began and perhaps grew to its fullest stature. As noted above, the Liturgical Movement, the first of the renewal's three branches, began at the Catholic Congress of 1919 in Mechelen. Its dynamic inspiration was my dear friend, Dom Lambert Beauduin, OSB, then of Keizersberg (Mont-César) Abbey in Louvain and later founder of the famous bi-ritual Abbey of Chevetogne. Dom Lambert so mobilized the Belgian bishops, and especially Cardinal Mercier, head of Belgium's hierarchy, that within a few years the movement won the whole country, both the Flemish and Walloon peoples. Soon the movement had penetrated schools, parishes, and seminaries, mainly by means of magazines, school manuals, missals, and leaflets covering all areas of Church life and filling every need for instruction, theology, and practice — for the movement was rooted in daily life, in Christian life as a whole.

Besides this popular formation, the institutes of higher Christian education in Belgium provided a strong scholarly undergirding for renewed thinking in a return to the Church's sources in the liturgy, the Fathers, and the great medieval philosophers. Almost all the seminaries and religious houses of formation in Belgium followed this awakening by the Spirit, but the Catholic University of Louvain (my alma mater) set the tone and made the deepest impact. Allow me to mention some of its greatest churchmen, my friends and teachers.

Gérard Philips, Professor of Dogmatics, was to become the principal author of the most important document of the Council, *Lumen Gentium*, on the Church. I still remember his "sayings of wisdom," akin to those of the Desert Fathers. An example: "They used to speak of the opposition between *ecclesia docens* (teaching Church) and *ecclesia discens* (learning Church). Your mothers certainly belonged to the latter, in their beautiful Christian humility. But let us be honest. Who has had the deepest impact upon your life of faith: the most outspoken pope or bishop, or your mother?" The answer and its implications were clear, but quite revolutionary. Another of his sayings: "If you need to know exactly the true heritage and teaching of the Church, where do you look first: at papal pronouncements, or the Fathers? I tell you, look at the Eastern Churches—what they teach, how they live, what they consider important—for they have kept the Early Church's Tradition, the heritage of Christ Himself."

Professor Albert Dondeyne of Louvain's School of Philosophy was a man of sincere humility and yet of deep, intellectual penetration into the problems of his time. He dared to take responsibility and persevered in it, including during the Nazi occupation when others, even high Church authorities, backed down in cowardice.[3] Albert de Meyer, Professor of Church History, a mentor for my doctoral work, was another remarkable man, for whom honesty and truthfulness were the only norm. What a joy and honor it was to learn from such great scholars, all eagerly committed to the sources of Christianity as a means of permanent renewal in the Church. Sadly, some of them, having researched and taught selflessly for years in preparation for the Council, were forced to witness, in deep pain, the perversion of truth that followed soon afterward.

The Benedictine and Norbertine abbeys in Belgium soon joined the movement and contributed strong leadership. The members of Loppem Abbey lived out the renewed theology and new liturgical spirit, following the example and teaching of their leader, Abbot Gérard van Caloen. In Tongerlo Abbey, Abbot Emil Stalmans was a spiritual leader to his own community and to countless priests and laypersons who found their way to Christian fervor under his direction. Among the Tongerlo brothers was Father Antoon van Clé, who bubbled over with the power of the Spirit and led various movements of young idealists. The leaders of the abbeys of Affligem and Keizersberg-Louvain collaborated with scholars and pastorally-motivated monks throughout Europe, especially by means of excellent magazines, manuals, and books; the Abbey of Maredsous joined them in biblical study. Regular study meetings in Keizersberg-Louvain, Tongerlo, and Heeswijk Abbeys (the latter in Holland) increased the movement's influence.

---

[3] Father Dondeyne recruited Father Boniface to serve as a priest to the Belgian Resistance movement and underground army during this time; see Appendix A.—Ed.

Another center of the renewal, though on a different plane, was the bi-ritual Abbey of Chevetogne, where the Roman and Byzantine rites beautifully coexisted. Its founder and soul, the aforementioned Dom Lambert Beauduin, was sent into exile in France early in this period because of his clashes with Bishop Michel d'Herbigny.[4] Nevertheless, Chevetogne's outstanding ecumenical work was invaluable, especially in the remote preparation of the Decrees *Orientalium Ecclesiarum* on the Eastern Churches and *Unitatis Redintegratio* on ecumenism. I assisted at Chevetogne's annual theological study-weeks from 1945, the year Dom Lambert returned from exile, until his death in 1960. One could not help loving Dom Lambert, and during those years a great friendship grew between us.[5] Chevetogne added to the preconciliar period a dimension that proved crucial for both the Church and my own life: an understanding of the Eastern Churches as *the* great source of true Church renewal.

Finally I must mention an outstanding scholarly and pastoral fruit of the movement: the *Liturgisch Woordenboek*.[6] This liturgical encyclopedia, perhaps the best ever written, was the fruit of top European scholars, most of them Dutch-speaking, as the Liturgical Movement arose primarily from Belgium and Holland. I served as one of its editors and contributed approximately one hundred articles.

2. Austria

Austria played an extraordinary role in the Liturgical Movement through its two gentle, soft-spoken spiritual leaders: Father Pius Parsch of Klosterneuburg Monastery near Vienna, and Father Josef Jungmann, a Jesuit scholar. Our meetings were suffused with a beautiful friendship which was the wellspring of action plans and scholarly exchanges for the good of the Church.

---

[4] This tragedy and its repercussions are described by Léon Tretjakewitsch in his work, *Bishop Michel d'Herbigny SJ and Russia: a Pre-Ecumenical Approach to Christian Unity* (Würzburg: Augustinus-Verlag, 1990). See also Sonya A. Quitslund's outstanding biography, *Beauduin: A Prophet Vindicated* (New York: Newman, 1973), which describes the spiritual environment in which Dom Lambert worked fervently despite the relentless opposition and persecution of some Church authorities.

[5] Louis Bouyer described Dom Lambert's warm personality well in his biography, *Dom Lambert Beauduin, un homme d'Église* (Paris: Casterman, 1964).

[6] *Liturgisch Woordenboek* (Maaseik, Belgium: Romen en Zonen, 1962–68 and other editions).

Father Parsch, whose personal motto was *"Mit zarter Zähigkeit"* (with tender toughness), was converted to the Liturgical Movement by his experiences as an Austrian army chaplain during World War I. There he saw that the soldiers, though good men, were spiritually starving around the richly-laden table of Bible and liturgy, for no one broke the bread for them: that is, no one helped them to actively participate in and profit from the Church's riches. Moved by this need, after the war Father Parsch founded, in Klosterneuburg Monastery, the fervent lay community Saint Gertrud Gemeinde, in which the liturgy and gospel were fully lived. From there he published the magazine *Bibel und Liturgie*, whose primary undergirding was the pioneering scholarly work of Maria Laach Abbey, which Father Parsch popularized in the German-speaking countries.

Father Josef Jungmann was perhaps the most respected scholar of all the renewers, yet so humble and self-effacing that he claimed not the slightest recognition for himself. A personal story shows his humility. When he and I first met, the first edition of his *Missarum Sollemnia* had just been published.[7] In it he had made a statement about the origin of the late Carolingian "Rhenish liturgical movement" in the eleventh century, a subject that was my specialty at the time.[8] When I said I disagreed and showed him the results of my study, he humbly accepted my arguments; in his next (1955) edition he integrated the whole correction "by that young Flemish scholar." Later in our friendship he confided to me: "I know you will understand this: I have always wanted to become a monk and consecrate my whole life to *celebrating* the liturgy. But, by an odd accident, I became a Jesuit. So I can *work for* the liturgy, but with the heart of a monk. And," he added triumphantly, pointing heavenward, "up there we'll make up for the loss!" Father Jungmann worked valiantly for true reform of the liturgy during and after the Council; we will meet him again later.

---

[7] This was published in English as *The Mass of the Roman Rite: Its Origins and Development* (New York: Benziger, many eds.). — Ed.
[8] See my book *De oorsprong van het gewone der Mis* (Utrecht-Antwerp: Spectrum, 1955), published in German as *Der Ursprung der gleichbleibenden Teile der heiligen Messe* (Maria Laach: Verlag Ars liturgica, 1961). [This 48-page book, rendered "On the Origins of the Ordinary of the Mass" in English, generated significant interest among scholars; see note in Appendix B. — Ed.]

3. Germany

Several excellent centers of renewal developed in Germany, including the Archabbey of Beuron, famous for its monastic, theological, and artistic productivity. Maria Laach Abbey, however, was the undisputed center of the Liturgical Movement and a center of spiritual renewal for all of Western Europe. On an average Sunday eighty busloads of spiritual seekers visited Maria Laach, magnificent in both its physical setting and its worship. The liturgy was celebrated there more beautifully than one can imagine: faultless yet naturally reverent, amidst a dignified yet sincere brotherly love. How often I heard visitors say, "This is heaven on earth; it couldn't be more beautiful."

Yet the beauty of Maria Laach was not sterile but highly creative and communicative. It was spread mainly through two channels: conferences that brought together the leading theologians and liturgists of Western Europe, and many scholarly publications, including the magazine *Archiv für Liturgiewissenschaft*, which documented the Liturgical Movement. Those who assisted at these conferences took the fruits back to their homelands, and the publications formed the spiritual food for their work.

As was true in the Belgian abbeys, at Maria Laach the impact of charismatic leaders carried the movement forward. One example is the enormous influence of Abbot Ildefons Herwegen and a group of confreres who worked out his vision. Foremost among them was Dom Odo Casel, "father" of the famous *Mysterienlehre*, the forgotten Eastern theology of the active presence of the objective Mysteries in the very celebration, later fully accepted by Vatican II.[9] Having worked his whole life for the restoration of the Easter Vigil, Dom Casel collapsed and died in joy while intoning the *Exultet* during the Easter Vigil in 1948.

After some years, however, a group of German liturgists, mostly secular priests, came to feel that Maria Laach's orientation was not pastoral enough. Led by the activistic Monsignor Johannes Wagner, they loudly proclaimed that "liturgy is to be led by the priest; hence priests, not monks, should run the movement." With the support of some German bishops, they set up in the city of Trier the *Liturgisches Institut*, mainly a school for higher

---

[9] Father Boniface began his scholarly work with a baccalaureate thesis on this teaching of Dom Casel, which he discusses later in this book. — Ed.

liturgical teaching, which became a center of activity rather than prayer and contemplation.

From the outset, there was painful rivalry between Trier and Maria Laach, largely due to the bad character of the *Institut*'s leader. It was especially distressing that the *Institut* made public statements against Maria Laach, Father Pius Parsch, and others including me, because a beautiful characteristic of the renewal was its members' friendship, mutual support, and respect, which this jealousy ridiculed or destroyed. (Monsignor Wagner later became a major force behind the *Novus Ordo* and was perhaps the most outspoken modernist in the liturgical commission after the Council.) Yet I gladly state that, in spite of this fraternal infighting, the *Institut* did make an indispensable contribution to the preconciliar renewal, especially through its school, publications, and workshops.

The attitude of "priests versus monks" is a lopsided presentation, for the Liturgical Movement was carried by — and such a movement must always consist of — two main currents. The first was a popular current toward practical, active participation, bringing worship back to the people (hence the movement's strong claim for the vernacular). The second, which nourished and guided the first, was an undercurrent of scholarly work at universities, *plus* the holiness of monasteries where the renewal was carried out and lived.

4. France

Before World War II the movement's Franco-Belgian leaders and publications familiarized France with the theological and liturgical renewal.[10] During the war the German movement, especially the work of Maria Laach and French translations of the Germans' thorough studies, truly opened the door to the movement in France. The war was hardly over when Père Pie Duployé, OP, set up in Paris his *Centre de Pastorale Liturgique* which, along with Maria Laach and Klosterneuburg, soon became a leader of a new parochial and pastoral direction in the Liturgical Movement. In France, unlike other countries, the bishops as a whole backed and even directed the movement with wise *Directoires*

---

[10] A century earlier, the Monastery of Solesmes had inaugurated the monastic renewal and restoration of Gregorian chant under the leadership of Dom Prosper Guéranger, Gabriel Beyssac, and others.

for celebrations of the sacraments and the Mass. In France the Liturgical Movement ran parallel with the Theological Movement, inspired by great theologians such as Jean Daniélou, SJ, Henri de Lubac, SJ, and Yves Congar, OP, who directed the renewal toward a return to the sources. Almost all of these theologians, together with the Belgian and German theologians and liturgists, were enlisted by the Council.

5. England and Ireland

In England and Ireland the preconciliar movement was preceded by the theological and liturgical scholars of the nineteenth and early twentieth centuries, including Cardinal John Henry Newman, Edmund Bishop, Francis Brightman, and R. W. H. Frere, plus the Henry Bradshaw Society and the Alcuin Club, publishers of liturgical and historical sources. The renewal, however, was outspokenly pastoral, with great support for the vernacular. Its most active center was the Benedictine Abbey of Glenstal in Ireland; and Father Clifford Howell, SJ, was an indefatigable "propagandist" for the Liturgical Movement. But the movement never became generally popularized in these countries.

6. United States

Remarkably, the renewal movement in the United States arose not from England but from Germany, primarily because its founder, Father Virgil Michel, and later Father Michael Marx, belonged to the German-Swiss Benedictine Saint John's Abbey in Collegeville, Minnesota. Also instrumental was Damasus Winzen, a monk from Maria Laach (in Germany), who founded Mount Saviour Monastery in upstate New York. The movement spread rapidly in the United States after World War II; the magazine *Orate Fratres* (now called *Worship*), founded by Father Michel in 1926 and edited by Father Godfrey Diekmann after 1938, attracted numerous liturgists as collaborators.

This predominantly liturgical movement in the United States soon linked with other movements, such as Catholic Worker and Grailville, born from a multifaceted need for updated catechesis and renewed theology. Annual congresses brought together their spiritual leaders: scholars and pastors, contemplatives and parish priests, artists and musicians — holy churchmen and women eager to fully live the liturgy and spiritual riches of the Church.

One of the great liturgical workers in America was my good friend, Father Michael Mathis, CSC, who in 1947 founded the Summer School of Liturgy at Notre Dame University in Indiana, where I was privileged to teach from 1951 to 1967. This Summer School drew hundreds of students, mostly on the graduate level, from the entire English-speaking world. Its great attractions were not only the sharing with scholars from Europe but also participation in the fullness of liturgical life and initiation into the sources of true Church renewal.[11] For us professors it was an unforgettable privilege and joy to develop deep, lasting friendships with like-minded colleagues from many nations.

To list all the great men I met at these liturgical conferences would be impossible, but I mention these because of their influence upon the Council or my friendship with them, or both:[12] Monsignor Martin Hellriegel who was patriarch of the whole movement in the United States, the great French theologian Louis Bouyer, Hans Reinhold, Reynold Hillenbrand, Gerald Ellard, Frederick McManus, Johannes Hofinger, Godfrey Diekmann, Damasus Winzen, Gerard Sloyan, architect Maurice Lavanoux, historian Tracy Ellis, and many others from monasteries and seminaries. I must especially mention Belgian monk Dom Ermin Vitry, OSB, professor of Gregorian chant for the Precious Blood Sisters in O'Fallon, Missouri. An extremely faithful friend, he was one of the most remarkable people I have ever met. What a joy it would be to sit next to him in the heavenly choir!

The optimism, anticipation, and excitement of those days, all of which intensified upon Pope John's announcement of the Council, was well captured by Father Godfrey Diekmann:

> 'Twas sheer bliss to be alive. We felt we were at the cutting edge of a profound renewal in the theology and spirituality of the Church. We could *smell* spring in the air. . . . Moreover, we discovered kindred souls, thousands of

---

[11] For a delightful recounting by one of Father Boniface's students at Notre Dame, see Ignatius Roppolo, "A Summer that Made a Difference," in Andriy Chirovsky, ed., *Following the Star from the East: Essays in Honour of Archimandrite Boniface Luykx* (Ottawa: Metropolitan Andrey Sheptytsky Institute of Eastern Christian Studies, 1992).—Ed.

[12] Sister Kathleen Hughes's book *How Firm a Foundation: Voices of the Early Liturgical Movement* (Chicago: Liturgy Training Publications, 1989) is a precious account of this pioneering period.

them, at the annual National Liturgical Weeks begun in
1940. There we rejoiced and sang together with gusto—
and stretched our hopes....[13]

Amidst the joys, this Church-loving movement in America met
with much opposition, especially from some reactionary elements
of the established Church that opposed any kind of change, no
matter how valuable or needed. For instance, the apostolic delegates to the United States at that time were quite reactionary, and
they in turn generally appointed outspokenly reactionary bishops.
Other bishops who might have supported the movement were
pressured by the apostolic delegates into opposing it; I remember
well one delegate's painfully threatening letters to godly bishops.

This exaggerated ultramontane bias of some Roman (and
American) dignitaries partly explains the equally exaggerated anti-
Roman reaction of some postconciliar renewers and theologians.
An innocent joke of those days comes to mind, one inspired by
this situation: "Do you know the conditions for being appointed
a bishop in America? First, be of male gender; second, be of
legitimate birth; third, be educated in Rome. They can dispense
you from the first two, but not from the third."

It is almost impossible for Catholics today in the deeply dissenting American Church to comprehend that in those years the
hierarchy in the United States—the country that would soon
lead the world into the new Church problems—was then so
very closed in matters religious. The authorities who opposed
the movement certainly acted with the best of intentions, which
I respect, yet I still regret their actions. In fact, I am convinced
that the present situation of the Church in the United States
would not be so tragic if her leaders at that time had listened to
the Holy Spirit working in these events.

It bears repeating that the deep impulse of the whole renewal
movement, including in America, was *a striving for true piety and
a return to the sources of Christianity*—completely the opposite of
the destructive resentment of today's dissenters. To my great sorrow I must report that many of the renewal movement's leaders

[13] "Vatican II Fading Away?" in *Saint John's Magazine*, Advent 1992. Sister
Kathleen Hughes's *The Monk's Tale: A Biography of Godfrey Diekmann, O. S. B.*
(Collegeville, MN: Liturgical Press, 1991) provides additional details about
the preconciliar period in America. It also chronicles some of the postconciliar tensions, from a rather liberal perspective.

in both the United States and Europe, some of whom were my dear friends, gradually lost the movement's original vision and no longer promote its goals. *Mais où sont les neiges d'antan.* How have the old dreams vanished.

ARTICLE 3: *AGGIORNAMENTO*, ACTIVE PARTICIPATION, AND THE CLIMATE IN ROME

When Pope John XXIII announced the Council, he clearly expressed his mind and intention regarding its work. His primary theme was the updating (*aggiornamento*) or renewal of the Church — *an updating in continuity with, and in restoration of, the true Tradition and spirit of the Early Church.* The specific needs Pope John identified were (1) the adaptation of canon law and church discipline to the needs of the time, and (2) the relative updating of the liturgy, built upon a deepening of faith and love among all members of the Church. A further desire of Pope John was the restoration of unity among all Christians, especially between Catholics and the Eastern Churches: this explains in part the Council's openness to Eastern Christianity and its Churches' deep impact on the Council.

THE TRUE MEANING OF *AGGIORNAMENTO*

Pope John XXIII's emphasis on *aggiornamento* (updating) as the Council's main goal has been purposefully twisted or at least misunderstood ever since he announced the Council, largely because his focus on restoration and continuity with the Early Church has been suppressed or overlooked. Dissenters and many historians of the Council have erroneously taken the emphasis on "updating" to be license for unlimited criticism of all Church spirit and institutions. The more traditionally-minded, on the other side, have been upset by the very idea of "updating," as well as by the criticism and upheaval after the Council. In our day, positions for and against Vatican II have become so acutely opposed as to seem irreconcilable. Much of this misunderstanding and polarization has resulted from what *appeared* to be contradictions, in addition to a failure to understand Pope John's real intentions.

The primary instance of apparent contradiction that led to misunderstanding was *aggiornamento* itself: updating the Church, bringing her into step with her time. What did Pope John really mean by this? Can the Church as a whole, as the mystery of redemption by Christ, as his Mystical Body, be out of step with her time? Is the Church not always the great counter-cultural witness in every period of her history, preparing the Lord's return? Is she not the light in the darkness, the salt of the earth, the leaven in the dough? Will the world not always hate and destroy the true followers of Christ? Did not Christ solemnly proclaim that we, like him, are *in* the world, but not *of* this world?

Answers to these questions are in Christ's words recorded in John 16:8–28, 17:23, and especially John 15:18–25 and 17:9–16. We must carefully meditate upon all these statements about the real position of the Church in the world, and we must take them as our obligatory way of thinking.

Dare we also fully accept all the consequences of Saint Paul's strong teaching on the wisdom of the Cross as opposed to the wisdom of the world (1 Cor 1:18–2:16)? Or Saint John's radicalism about concupiscence as all that the world can give (1 Jn 2:15–17)? Or the serious injunction not to be conformed to this world but to be transformed by the renewing of our minds, that we may know what is perfect (Rom 12:2)?

The Church has the task of witness, of love and salvation, in the world but she does not belong to it. How then could her most solemn gathering, an Ecumenical Council, be called together in order to "update her with her time"? In answering this question we must clearly distinguish between two elements of the Church's heritage.

The first element is the everlasting core of the Church, that which belongs to divine Revelation and is the life-giving presence of the Holy Spirit in the Church, in the form of her liturgy, Holy Tradition, Holy Scripture, and the Fathers. In short, it is the heritage of Christ, the apostles, and the Early Church: the object of divine Revelation. All this divine heritage, as the core of the Church, is by definition unchangeable, as God himself is unchangeable.

Because this core of Revelation is meant to be lived out by man in his culture, the second element is that this divine heritage (Revelation) must be presented in a form man can digest in his own life. It must be incarnated into cultural patterns and time-bound expressions that are by definition adaptable to varying stages and shapes of culture. This is the task of theology, Christian art, music, language, adaptation of the liturgy, and adaptation of catechesis to the understanding of those catechized.

It is into this second element, and not the first, that the *aggiornamento* of Pope John enters. *Aggiornamento* does not, and cannot, apply to the first element. An understanding of this distinction is absolutely essential to a correct understanding of the Council. The external expression of divine Revelation and of the Church's core of Holy Tradition and worship must be adapted to the comprehension of those who practice it: divine Revelation must be translated into their lives. But at the same time Revelation's original content and divine consistency must be zealously preserved intact, just as Jesus and the apostles handed it down to the Church.

Hence, *aggiornamento means an essentially limited adaptation of the unchangeable, permanent core of divine Revelation to modern man's culture.* The core remains the essence and goal of the process; *aggiornamento* is only an adapted expression of the core. Pope John XXIII understood this well and intended it so, but not all those who publicized and implemented the Council wished to accept it.

A further element must be mentioned here. Upon his return to the Father, our Lord entrusted to the Church's leadership (the apostles and their successors) the task of the continued incarnation of his divine and redeeming heritage into the changing cultures. See John 20:21–23 and Luke 10:16: "He who hears you hears me." We will discuss later how this heritage or Revelation is not to be wrapped up and engrossed in these cultures but rather the very opposite: Revelation must penetrate the cultures.

This expanded but analogous incarnation process entrusted to the Church's unanimous hierarchy requires the Holy Spirit to be its divine Warrantor as an extension of the guarantee of the initial, historical core of Revelation (even though that core was closed by the last apostle's death). Therefore Pope John saw the Council as a "new Pentecost," and every session was opened with a solemn appeal to the Holy Spirit.

It was precisely at this critical point of the objective presence and guarantee of the Holy Spirit that the misunderstanding of the Council began. After the Council a rift began to grow between the true objective meaning of Revelation and a subjective, self-centered interpretation (*Hineininterpretierung*) of it. It is a fact that as soon as one lets go of the objective nature of Revelation, one falls into all kinds of subjective exaggerations. And so it happened after the Council: theologians and scholars infected with a spirit of *Hineininterpretierung* rather than the Holy Spirit began to abandon the objective Revelation in favor of their own subjective ideas.

In later chapters I will document and analyze many consequences of this subjectivism. Here I will briefly state but three:

1. The essence of the priesthood has been distorted, so that the priesthood of all believers has been unduly elevated while the ordained ministerial priesthood has been degraded to the point of being considered superfluous.

2. The true nature of liturgy has been perverted, resulting in social, man-centered, desacralized "services" in which awe and reverence for God's holiness have all but disappeared.

3. Even the most basic Christian teachings, part of Holy Tradition, such as the Resurrection, have been rejected by those calling themselves Catholic "Bible scholars" and theologians.

These distressing examples reveal that in the heart of the Church today there exists a decay precisely the opposite of the goals of both the Council and the preconciliar renewal movement. Why was it that Christians in the decades before the Council thronged to the European abbeys that were hearts of the renewal? Was it to be entertained by popular novelties or have their ears tickled by new teachings? No; they came to share in true worship, enlivened by a solid hunger and respect for the holy, for reverence, and for objective authenticity. By participating in reverent worship and embracing objective truth, the people were freed from their unredeemed subjectivism and the often-prosaic banality of daily life.

THE TRUE MEANING OF ACTIVE PARTICIPATION

In the first article of this chapter I noted that many of my friends in the renewal movement were appointed to the Council's Preparatory Commissions. Indeed, most of the movement's leaders eventually participated in the Council's various commissions, because the work of the Council was largely a continuation of that renewal.

A significant example of this similarity of purpose was the desire of both movement and Council to bring the faithful to *full and active participation in the Mass*. Precisely what is meant by "active participation"? Because this crucial term has been as misunderstood and abused as *aggiornamento*, let us briefly delve into its correct meaning.

As I noted above, Pope Pius X, in his solemn statement on sacred music, *Tra le sollecitudini* (1903), wrote that the purpose of active participation is *to draw life from the main source of the true Christian spirit, by means of personal and communal prayer.* He further said that "the first and most indispensable source of the true Christian spirit is the active participation of the faithful in the Sacred Mysteries of the Altar."

Pope Pius XII, in *Mediator Dei* (1947), distinguished two elements of this active participation, both of which are essential: (1) *interior* participation and (2) *exterior*, expressed participation. Generally speaking, in the context of the Mass, *interior participation is that inward assent and attitude in which the worshipper prayerfully unites himself with the priest in the holy Sacrifice (or prayers and readings).* Exterior participation refers to such liturgical actions as singing, speaking, kneeling, standing, and making the Sign of the Cross. It is not proper to pray out one's interior participation in opposition to external participation. *Nor is solely external participation, without an inward prayerful attitude, truly "active."* One type cannot exist without the other, for each fertilizes the other.

As the reader might guess, the grave error of our day is an overemphasis on exterior participation to the exclusion of the interior. This misunderstanding of the true nature of "active participation" has resulted in the virtual elimination of an attitude of prayer and reverence within Catholic worship, to the great detriment of the faithful.[14]

The Liturgical Movement before the Council greatly desired true, full, active participation for the people. It fully agreed with Pope Pius XI, who asked, "Is it not a shame to see our people [spiritually] starving around the altar covered with food?" The renewers said, "There are the people, and here are the documents of the popes; let us implement them for the nourishment of the faithful." The renewal movement made great progress in this regard; interior participation was especially strong. Yet, due to certain liturgical practices of the time, it was unable to fully implement the exterior, express, sacramental participation needed to balance the interior.

To understand this situation, we must look at the opposition to the renewal. This will ensure also that we do not have an overly-rosy picture of the preconciliar period.

---

[14] See a delightful little article on this subject by Msgr. Richard Schuler, president of the Church Music Association of America, in *Adoremus Bulletin*, October 1996, p. 3.

Opposition to the renewal movement and to the Council itself came mainly from two sources: people and practices. The first consisted of a small number of obstinate, yet sincere, conservatives— Vatican officials as well as local churchmen. We met some examples already and will meet more when we discuss the situation in Rome.

The second source consisted of inveterate customs and abuses, quite widespread in some circles, on the levels of life in the parishes, teaching in the seminaries, and runaway devotions. These included self-centered piety, disaffection for the Divine Office, impersonal catechesis, loss of the sense of belonging, soul-less administration, disappearance of the permanent diaconate, and a weakening of collegiality.

Although these forms of opposition moved separately and on different levels of authority, they nurtured and supported each other. Taken together, they easily gave an impression of representing the "real Church," making it difficult even for Pope John XXIII to break through this inertia to "sell his Council," as some disparagingly said.

We cannot discuss here each of these kinds of opposition. It is imperative, however, that we look at the state of the liturgy before Vatican II. Thus we will become more aware of the necessity of the reform offered by both the preconciliar movement and the Council.

THE LITURGY BEFORE THE COUNCIL

Because so much has changed since then, it is almost impossible for today's younger orthodox Catholics to imagine the situation of the liturgy in the first half of the twentieth century. In those years when the Tridentine Mass was the only rite used, the Mass, although beautiful, was not really part of the life of the clergy and people. The people *attended* the Mass and other liturgical services with great faithfulness, but they were unable to truly *participate* in them. One reason was, of course, that everything was in Latin, which most people did not know. But even those of us who knew Latin could barely understand it, for it was mumbled far away, at the altar, without any concern for active participation by the people, and without any contact with them.

In the "old countries" of Europe, on big feasts of the liturgical year everyone went to Mass, Vespers, and Compline, and sometimes two Masses. The services lasted for hours, and the people understood not a word. Yet they did not protest, for the concept of active participation was then unknown. Their participation in the feast was accomplished in other ways, especially by the custom of gathering after Mass for a solemn family meal. The New World countries, however, generally did not have this family custom.

In the earlier years the faithful prayed the Rosary during the Mass. Later there were prayer books. One of the main works of the Liturgical Movement was to produce and spread all kinds of literature, including Missals, to help the faithful understand the Mass and to bring the liturgy into the whole of the people's lives.[15] By the 1940s most Catholics in Europe and America had Missals and took them to church. During the Mass, while the priest was far away at the altar, they read their Missals, and they felt satisfied, because they knew what the priest was doing. But they did not *celebrate* the Mass; there was no exterior communication with the priest and with the mystery.

Added to this lack of communication were serious liturgical abuses. Here is an example from my early years.

In the 1920s through 1940s, it was almost impossible for communicants in parishes of the old countries to receive Holy Communion *during* the Communion of the Mass, as we do today. Instead, Holy Communion was distributed *only* at the Offertory. Every Sunday the priests consecrated a big ciborium full of Hosts for the whole week, as a big reservoir for a pious exercise — reception of Holy Communion — that stood totally apart from the Mass itself.[16] "Black Masses" (Requiem Masses for the deceased) were sung or unintelligibly rambled through every day of the year, a few big feasts excepted. In the monasteries, private Mass in the morning was the unbreakable custom; concelebration was nonexistent. Exceptions to this sad state of affairs were some renewal-minded Jesuit colleges, one of which I was privileged to attend.

---

[15] I was delighted to locate and purchase one such Missal (Dutch, hardbound, 291 pages) in which our author collaborated: Bonifaas Luykx, Placidus Bruylants, and Ambrosius Verheul, *Gebedsoproepen voor Aktieve Deelname aan de H. Mis* (Leuven: Liturgisch Centrum, Abdij Keizersberg, 1963). The authors represented Postel, Keizersberg, and Affligem Abbeys, respectively. The Imprimatur was granted by Cardinal J. E. van Roey, Archbishop of Mechelen, in October 1959, just months after Pope John XXIII announced the Council. — Ed.

[16] Saint Thomas Aquinas called such a situation *stultitia*: "It is stupidity to receive Holy Communion from gifts consecrated in the previous Mass."

My family (I was one of eleven children) was active in the Liturgical Movement that arose from the Belgian abbeys. We knew that the prevailing custom regarding Holy Communion was not correct. One time our family decided to begin going to Holy Communion at the Communion of the Mass rather than at the Offertory. Were we successful? No; the priest left us kneeling at the communion rail until the Offertory of the *next* Mass, for that was the only moment when Communion was given! If no Mass followed, we could not receive Holy Communion at all. All this, of course, caused great scandal in the parish, so we gave up; otherwise we'd be kneeling there till now!

Such a practice constituted a real destruction of the essence of the Eucharist, for the Eucharist is a sacrifice that is given as a meal to those who participate; such participation was generally impossible at that time. Although the preconciliar renewal was able to ameliorate the effects of some such abuses, the authoritative action of a Council was needed for a full and complete reform of the liturgy.

THE SITUATION IN ROME

The preconciliar renewal had both proponents and opponents in Rome. Among its active supporters were several Curia cardinals including Augustin Bea, and Pope Pius XII himself. The movement made its way into several schools in Rome, including the Gregoriana under professors Herman Schmidt, SJ, and Ferdinando Antonelli, OFM. Its influence was especially felt at *Ephemerides Liturgicae*, the leading liturgical magazine in Rome, and in the work of Josef Loew, CSsR, whom we will meet later. We owe to all these scholars several remarkable theological, biblical, and liturgical initiatives backed by Pope Pius XII: for instance, the restored Holy Week and the new Code of Rubrics.[17]

Opposition to the renewal from the Curia has been much exaggerated in the dissenters' accounts. But there was opposition, not from the popes and their immediate collaborators but from some subalterns. The greatest opponents were two religious who did not belong to the Curia but worked for it. Their zeal for orthodoxy was admirable, but at that time they were also paradigms of what

---

[17] The restoration of Holy Week was approved by Pope Pius XII's decree *Maxima Redemptionis* (1955), and the Code of Rubrics was promulgated by Pope John XXIII's motu proprio *Rubricarum instructum* (1960).

Rome should not be, tarnishing her image of "presiding in love," as Saint Ignatius of Antioch wrote. Perhaps they had misgivings due to imprudent actions by some renewers; I do not know and therefore do not want to judge their intentions.

An incident in which I was involved exemplifies the difference between the popes and some members of the Curia during this period. In 1956 one of the Roman canonists wrote a scholarly article about the pope as the only real and full bishop in the Church. He argued that the pope has ordinary jurisdiction over the whole Church, all other bishops being only his managers in this worldwide diocese.

A group of our movement's theologians met in Chevetogne to discuss the article, and I was asked to write against this manifest heresy. My article reached Pius XII, who sent me a solemn letter of approval, saying that my study about the primary task of the bishop as successor of the apostles was the correct teaching of the Church—not the canonist's.[18] This event was to have a positive impact on the Second Vatican Council's teaching on collegiality and the meaning of the bishop in the Church.

The main deficiency of the "secondary Rome," an overly-conservative element of the Curia, was that it seemed unaware that we were experiencing at that very moment the decisive end of the Baroque and even of the Constantinian Era, as I said in the Introduction.[19] The reason for this end of the Constantinian Era follows from a deeper anthropological principle, which I will explain briefly.

One of the characteristics of the cycles of culture is that, at certain creative conjunctures, the life-giving inner core bursts out into concentric waves of expression. These waves are the different forms of culture, outwardly expressing the core and inwardly nourishing it in return. These outward forms of culture gradually wear out, in the form of sclerotic institutions that start living for their own sakes, having lost vital contact with the life-giving inspiration of the core. Thus instead of being the core's expression and nourishment, the institutions become stagnant and choke it.

---

[18] My study was published under the title "De l'Évêque (On the Bishop)," *Les Questions liturgiques et paroissiales* 37 (1956): pp. 191–205.
[19] I explained this situation in my study, "Het einde van de Barok en de huidige Kerkvernieuwing (The End of the Baroque: Present-day Church Renewal)," *De Maand* (1960): pp. 602–9.

The three Popes Pius seem to have felt the existence of this sclerosis when they issued their strong statements about the three related subjects I noted before: (1) the starvation of the faithful around the richly-laden table of the liturgy, (2) the need for a return to the primary sources of the true Christian spirit through active participation in the liturgy, and (3) the need to return to the ancient sources in Bible study and theology.

It is clear that these concerns were behind Pius XII's work to update the rubrics. But the resulting Codex (1960) was outdated even before it was published, because the inner core of the liturgy as the celebration of Christ's Mysteries by an actively participating people demanded a deeper overhaul of the very theology of liturgy itself. The earlier restoration of the full observance of Holy Week has been retained until now precisely because it restored the very core of the liturgy: the Paschal mystery. We know that the Eucharist is the "primary source of Christian life." But if we cannot fully participate in it, because of prohibitive and unfamiliar language or individualistic rubrics, this source is blocked and its fruitfulness halved.

Once again I emphasize that the approach proposed by the Popes Pius and the preconciliar movement — and the Council — contains not the slightest suggestion of an *aggiornamento* (updating) of the *core* of divine Revelation and hence of its theology, its celebration in the liturgy, its teaching in catechesis, or its living-out in Christian life. The renewers knew that this core is by definition unchangeable and not subject to human alteration, because it comes from the eternal Way, Truth, and Life (Jn 14:6). They sought only the incarnation of this core into cultural patterns and expressions, such as language, music, and art, that are by definition adaptable to the variations of culture.

The renewers knew well, too, that in this incarnation or adaptation a *continuity* of fundamental cultural forms must be maintained, as must those forms' links with the permanent inner core. The Second Vatican Council's Constitution on the Sacred Liturgy therefore would insist that new forms must develop organically out of existing ones and that liturgical books in the vernacular must strictly follow their Latin models. We will develop these subjects more fully in the coming chapters.

For the sake of completeness I must add a final note. The members of the preconciliar movement were highly orthodox in their thinking, as I have explained before. But, as happens in every widespread movement of great depth, there were a few inevitable exaggerations, either in relativizing the permanent core of Revelation and overdoing its adaptability, or in emphasizing the gospel's permanent newness to the point of subjecting it to one's own creativity. Some theologians went overboard in specific areas while remaining orthodox on the whole. Rome was forced to censure some writings of such men—Yves Congar's *Vraie et fausse réforme dans l'Eglise* (True and False Reform in the Church) and the works of Teilhard de Chardin come to mind—without rejecting the entirety of their work. As is the case in any community, the Church must pay the price of growth, in understanding and possible misunderstanding. But I repeat that the vast majority of the renewers remained firmly within the proper boundaries set forth above.

* * *

By now the reader should have a good sense of the true situation in the Church before Vatican II. The preconciliar period was marked, on the one hand, by the renewal movement's work to restore the creative new spirit of the Early Church by a return to the Fathers and the heritage of Christ. On the other hand, it was constricted by a girdle of dead or antiquated practices that prevented that spirit from blossoming into adequate forms for the nourishment of the faithful. The reader should also understand clearly that Vatican II was not just a genial intuition of Pope John XXIII, but the confirmation of a profound renewal movement in the Western Church. The geniality of "good Pope John" and his repeated invoking of the Holy Spirit's special assistance were based precisely on his discernment of this renewal as the *kairos* (opportune moment) of the Holy Spirit in his Church. Therefore Pope John sweetly yet strongly acted accordingly, in spite of real opposition and resistance by some in the Vatican.[20]

---

[20] The new pretentious *History of Vatican II* (Giuseppe Alberigo and Joseph A. Komonchak, eds. [Maryknoll, NY: Orbis]), which is being promoted as the definitive history of the Council, has given a false, grossly exaggerated *negative* picture of Church leadership before the Council, citing one-sided sources. [Note: Volume I of this *History*, subtitled "Announcing and Preparing Vatican Council II," was published in 1996, and Abbot Boniface added this critique in early 1997.—Ed.] On the opposite side, Father Annibale Bugnini paints a very *positive* picture in his book, *The Reform of the Liturgy 1948–1975* (Collegeville, MN: Liturgical Press, 1990), which extols a sincere openness and collaboration among the Roman Curials before, during, and after the Council. The truth, in fact, probably lies in the middle of these two extremes.

The Council was thus truly the fruit of a Spirit-led growth in the Church, at a time when the Church was ripe for it. The renewal movement, reciprocally, needed the authoritative expression of a Council, for three reasons: first, to break through the opposition that kept the movement from maturing; second, to help the whole Church profit from the movement; and third, to purify the movement from some all-too-human imperfections.

That the Council was the organic expression of a widespread, active longing for renewal explains the enthusiasm with which Pope John's announcement of the Council was received, both within the Church and without. There were exceptions to this enthusiasm, especially in Rome, but they could not dim the general positive reception, which was truly a sign from heaven. Vatican II, although primarily a gathering of the Roman Catholic Church, thus truly became an "ecumenical council," with the spiritual participation of the whole Church in prayer, with active cooperation of the Eastern Churches (and even some western Protestant groups). The countless publications that accompanied and reported on the Council confirm the widespread interest in its work.

In his address to the Plenary Assembly of the Congregation for Divine Worship and Discipline of the Sacraments on May 3, 1996, Pope John Paul II summarized the importance of the preconciliar period as the immediate preparation of Vatican II. He pointed out that, in order to revive the true spirit of the liturgy, the Church had needed a profound renewal, as the preconciliar movement had proposed:

> It was obvious that the spirit of the liturgy could not be restored by means of a mere *reform*. A true, profound liturgical *renewal* was necessary....
>
> The Second Vatican Council responded to the expectations of the people of our time, calling believers, as I mentioned in the Apostolic Letter *Orientale Lumen*, "to show in word and deed today the immense riches that our Churches preserve in the coffers of their traditions".[21]

Let us now move on to the Council itself, beginning with the work of its Preparatory Commissions.

---

[21] For the complete text of Pope John Paul's address, see *Inside the Vatican*, June–July 1996, pp. 10–12.

CHAPTER 2

The Preparatory Commissions and Council Sessions

Glorify the LORD with me.
Together let us praise his name.
—Psalm 33/34:4

ARTICLE 1: THE PREPARATION BEGINS

The work of the Second Vatican Council began on the eve of Pentecost, May 17, 1959, with the institution of the general Antepreparatory Commission. This "pre-preparatory" commission, led by Cardinal Domenico Tardini as President and Pericle Felici as Secretary, consisted almost entirely of the prefects and secretaries of the Roman Congregations. Its main—and massive—task was to contact all the Ordinaries, Superiors General, and Catholic faculties of the Church throughout the world—2,700 in all—requesting that they promptly submit their suggestions and *vota* (proposals) for the Council's work.

Soon the *vota* began to arrive—an enormous number! Of course there were many duplications, but at least 2,000 different responses were submitted.[1] Pope John XXIII had given absolute and total freedom to the 2,700 consultees as to the content of their suggestions, and this proved a great blessing. The high quality and ecclesial dimension of the responses showed that giving this freedom—committing the matter to the guidance of the Holy Spirit from the very beginning—was the correct way to assure the charismatic and supernatural character of the Council.

The responses showed, too, that the Church had already long been craving a Council as *the* instrument for a deep and general

---

[1] The *Acta et Documenta* and *Acta Synodalia* of Vatican II—sixty-two volumes of primary documents—have been digitized by Matthew Hazell. The actual *vota*, by geographic region, are contained in Volume II of the Antepreparatory Period documents. See https://archive.org/details/second-vatican-council or https://www.newliturgicalmovement.org/2023/04/the-acta-of-second-vatican-council-now.html.—Ed.

reform. As Emile Guerry, the famous archbishop of Cambrai, France, wrote at that time:

> The Council is a privileged moment: the Church is now gathering in the person of her spiritual leaders, to make an honest examination of conscience, to "reorient" herself anew, to decide which of her human structures, methods and customs (of course, excluding her divine institution, given by Jesus Christ Himself and hence unchangeable) need purification, change and adaptation to the apostolate of our time.[2]

The next task was assigned to the Council's Central Preparatory Commission, composed of members of the Curia and numerous archbishops. This Commission sifted through all the responses, prioritized them, organized them according to key themes, and submitted them to Pope John.[3] The material was then assigned to ten specific Preparatory Commissions created by Pope John on June 5, 1960: Commissions for Theology, Bishops and the Government of Dioceses, Discipline of Clergy and Faithful, Religious, Sacraments, Sacred Liturgy, Studies and Seminaries, Oriental [Eastern Catholic] Churches, Missions, and Laity. Participants in the preparatory work were appointed to these specific commissions.

Each Preparatory Commission was led by a President (a cardinal or bishop) and Secretary (usually a specialist in that commission's field) and composed of Members and Consultors.[4] As a general rule, the bishops were Members and priests were Consultors, but these categories often overlapped. The Consultors (*viri rei periti*, "experts in the matter," usually just *periti*) provided scholarly information to the Members (*viri praeclari*, "outstanding men"), who by voting made the final decisions. In practice,

---

[2] The author did not provide a source for this quote and I was unable to find it. —Ed.
[3] See Mathijs Lamberigts and Claude Soetens, eds., *À la veille du Concile Vatican II: vota et réactions en Europe et dans le catholicisme oriental* (Leuven: Bibliotheek van de Faculteit der Godgeleerdheid, 1992).
[4] A list of the Preparatory Commissions' participants is included in the Vatican's Acta Apostolicae Sedis (AAS) 52 (1960), pp. 839–56, accessible at https://www.vatican.va/archive/aas/documents/AAS-52-1960-ocr.pdf. Participants in the Preparatory Commission for Liturgy, including Father Boniface Luykx, are listed at pp. 846–48. This entry in the AAS is not dated and the list is not complete: for example, some additional participants are named in entries dated in November 1960 at pp. 994–96. —Ed.

however, the distinction between the Consultors, who actually did the work, and Members, who listened and voted, was often abandoned. The pope gave full freedom to the commissions to operate as they wished.

The spirit of openness and collaboration between Consultors and Members, between priests and bishops, was generally quite good. This was a revelation to them all, showing that charism, wisdom, and skill are as important in running the Church as they are in society. Despite the inevitable clashes and antagonisms, this overall spirit of cooperation is one of my dearest remembrances of the Council.

The Preparatory Commissions consisted almost entirely of clergy. Several Catholic laymen, including the French author Jean Guitton, served as Advisors, which was a third category of participants, ranking below the Consultors. A number of Orthodox and Protestants (for instance, from the Taizé community in France) also had advisory roles. But very few laymen or women were involved. In retrospect one might regret especially that they were not included in those commissions whose work affected their lives. At that time, however, the subject of lay participation was brought up only rarely, and then mostly in the secular press. The laity in the Western countries was not then fully "emancipated"; if Vatican II had taken place in the 1990s, many laymen and women certainly would have assisted.

The Preparatory Commission for Liturgy, in which I participated, consisted of twenty-three Members and thirty-five Consultors: twelve bishops, twenty-seven secular priests, and nineteen religious priests. Fourteen were from Rome and Italy, the rest from all parts of the world, especially the old Christian countries of Europe. My bishop, Joseph Malula of Kinshasa, was a Member, and I was a Consultor; later I will describe our work together.

Cardinal Gaetano Cicognani, Prefect of the Sacred Congregation of Rites, was our President. An especially kind man, he often honestly said to us, "You know, I am no liturgist; you have to do the work. And with the grace of the Holy Spirit, we will decide for the good of the Church." Father Annibale Bugnini, editor of the journal *Ephemerides Liturgicae* and professor at several Roman institutes, was our Secretary. He was a very capable man and an adroit politician with a special charism for bringing people together and bridging oppositions. As we will see in the pages to come, he exerted a strong (and often problematic) influence in the liturgical developments during and after the Council.

The spirit of friendly collaboration in our Preparatory Commission for Liturgy was truly outstanding; this is, no doubt, the primary reason why our commission did such excellent work. Most of us Members and Consultors had known each other for years, as participants in the Liturgical Movement. As such we had met regularly at international meetings, published in the same magazines, experienced the same enthusiasms and setbacks, and learned how to work well together.

Clergy who lived in Rome naturally exerted a special impact upon the Council's decision-making processes. The popes of the Council watched carefully to ensure that the universal character of the Council be maintained and that it not become a "Roman affair." But the influence of those in Rome remained strong—and not always positive. For instance, both before and during the Council there was, mostly in the Curia and behind closed doors, a strong resistance to "that Council of John." Its four most active leaders were two cardinals, one of whom was President of the Preparatory Commission for Theology, and the two religious who worked for the Curia as mentioned in the previous chapter, one of whom was a Consultor to the Central Preparatory Commission. These men worked relentlessly to prevent the Council, and then to sabotage it once it had begun. In retrospect, to their credit, I think they may have opposed the Council because they foresaw problems on the horizon.

Well I remember one incident regarding their opposition. It was a wonderful spring day in 1961, as wonderful as can happen only in Rome. I had just flown from Africa to Rome for the second session of the Preparatory Commission for Liturgy. As was my habit, I had arrived a day early to make prayerful visits to the four old major basilicas.

Coming out of Saint Peter's at noon, I crossed the square and entered the Via della Conciliazione to the right. Suddenly, from the left, near the stately building of the Oriental Congregation, someone called my name. I turned and saw a group waving at me to join them: Herman Schmidt of the Gregoriana in Rome, Godfrey Diekmann of Saint John's Abbey in Minnesota, and Frederick McManus and Johannes Quasten of the Catholic University of America. What a joy to meet old friends again!

After the usual greetings they were eager to tell me the big news. The day before, the cardinals and theologians mentioned above had hatched a plan to impeach Pope John XXIII for heresy, so the Council could be cancelled. We all laughed at such a show of bravado. Of course nothing came of the plan. But this incident shows the atmosphere in some Roman circles before the Council.

We did not doubt that these men had good intentions. Yet, sadly, their actions dampened some of the beautiful enthusiasm Pope John had been able to arouse in the Church.[5] In fact, the much-reported turbulence in the Council's first session in 1962 was caused largely by some of these insiders who gained official positions, even as presidents of the daily sessions (called "congregations"), in order to disrupt the Council. In the next article I will recount how Cardinal Suenens, the famous Archbishop of Mechelen-Brussels (Belgium), intervened in this situation.

The first session of the Preparatory Commissions took place in Rome, November 11–14, 1960. This was not a working session but a time for each commission to set up *sub*commissions and assign their work, and for participants to become better acquainted with each other.

Within the Preparatory Commission for Liturgy, thirteen subcommissions were established to deal with various aspects of the liturgy. (One of these was *De lingua Latina*; later I will relate why it was eventually dissolved.) Due to my previous publications in their areas, I was assigned to two subcommissions: Sacraments and Sacramentals, and Adaptation. As the only practicing anthropologist in our whole commission, from the beginning I, along with Bishop Joseph Malula, also handled the topics of religious anthropology and spirituality, for which no specific subcommissions were established.

The work given to us at the first session of all the Preparatory Commissions was the texts of the *vota* (proposals) received from the world's episcopates, superiors, and Catholic faculties. Our urgent task was to comment upon the *vota* and to digest both their contents and our comments into individual *fiches* (cards). We returned these *fiches* to our Preparatory Commission Members

---

[5] Further details about such incidents in the decisive days immediately preceding the Council are recorded in Hughes, *The Monk's Tale*, especially pp. 183–220. The secular press in Europe also paid some attention to these internal tensions.

in Rome, who compiled them and passed them along to the Central Commission of the Council. From this early stage until the presentation of our schemata (draft documents), the work of each Preparatory Commission was reviewed and approved (or rejected) by this Central Commission.

I must relate here an incident during the first meeting of the Preparatory Commission for Liturgy. At one point, Secretary Bugnini called into his office some Members and Consultors, including me, to give us a friendly yet serious "warning" about our activity in the Liturgical Movement. What he said was quite erroneous. So when he had finished, I told him so and got up to leave, saying, "I did not ask for this appointment to the Council; I am ready to leave right now." He was surprised, and said in a conciliatory manner, "I did not mean to lecture you. You are very precious to us, and we are very glad you are willing to work with us." From that moment of reconciliation we became good friends — until we became estranged after the Council, for reasons to be recounted later.

During the next year and a half, our Preparatory Commission for Liturgy worked diligently to prepare the schema (draft) of what would become the Constitution on the Sacred Liturgy (CSL). Three times we all gathered in Rome for intense working sessions of about two weeks' duration. During these sessions, we were often given draft texts and asked to bring back our corrected and approved versions of them the very next day. We were also given assignments to be completed at home before the next session. One example is CSL's Articles 37–40, on liturgical adaptation: Bishop Malula and I were given a rough draft of this section and asked to work on it at home in Africa. When we next returned to Rome our work was discussed, revised, and eventually approved by the Preparatory Commission for Liturgy.

Each section of the future CSL was approved internally in this manner until the schema was completed in early 1962. It was then delivered to the Central Preparatory Commission for preliminary approval before its presentation to the Council Fathers. Ours was one of only two schemata that were ready by the opening of the Council in October 1962 (the other was on the media). This was in part because our commission had a great advantage: most of the problems with which we had to deal had already been formulated, and often solved, at the congresses of the Liturgical Movement before and after World War II. We will see later in this chapter that the timely completion of our schema was to have a great impact on other Council documents.

ARTICLE 2: PEOPLE AND ENCOUNTERS

The first session of the Preparatory Commissions ended with a glorious inauguration in Saint Peter's Basilica on November 14, 1960. Quite remarkably, Pope John XXIII celebrated this event with a solemn Byzantine Liturgy. I was sitting in an excellent balcony vista point, opposite the balcony of the *schola*, and enjoyed every minute of it. The anti-curial press reported this liturgy as a big show of curial pomp, at which the "Council people" were crowded far away against the organ in the apse but I, an eyewitness, know that not to be the case.

Pope John was to later treat us to another Byzantine Liturgy in the Sistine Chapel, for the episcopal ordination of Archbishop Acacius Coussa of the Syrian Melkite Church. During that liturgy I stood right next to the altar and saw Pope John's great piety and enjoyment of the celebration. Because I was able to sing much of the liturgy, our eyes often met. His gaze was fatherly and prayerful, and his smile was holy.

During both the preparatory period and the Council itself, as mentioned above, I was the faithful companion and *peritus* of Bishop Joseph Malula, auxiliary of Archbishop Félix Scalais of Kinshasa, the capital of the Belgian Congo (Zaire). We flew to Rome together on several occasions before and during the Council. Our travel was made quite comfortable by the flawless Belgian protocol that treated us both as VIPs. When our plane arrived in Rome at night, the pilot regularly flew low over the city before landing, to show his VIPs the fantastic illumination of the Eternal City.

Once in Rome, I received further VIP treatment. My Abbot General, Monsignor Hubert Noots of the Premonstratensians (Norbertines), had his driver on alert to pick me up from the airport at any time, day or night, and take me to his Procure at the Viale Giotto, where I was treated with great deference because of my work for the Council. If I remember well, only three Norbertines had been appointed to the Preparatory Commissions, including the Abbot General himself. He regularly invited his friends from the Curia (mostly non-Italian cardinals) to enrich my knowledge of the milieu in which I was working. One of these was Cardinal Eugène Tisserant, Dean of the Sacred College of Cardinals, whom I came to respect highly for his enormous personal experience of Churches all over the world, his love for the Eastern Churches, and his absolute honesty and allergy to compromise.

Between the sessions, at home in Africa, Bishop Malula and I worked diligently on the documents entrusted to us. My work was twofold. I had my own scholarly work as an appointed Consultor. In addition, as the Bishop's secretary (*peritus*), I prepared all his reports, answers to questionnaires, and other papers for the Preparatory Commission and for the entire four years of the Council. My schedule was already extremely full, as I was both an assistant to the bishops and Professor of Liturgy at the Jesuits' Lovanium University in Kinshasa. But working for the Council was a great honor, and I gave myself wholeheartedly to the task.

AFRICA AND ADAPTATION

To help the reader understand the work Bishop Malula and I did for the Council, I must digress to describe our work for the Church in Africa.

Bishop Malula and I became close friends shortly after my arrival in Africa in January 1960, in large part due to our common interest in Christian music and worship. My main work in Africa—as Director of the Center for Pastoral Liturgy for Central Africa—was the inculturation of Christianity into the African soul and society. My other main labor in Africa, undertaken at the urging of some missionaries and with the blessing of my superiors, was the founding of a truly African monastery in the Eastern Christian tradition, but that is a story for another book.[6]

The starting point of my work with Bishop Malula was African liturgical music. When I arrived in Africa, its Church had little more music than a few unfortunate Western songs with African words. During my eleven years there, I notated and published more than 200 truly African liturgical compositions covering all facets of the liturgy, most of them written by Bishop Malula. (He would often urgently call me over to notate a musical inspiration before he forgot it!) These songs are still sung throughout Central Africa, especially where Lingala is spoken.[7] The *Messe Zaïroise* (the

---

[6] Details of these years are contained in *Following the Star from the East*, pp. 17–20; a few are included in Appendix A, About the Author. —Ed.

[7] Published as *Nzembo na Mindule* (Kinshasa: Centre Pastorale, 1965). One

Zaire Rite of the Mass) now celebrated in several countries was also the result of our collaboration.[8]

Bishop Malula was a man of many gifts beyond musical composition. He was a perfect dancer in the dignified African liturgical style, a skilled conductor of immense churches filled to the brim, a stirring preacher who could bring the whole assembly to lively dialogue. The relationships of this loving pastor were permeated with noble kindness and self-sacrifice. In short, he was a true African and a perfect bishop after the model of the great Church Fathers. During his entire formation, Bishop Malula never left African soil: he was the fruit of the Scheut Fathers' excellent training and the fatherly assistance of his predecessor, Archbishop Scalais. I believe he had never spent any length of time in Rome until his work for the Council. Official acknowledgment of Bishop Malula's greatness came when in 1964 he was appointed the Archbishop of Kinshasa. He died from cancer in 1989, and his funeral was a triumphal celebration as of the greatest chief Africa has ever had, in all the beauty of African ancestral ritual. I consider it an honor to have worked closely with such a beautiful man of God.

Back in Rome, due to my background in worship and anthropology, and my work with adaptation in Africa, I was involved with the Preparatory Commission for the Missions, though not officially appointed to it — for adaptation was, and still is, one of the main problems in the missions. This commission's president, Tarcisius van Valenberg, a retired Capuchin bishop from Indonesia, was a most gentle and capable man, and we quickly became friends. He asked me to attend his commission's meetings as often as possible because I was the only actual missionary in the whole group — a deficiency he strongly regretted.

What exactly is adaptation? *Adaptation is the limited modification of the liturgy to the genius of the peoples.* The universal Church expected the Council to grapple with this subject and provide much-needed guidance. As I wrestled with the work assigned to

---

of these songs is "The High-Feast of Christmas," with short verses narrating the Christmas story and the oft-repeated refrain: *Tosepela, toyembela: Eyenga ya Mbotama!* (Let us rejoice, let us sing: the High-Feast of Christmas!). We sang this in the refectory at Mount Tabor Monastery every Christmas, in Lingala, with Abbot Boniface intoning the verses. — Ed.

[8] The Zaire Rite, under the title *Roman Missal for the Dioceses of Zaire,* was formally approved by Rome in 1988 for celebration in what is now the Democratic Republic of the Congo. — Ed.

me, I gradually came to this crucial realization: *adaptation, with all its ramifications, was one of the seminal and fundamental problems of the entire Council.* (Adaptation is often, but less aptly, called inculturation; we will return to this topic.) As over the years I have looked back upon the postconciliar evolution, my intuition has been confirmed: the problem of adaptation came more and more to the forefront as time progressed.

THE VERNACULAR

In between sessions of the Preparatory Commissions, while most of us were working on our assigned tasks in our home countries, certain men in Rome were also busy, but in a less honest way. Some of them, thinking they had the field free for their obscure operations, went so far as to change the conclusions reached by the Members at previous sessions. In our Preparatory Commission for Liturgy, we strongly suspected a certain monsignor of doctoring texts that the Commission had approved but were not to his liking. In the aftermath, some have seen this underhanded activity as part of a general plot, but it has not been proven.

The vernacular was one area of much maneuvering during this period. Use of the vernacular had become, for sound theological reasons, a symbol of the preconciliar renewal movement, and most in our Preparatory Commission were convinced of its necessity. (We were *not* promoting a wholesale abandonment of Latin; we will discuss this later.) Yet, strange as it may seem today when the vernacular in worship has become self-evident, some wanted to prevent its use at almost any cost. The influential Monsignor Higini Anglés of the Music Institute and his allies represented this element in our Preparatory Commission. Early in our work, every time the subject of the vernacular arose, they interrupted and alleged that higher authorities had forbidden discussion of the topic.

After several such interruptions, the indomitable Bishop Malula could restrain himself no longer. He became so angry that he slammed his fist on the table and asked, in his beautifully broken Latin: "*Quae est haec auctoritas? Quis in Ecclesia prohibebit episcopos loqui de hac re?*" ("Who is this authority? Who in the Church will forbid bishops from speaking about this topic?") Then he stood up and said in a loud voice, "I will go to the pope and ask him."

And indeed he did. The next morning, Bishop Malula triumphantly entered the meeting, waving a handwritten message from the pope. Then he told us the story. John XXIII had received him cordially and had strongly assured him that any prohibition regarding the vernacular did not come from him at all; rather the opposite. "Wait a bit," the pope had said. He reached for a used envelope in his wastebasket and wrote on it these decisive words: "It is my decision that all topics should be freely discussed — also the vernacular." This message on the used envelope was Bishop Malula's banner of triumph; it was a message which proved critical for both the Council and the Church.

As a result of this incident, it was decided that the problem of language should be treated within each particular topic — Eucharist, Office, Sacraments — where it truly belonged. Thus the *De lingua Latina* subcommission was dissolved.[9]

This was the only solution to be found. Many commission Members could not imagine that the "unchangeable" Roman liturgy could become "contaminated" by any vernacular, therefore use of the vernacular had to be pleaded in each particular application. Perhaps if today's abusers of the vernacular knew how dearly its original advocates paid to obtain just a precious bit of its use, they would cease corrupting it.

Another incident may be of interest. Our commission was discussing liturgical music and we were at an impasse: the same group was stubbornly denying the possibility of liturgical music in the vernacular. I was at my wits' end, as was Bishop Malula, so to give a counterproof I suddenly asked the bishop to sing for us the "Our Father" he had composed. He was extremely embarrassed: imagine, an African bishop singing in front of these white critics who might ridicule him to death!

But finally he closed his eyes and solemnly began to sing. A holy shiver ran through everyone present. When he had finished, a full minute of enthusiastic applause filled the room. This event inaugurated our first victory in favor of the vernacular. The dear Bishop Malula never forgave me for having "used" him in what was dearest to him — his African prayer, especially the Our Father — even though it was used as a means to win our cause. But it was worth it!

---

[9] Yves Chiron, in *Annibale Bugnini: Reformer of the Liturgy*, p. 71, describes these discussions and includes this insight provided at the time by our author: "Another consultor, the Belgian Norbertine Fr Boniface Luykx, pointed out that 'in mission territories a broader use of the vulgar tongue must be granted. Most often the Latin language is perceived as a vestige of colonialism.'"

Another of our commission's successful efforts for the vernacular pertained to the Divine Office. For many years, in the United States and other countries of new Christianity where Latin was little known, the obligation for priests to pray the breviary in Latin had become an almost unbearable burden, and disaffection toward the Latin breviary was becoming ever more evident. Some solution *had* to be found, and the Preparatory Commission for Liturgy was the proper forum.

A long study of mine on the Divine Office, appearing in the Festschrift for Dom Lambert Beauduin, had prepared the ground somewhat for this discussion.[10] My thesis, supported by history and theology, was that the Divine Office is essentially not merely a priestly work but a work of the whole Church, including the laity. Because of the urgency of the situation, the Members of our commission took the significant step of accepting the *principle* of the vernacular in the Divine Office, for pastoral reasons and as far as it was necessary. But Latin was, fortunately, to remain the "mother language" of the Roman liturgy, not only in principle and for historical reasons, but also in practice. One significant reason for retaining Latin was to preserve the beautiful Gregorian chant, one of the most precious inheritances of the Western Church.

The reader should not gather from these stories of conflicts that the atmosphere in our Preparatory Commission for Liturgy was always tense. Often it was rather the opposite. I remember, for instance, the intervention of Monsignor Joaquim Nabuco from Brazil about the pontificals (episcopal attire) for abbots. He was dead set against them, and used as one of his arguments — in Latin, of course — the old saying, "Pontificals are in an abbot as genitals in a mule."[11] We all burst out laughing. But the saying did not help the good monsignor's cause: the abbots kept their pontificals, and for good reasons.

THE INFLUENCE OF THE CHRISTIAN EAST

While in Rome for our working sessions, I made numerous visits valuable to my work for both Africa and the Council. Archbishop Pietro Sigismondi, Secretary of the Congregation for the Propagation of the Faith, was quite interested in our work in

[10] "Prière de l'Église et participation active," *In Memoriam Dom Lambert Beauduin* (Chevetogne: J. Duculot, 1960).
[11] A clue for the city-bred reader: mules are not capable of reproducing!

Africa. So too was the kind and pious Cardinal Gregorio Agagi-
anian, Prefect of the same congregation. But he, highly Western-
ized as he was, could not understand why we had replaced the
wonderful Latin songs (he sang *Adoro te devote* for me as proof)
with African music (and he drummed on his desk).

Perhaps my most significant visits in Rome involved the Eastern
Christian Churches, which exerted a great influence on the Council. As I mentioned above, when Pope John XXIII announced the
Council, he spoke of a theme particularly dear to him: the unity
of the Churches. He especially desired unity between Catholics
and the Eastern Orthodox, with whom he had lived for several
years in Bulgaria and with whom he maintained many friendships.
I stress this because it partly explains the openness of the Council to Eastern Christianity, and why the Eastern Churches had
a much deeper impact upon the Council than one would have
expected, given their small number of representatives.

This brings us to a highly significant but lesser-known fact:
both in the Preparatory Commission for Liturgy and on the Council floor,
when the Council Fathers came to an impasse, very often the problems were
finally resolved according to the Eastern Christian tradition. The reason
for this, quite apart from the influence of Pope John, is that *the*
Eastern apostolic Churches have always preserved and remained close to
the gospel and the early Christian heritage. Use of the vernacular, the
Divine Office as the work of the faithful, the permanent diaconate,
concelebration, and especially the "revolutionary rediscovery"
of collegiality on all the levels of governance were accepted at
the example of the Eastern Churches, who had preserved the
Apostolic Tradition in these matters.[12]

This sensitivity to the Apostolic East also explains the pre-
eminence of some Council documents, such as *Lumen Gentium*
on the Church, *Orientalium Ecclesiarum* on the Eastern Churches,
and *Unitatis Redintegratio* on the union of the Churches. The latter
two documents did not receive the attention they truly deserve,
in this activistic postconciliar Western world.[13] But postconciliar

---

[12] See my survey on the genesis and content of the Council's decrees on
Ecumenism and the Eastern Churches: "An Eastern View," *Communio*
(1990): pp. 211–13.
[13] See my extensive study on these documents: "Thirty Years Later: Reflections on Vatican II's *Unitatis Redintegratio* and *Orientalium Ecclesiarum*,"
Logos 34 (1993): 364–87.

neglect of the ecumenical thrust of Vatican II does not undo the substantial impact the Eastern Churches had upon the preconciliar renewal, the Preparatory Commissions, and the Council itself—where the awareness of Eastern theology, though in the background, was very much present.

My most profitable contacts in Rome included Patriarch Maximos IV Saïgh of the Melkites, a Byzantine Church of the Near East. Among his group were Archbishop Néophytos Edelby, my old friend from Chevetogne Abbey, and Archbishop Joseph Tawil, the future Ordinary of the Melkites in the United States. These men, who were largely responsible for the Eastern Catholic Churches' significant contributions to the Council, brought a message for the whole Church, because the Eastern Church still *lived* the blessing that the West was struggling painfully to apply. (In Chapter 6 I will expand upon this subject.) My other main contact was Maxim Hermaniuk, CSsR, the Ukrainian Metropolitan of Winnipeg (Canada), who had been a classmate of mine at the University of Louvain. A gifted theologian, he was one of the principal architects of the restored theology of collegiality.

Many of the Eastern Churches were at that time in slavery behind the Iron Curtain. An event during the Council made the Council Fathers acutely aware of this: by the concerted action of Pope John XXIII and President John F. Kennedy, Josyf Slipyj, the Major Archbishop of the Ukrainian Catholic Church, was liberated after eighteen years in Russian prisons. News of Archbishop Slipyj's release brought great joy to not only the Ukrainian colony in Rome but all at the Council.[14]

While in Rome I also regularly took Bishop Malula to the Ethiopian College in Vatican City. He thoroughly enjoyed this bastion of African Christian culture, especially their Eastern style of liturgy, and became convinced that the Ethiopian liturgy should be adopted by all of Africa. How often he reproached me—or rather the Western Church I represented—saying, "Why did you not give us *this* [Ethiopian] liturgy? Why did you impose upon us a [Western] way of celebrating that will always remain foreign to us?" In fact, I was already working hard to make the Ethiopian

---

[14] Archbishop Slipyj, later named a cardinal, was a spiritual giant and one of the greatest men of this century. See Jaroslav Pelikan's excellent book, *Confessor Between East and West: A Portrait of Ukrainian Cardinal Josyf Slipyj* (Grand Rapids: Eerdmans, 1990).

liturgical and monastic heritage known wherever I could. But Bishop Malula and I felt like "voices crying in the wilderness." Will his cry on behalf of the African people ever be heard?[15]

THE AFRICAN CELIBACY ISSUE

After the exhausting sessions of the Preparatory Commission for Liturgy all morning and afternoon, I frequently stayed behind in a small workroom of the Vatican Library in the evening. Often I could hear someone talking in the room next door. One day the door opened and a small-built Redemptorist came into the room. He introduced himself as Father Josef Loew, and I responded that I knew of him from his excellent articles. In his wonderful Austrian accent, he said he knew me, too, and he humbly invited me for a talk. Thus began a remarkable friendship, one of my life's great treasures for which I am grateful to the Lord.

Father Loew, who was a personal friend and advisor to Pope John, soon invited me to join in a plan that could have revolutionized the Church. "Since you live in Africa and know the situation of the clergy there, could you help the pope in realizing a plan of his regarding Africa?" he asked. I responded that, of course, I would be honored. Father Loew explained that Pope John was deeply concerned about priestly celibacy and how the Holy Spirit wanted to lead the Church in this area. The pope had heard that in Africa a great number of priests are married, privately and tribally, because, as (spiritual) chiefs, they have that right. "So," Pope John had proposed, "why not recognize such marriage of priests that is protected and guaranteed by strict tribal morality? Thus Africa could become the testing ground for the permission of married clergy for the West, just as the Churches of the East have kept the custom of married clergy from ages past." Pope John had asked Father Loew for help, and upon hearing that an African missionary was in Rome, he had instructed Father Loew to contact me.

Father Loew and I decided to quickly consult as many African bishops, priests, and missionaries as we could, as a private

---

[15] In a 1990 interview, Father Boniface stated categorically: "The Western form of Christianity is not for the Third World, and can certainly not serve as the matrix for a truly incarnated Christianity there. Only the Eastern Church—Byzantine or Ethiopian—can fulfill that role of a matrix for a true African Christianity. Otherwise we'll have there the same tragedy as in South America, where undigested 'paganism' goes on living underneath an imposed Christian veneer." *Following the Star from the East*, p. 19.—Ed.

initiative. The result was a surprise. Almost all the missionaries in Africa, who had both long experience of the concrete life of the African clergy and deep insight into the African soul and anthropology, agreed that married clergy could be a solution. The Africans themselves, on the contrary, said that if the African clergy could be married, this would become a cause for discrimination against them, because the white priests would not be married. They were concerned also that marriage could cause the priests to become enmeshed in the palavers of the village or tribe.

Finally, I gathered together Bishop Malula and all the African priests and seminarians studying in Rome. The discussion proceeded painfully until finally the bishop said, "Aren't you a white man? Well, what you whites are able to do, why not we Africans? Stop this discussion; I do not want to hear of it anymore!"

The next day I took the news to Father Loew, who communicated it to Pope John. The pope was deeply disappointed. But perhaps he was being unrealistic at that point. Bishop Malula certainly knew his African priests and people better than anyone else did—and why should they be made a test case for the West? Moreover, a married priesthood can survive and excel only if thoroughly supported by a Christian culture and long tradition, as is the case in the Eastern Churches. Therefore, contrary to appearances, Bishop Malula perhaps prevented a decision for which the Church was not ready.

Some days after my work with Father Loew, Pope John presided over one of our commission's sessions, and each of us was personally presented to him. He took my little hand in his large fatherly hands and gazed at me for a long time as if to look through me. "So you are from Africa. A very hard life, isn't it?" he asked, as one who knew and understood.

CARDINAL SUENENS'S ROLE

As a Belgian, I was especially interested to see what role Cardinal Leo Jozef Suenens, the Archbishop of Mechelen-Brussels and my former Vice-Rector at Louvain, would play in the Council. It proved to be a highly significant one.

Before the Council began, Cardinal Suenens was aware that, as I noted above, a handful of "old guard" Roman Curials was quite upset with the course the Council threatened to take. He knew, too, that they had maneuvered to have three of their friends—men who were determined that the Council should fail—appointed as presidents of the daily sessions.

In the spring of 1962, after the Council Fathers had been presented with several unsatisfactory drafts of *Instrumenta Laboris* (working instruments) for the Council, Cardinal Suenens realized that the Council was in a tragic situation. So, together with Cardinals Josef Frings of Cologne and Giacomo Lercaro of Bologna, he went to Pope John and proposed an alternative agenda for the Council. The pope responded by appointing *these* three cardinals as alternate presidents of the daily sessions.

More important was that Pope John accepted Cardinal Suenens's proposed agenda. His proposal was that the Council's focus be two-pronged: internal reform of the Church on one hand, and engagement with the modern world on the other. This proved a decisive turning point for all the further deliberations of the Council.

Cardinal Suenens remained one of the Council's main leaders and, working with Pope John XXIII and later Pope Paul VI and John Paul II, became one of the fathers of the late twentieth-century Western Church. A couple of times the postconciliar euphoria brought him into conflict with his friend Paul VI: that delicate Italian diplomat was not always comfortable with Suenens's Flemish frankness.

I must note that by the mid-1970s Cardinal Suenens began to worry about the direction some reformers and dissenters were taking—a direction contrary to the one he had spearheaded at the Council—especially in matters pertaining to the liturgy and the religious life. He is reported to have said, "I have written the book *The Nun in the World*. But now what are we going to do to get the world out of the nun?" This disappointment brought him to clarify his position. "Conservatives are confusing Tradition and traditions," he said, "and progressives are confusing liberty and anarchy. Between the extremes, we must try to keep the middle of the road." He certainly always tried to stay in the middle, until his death in 1996.

Among all these people and encounters—people great and small, encounters intimate and official—my friendships with Americans provided some of my best memories. Our commission's most productive meetings were held at the lunch table, often in a small restaurant in the Via del Rinascimento behind the colonnade to Saint Peter's. The food was good, cheap, and plentiful, three conditions important for a clerical wallet. I must gratefully acknowledge that my American friends always footed the bill for this poor African missionary. These lunches with friends were the perfect intermezzo between the morning and afternoon sessions, as occasions not only to talk things over but also to refresh our minds between heavy meetings full of intense discussions.[16]

ARTICLE 3: ON THE COUNCIL FLOOR

The Council itself opened on October 11, 1962, with a grandiose Mass attended by representatives of eighty-six governments and international bodies. The Council Fathers, resplendent in their ecclesiastical attire, were there: the bishops, archbishops, and cardinals of the Roman Catholic Church, plus a lesser number of hierarchs of the Eastern Churches united with Rome — about 2,500 in all. It was a time of great joy, optimism, and anticipation of what the Holy Spirit had in store for his Church.

As I said above, our Preparatory Commission for Liturgy was the first commission to finish its schema, its draft. Thus the document on the liturgy was the first to be considered by the Council Fathers, and, as such, it set the pace and determined the spirit of the Council. But for this accomplishment our commission paid a heavy price at the hands of the reactionaries. These men had not joined in the rejoicing over the Council's opening; in fact, they were still plotting to derail it. They especially considered our schema too advanced and thus were determined that it should not be considered.

Hardly had the Council begun when they ventured their coup: they maneuvered the situation to the extent that our whole Preparatory Commission for Liturgy — Members, Consultors, and Secretary Bugnini — was deposed and officially reproached on the Council floor.[17] Before this coup, and indeed before the Council began, our Commission's president, Cardinal Cicognani, had died, in February 1962. He was succeeded by Cardinal Arcadio Larraona of the Congregation for Religious, a man filled with goodwill but unskilled in matters liturgical. During this upheaval,

---

[16] For more descriptions of such encounters see Robert Blair Kaiser, *Pope, Council and World: The Story of Vatican II* (New York: Macmillan, 1963); and Alberic Stacpoole, *Vatican II Revisited: By Those Who Were There* (Minneapolis: Winston, 1986).

[17] These events are detailed in Yves Chiron, *Annibale Bugnini: Reformer of the Liturgy*, pp. 83–86. — Ed.

we greatly missed the gentle Cicognani, who certainly would have been our great defender.

Because of the press of my duties in Africa, I was not in Rome when this coup occurred. On my next trip, I visited the ignominiously-deposed Secretary Bugnini to comfort him. He was still so affected by the events that he wept on my shoulder! As a token of appreciation for my concern, he gave me a bottle of excellent liqueur his brother had just brewed, to feed our friendship.

But our commission's work was not in vain, for our schema on the liturgy continued to be discussed on the Council floor. Nor was our work over. After we were deposed, Pope John XXIII himself quickly intervened and, in his subtle, fatherly care, he reappointed us all, during the first session of the Council, as Members (a higher level than Consultors) of his newly-established Consilium for the Authentic Interpretation of the Constitution on Liturgy.[18] This Consilium of Pope John functioned during the Council (1962–63) and preceded Paul VI's Consilium established in January 1964. Our work for Pope John's Consilium actually proved more important than continuing in the tracks of the Preparatory Commission: as the Council Fathers discussed our schema on the liturgy in the 1962 and 1963 sessions, we were at their service, responding to questions and reworking the text.

The Council Fathers began discussion of our schema during the fourth daily session ("congregation"), on October 22, 1962.[19] Over the next three weeks, each of the eight chapters of the schema was debated in detail on the Council floor. On November 14, 1962, the Council Fathers voted by an overwhelming majority to approve the liturgy schema in principle. But this was not the final vote: our Consilium was directed to work on various proposed amendments, which would then be submitted to the Fathers for further voting.

---

[18] The Secretary of this Consilium, more commonly called the Conciliar Liturgical Commission or Conciliar Commission for Liturgy, was Father Ferdinando Antonelli, OFM, then in leadership at the Congregation of Rites. Father Bugnini was appointed as a peritus to this commission but had no leadership role. — Ed.

[19] Father Boniface provided very few details in this section. Consequently, in 1997 I drafted these three paragraphs based on other sources he had provided to me. He never responded to approve them before our work together ended, so they should be taken as such. — Ed.

Some of these amendments were completed and accepted by the Fathers before the Council's first session closed on December 8, 1962. The majority of them, however, were worked out and accepted, one by one, during the Council's second session. In each vote, our work received a huge majority of votes *placet* (in favor).

Finally, on November 22, 1963, near the end of the Council's second session, the Council Fathers voted on the entire schema on the liturgy. They approved our work almost unanimously — the official vote was 2,147 to 4 — and on December 4, 1963, *Sacrosanctum Concilium*, the Constitution on the Sacred Liturgy, was promulgated.

In the meantime, on June 3, 1963, before the Council's second session, the eighty-one-year-old Pope John XXIII went to his eternal reward. His successor, Pope Paul VI, elected on June 21, decided to continue the Council "in the same spirit." My personal impression, however, was that the initial optimism Pope John had kindled in the Church was somewhat dampened by the rather businesslike approach of his successor. Yet perhaps this approach was necessary for the good results of such an enormous enterprise as an Ecumenical Council.

ARTICLE 4: CONTEXT OF THE CONSTITUTION ON THE SACRED LITURGY

Before focusing on the Constitution on the Sacred Liturgy (CSL) itself, as we will in the next article, we must place it in context among the sixteen primary Council documents. In this book I will assume that the reader is somewhat familiar with these documents; here is a rapid overview.[20]

The main purpose of the Council was dual: to update the Church into modern times, but to do so by preserving her essential constitution as given in her divine heritage: the primitive sources, namely Scripture and Holy Tradition. The Council documents reflect both aspects of this dual purpose.

The first aspect, updating the Church, is covered in the Pastoral Constitution on the Church in the Modern World (*Gaudium et*

---

[20] In this manuscript Abbot Boniface quoted solely from Austin P. Flannery, ed., *Vatican Council II: The Conciliar and Post Conciliar Documents* (Grand Rapids: Eerdmans, 1987); he also recommended *The Sixteen Documents of Vatican II* (Boston: Daughters of St. Paul, 1967). Translations in multiple languages may be found on the Vatican's website: https://www.vatican.va/archive/hist_councils/ii_vatican_council/index.htm. — Ed.

Spes); the Decrees on the Up-to-Date Renewal of Consecrated Life (*Perfectae Caritatis*), the Church's Missionary Activity (*Ad Gentes Divinitus*), the Apostolate of Lay People (*Apostolicam Actuositatem*), and the Means of Social Communication (*Inter Mirifica*); and the Declarations on the Relation of the Church to Non-Christian Religions (*Nostra Aetate*) and on Religious Liberty (*Dignitatis Humanae*).

The second aspect, preserving the Church's heritage, is addressed in the Dogmatic Constitution on the Church (*Lumen Gentium*), the Dogmatic Constitution on Divine Revelation (*Dei Verbum*), and the Decrees on the Catholic Eastern Churches (*Orientalium Ecclesiarum*) and Ecumenism (*Unitatis Redintegratio*).

In between these two groups lie other documents dealing with both aspects: the Constitution on the Sacred Liturgy (*Sacrosanctum Concilium*); the Decrees on the Pastoral Office of Bishops in the Church (*Christus Dominus*), the Training of Priests (*Optatam Totius*), and the Ministry and Life of Priests (*Presbyterorum Ordinis*); and the Declaration on Christian Education (*Gravissimum Educationis*).

ASSESSING THE COUNCIL DOCUMENTS

Now let us consider the documents according to another assessment, with which I agree. It is offered by two Orthodox theologians, Nikita Struve and Olivier Clément, professors at the Sorbonne and Saint Serge, both in Paris. These Eastern scholars suggest that the Council documents fall into two groups, each inspired by a quite different spirit: first, the "God-centered" or vertical group; and second, the "man-centered" or horizontal group.

Struve and Clément list among the "God-centered" documents the Constitution on the Sacred Liturgy, the Decrees on Ecumenism and on the Eastern Catholic Churches, and especially *Lumen Gentium*. All four of these have a common inspiration, and, significantly, an *organic continuity with the preconciliar renewal movement*. This common inspiration grew organically out of Holy Tradition and its sources as they live on in the Church — the Church Christ founded and will sustain until his return in glory.

These God-centered documents, then, must be interpreted in reference to both their preconciliar sources and each other. For example, the theology behind the Constitution on the Sacred Liturgy is also the theology of *Lumen Gentium* (or vice versa), with which the preconciliar movement was pregnant as well. In addition, because of its implicit reference to the Eastern Churches, CSL could propose a revolutionary (at that time) yet vital return to Holy Tradition in areas such as the permanent diaconate, concelebration, the vernacular, and *lectio continua* in the Eucharist and Divine Office.[21]

The "man-centered" documents, according to the Orthodox theologians, include *Gaudium et Spes*, the Constitution on the Church in the Modern World, and *Dignitatis Humanae*, the Declaration on Religious Liberty. These two are especially dear to many Americans, because of the active role played in them by several U. S. bishops and John Courtney Murray, SJ, and also because these documents reflect the necessity for a serious adaptation of the Church in America to the demands of this changing world.

Struve and Clément, however, are of quite the opposite opinion. As do many Orthodox, they accept almost the whole Council *except* these two documents. They object to some one-sided exaggerations in their presentation, and to the excessive importance given to the man-centered vision in the work of salvation, which inevitably leads to aberrations. They object also to another aspect of these man-centered documents: their *ambiguous wording*. As language is a crucial element in the interpretation, or misinterpretation, of the Council documents, let us explore this subject before proceeding.

The language used in the sixteen primary Council documents varies significantly between the two groups mentioned above. In general, the God-centered documents, especially CSL, were written in clear, unambiguous, theological and practical language. Many of the man-centered documents, on the other hand, contain unclear, ambiguous, ostentatious wording that made them ripe for misinterpretation, as we shall see. Some readers may question this assessment, so I will make a further distinction for clarity's sake.

There is a crucial difference between the *ambiguous* language purposefully used in some man-centered Council documents and the *general* language that is appropriate to all documents of an Ecumenical Council. Documents of a Council must be general, for their role is to state *principles* which are later to be worked out in practical *applications*. But their wording should be clear and unambiguous, and thus not subject to misinterpretation.

---

[21] An interview with Cardinal Franz König in *30 Days*, no. 10, 1992, pp. 12–17, explains very well the atmosphere wherein these documents originated. See also my study, "An Eastern View," in *Communio*, referenced above.

The Constitution on the Sacred Liturgy gives a good example of this distinction. We who wrote CSL, and the bishops who approved it, purposefully stated its principles in general terms, for we knew that it was the role of the ordinary magisterium (the bishops in union with Rome) to take care of the details. For instance, we stated in CSL that the vernacular could be used where and when needed; and we made a provision that later on the bishops — the leaders of the Church — would make these determinations. So we stated a general principle, but we did so in clear wording.

A deceptiveness regarding language lies at the heart of the postconciliar decay. It is said that when Edward Schillebeeckx was asked why many of the Council documents were written in ambiguous language, he answered to this effect: "That was done deliberately so that after the Council we, the theologians of the Council, could interpret them in the manner we saw fit."[22] Whether or not Schillebeeckx said these words, such a basically dishonest attitude perhaps lies at the heart of the postconciliar appeal to the "spirit of Vatican II" — *an appeal that is in essence invoked not in favor of the Council and its documents but rather against them.*

LITURGY: THE HEART OF THE COUNCIL

Having discussed CSL's place in the God-centered Council documents, we now must consider its importance. The reader may feel that I am focusing the entire problem of *aggiornamento* (updating) one-sidedly on the need to renew the liturgy. I do not think the *whole* problem lies in the liturgy; however, I do think, and have explained in many conferences and courses, that the liturgy stands at the heart of both the Council and the Church's present problems.

The Constitution on the Sacred Liturgy itself, speaking for the overwhelming majority of the Council Fathers (recall that the vote was 2,147 to 4), solemnly proclaimed the primacy of the liturgy. In its Article 10, a theological text of utmost importance, CSL states that, in spite of the importance of the "active" apostolate of the Church, the liturgy is both "the summit toward which the activity of the Church is directed" and "the fount from which

---

[22] The author originally added here, but without providing a source, that the following is an exact quote of Schillebeeckx made in an unguarded moment in an interview: "We have used ambiguous terms during the Council and we know how we shall interpret them afterwards." — Ed.

all her power flows." I encourage the reader to bear this text constantly in mind:[23]

> 10. Nevertheless the liturgy is the summit toward which the activity of the Church is directed; it is also the fount from which all her power flows. For the goal of apostolic endeavor is that all who are made sons of God by faith and baptism should come together to praise God in the midst of his Church, to take part in the Sacrifice and to eat the Lord's Supper. The liturgy, in its turn, moves the faithful filled with "the paschal sacraments" to be "one in holiness"; it prays that "they hold fast in their lives to what they have grasped by their faith." The renewal in the Eucharist of the covenant between the Lord and man draws the faithful and sets them aflame with Christ's insistent love. From the liturgy, therefore, and especially from the Eucharist, grace is poured forth upon us as from a fountain, and the sanctification of men in Christ and the glorification of God to which all other activities of the Church are directed, as toward their end, are achieved with maximum effectiveness.

The Constitution on the Sacred Liturgy, the first document the Council approved, implicitly contained the entire further work of the Council. This was true not only in theory but also in actuality: after two full sessions of the Council, CSL was still the only document approved by the Council Fathers; the other fifteen were waiting at the door.

First to profit from CSL was *Lumen Gentium*. Father Godfrey Diekmann reports that CSL twice saved *Lumen Gentium* from insignificance (once through the intervention of Cardinal Wojtyła, the future Pope John Paul II),[24] making CSL second in importance only to *Lumen Gentium*. As Archbishop Martin said in his intervention at the Council in the name of the French hierarchy, "The ecclesiology contained in the document on the liturgy [CSL] . . . has been sanctioned in the name of the whole Church."

The Constitution on the Sacred Liturgy saved not only the new ecclesiology of Vatican II but also the liturgy's vital links with all of church life. I will give some examples.

---

[23] In the original manuscript the author consistently referred to the numbered sections of CSL as "canons," but I have used the word "articles" because the official English translation of CSL identifies them as such. — Ed.

[24] Godfrey Diekmann, "Vatican II Fading Away?"

Good liturgy is impossible without good catechesis. Both liturgy and catechesis must be rooted in correct theology and in the Church's sources in Scripture and the Fathers; only thus will liturgy become the primary source and norm of the true Christian spirit, as Pope Pius X wrote in *Tra le sollecitudini*. Good liturgy requires full participation by the faithful, which requires at least some vernacular. Further, once its primary source and norm are regained, liturgy must be freed from later disfiguring accretions (such as those I recounted from my youth); the ritual expression of the re-enacted Mysteries of Christ must be strong and real. Concelebration, Communion under both species, and the permanent diaconate, which aid in this, are therefore necessary. The clergy must be well-trained in love for these sources and norms in the Early Church. The bishops, as successors of the apostles, must be the primary ministers and instructors of the liturgy, yet bound to Holy Tradition. Above all, the atmosphere of the celebration of the liturgy must be holy, clothed in awe and reverence, as befits the redeeming Presence of God's Majesty and our answer to this Presence.

So we see that the whole of Vatican II is present in CSL. The renewal of the liturgy and its extension into all of life, which was the primary objective of the preconciliar renewal movement, was strenuously and effectively taken up by the Council.

ARTICLE 5: AN INSIDER'S LOOK: WHAT CSL'S AUTHORS REALLY MEANT

I was privileged to be an active collaborator in the Constitution on the Sacred Liturgy from its inception to its completion. Because CSL and the changes it occasioned have so deeply affected the Western Church, and because CSL has been so often misconstrued, I offer here some "inside" insights, to help the reader attain a proper understanding of it. I will attempt to present this material objectively, not reading my own wishes or views into it, as some do in order to justify postconciliar abuses.

During this analysis, we must bear always in mind both CSL's membership in the God-centered group of documents and its affinity to the other documents in that group: *Lumen Gentium* and the Decrees on Ecumenism and on the Eastern Catholic Churches. In addition, in order to understand CSL aright, we must distinguish between its strong *theological undergirding* and its *practical application* to the need for reform in the various areas of liturgical life, the latter being the work assigned to the postconciliar subcommissions.

THEOLOGICAL UNDERGIRDING

The Constitution on the Sacred Liturgy contains 130 articles of one or more paragraphs each, grouped into seven chapters, as follows:

I. General Principles for the Restoration and Promotion of the Sacred Liturgy (Articles 1–46)
II. The Most Sacred Mystery of the Eucharist (Articles 47–58)
III. The Other Sacraments and the Sacramentals (Articles 59–82)
IV. The Divine Office (Articles 83–101)
V. The Liturgical Year (Articles 102–111)
VI. Sacred Music (Articles 112–121)
VII. Sacred Art and Sacred Furnishings (Articles 122–130)

The theological principles underlying all of CSL are rich, vast, and of utmost importance. One cannot properly *understand* CSL without grasping these principles. Further, it is impossible properly to *apply* or to *implement* CSL without a correct grasp of them. Unfortunately, these theological principles have been generally neglected after the Council in both practice and teaching, for two main reasons: (1) the postconciliar subcommissions appointed to implement CSL gave more attention to practical recipes and elaborations than to CSL's theological basis, and (2) CSL was promulgated in an unprepared and even heedless, irresponsible way, without due regard for these principles. This neglect continues into the present because most seminaries and departments of theology fail to teach this theological foundation. Even in some essentially good liturgical courses and studies, these vital principles are divorced from their practical applications, and vice versa.

Let us look at these principles, not in their entirety, for that would take a whole volume, but only some key points and examples. I hope that from this starting point the reader will delve into the entire Constitution. It behooves all Catholics to read it, for they will find it a treasure of knowledge and insight, and a source of clarity in this time of liturgical confusion.

We will begin at the beginning. The first and second articles of CSL deal with the nature of the sacred liturgy and its importance in the life of the Church. Setting the tonality of the whole Constitution, they comprise a profound and beautiful text, almost like a word from the Church Fathers, built totally upon Scripture and expressing the constant teaching of Holy Tradition, from the Early Church to the present. Here are CSL's Articles 1 and 2:

> 1. The sacred Council [*Sacrosanctum Concilium*] has set out to impart an ever-increasing vigor to the Christian life of the faithful; to adapt more closely to the needs of our age those institutions which are subject to change; to foster whatever can promote union among all who believe in Christ; to strengthen whatever can help to call all mankind into the Church's fold. Accordingly it sees particularly cogent reasons for undertaking the reform and promotion of the liturgy.
>
> 2. For it is the liturgy through which, especially in the divine sacrifice of the Eucharist, "the work of our redemption is accomplished," and it is through the liturgy, especially, that the faithful are enabled to express in their lives and manifest to others the mystery of Christ and the real nature of the true Church. The Church is essentially both human and divine, visible but endowed with invisible realities, zealous in action and dedicated to contemplation, present in the world, but as a pilgrim, so constituted that in her the human is directed toward and subordinated to the divine, the visible to the invisible, action to contemplation, and this present world to that city yet to come, the object of our quest. The liturgy daily builds up those who are in the Church, making of them a holy temple of the Lord, a dwelling-place for God in the Spirit, to the mature measure of the fullness of Christ. At the same time it marvelously increases their power to preach Christ and thus show forth the Church, a sign lifted up among the nations, to those who are outside, a sign under which the scattered children of God may be gathered together until there is one fold and one shepherd.

Some basic principles follow from this seminal text.

1. The Realism of the Mystery in the Celebration

The principle of *the realism of the mystery of salvation in the actual celebration*, the *Mysterienlehre*, is one of the foundations of all liturgical theology. Because it is little understood in current Western culture, some explanation is necessary.[25]

Let us first describe what this principle is *not*. Among the non-apostolic Christian Churches of our day, worship services and even liturgical celebrations are considered merely occasions in which we *horizontally* evoke a historical event before our eyes and minds as the object of subjective meditation and prayer. For instance, according to this view, on Palm Sunday we remember Christ's triumphant entry into Jerusalem; on Easter we rejoice over his Resurrection; on Pentecost we reflect upon the coming of the Holy Spirit in the Upper Room. In such thinking, these events in the life of Christ and his Church are merely historical events — powerfully important events, to be sure, but ones that took place nearly 2,000 years ago and are not present realities. Such a view, which limits the actions of Christ to their historical time frame, is woefully inadequate and robs the liturgy of the spiritual power intended by God to spill over from the liturgy into our daily lives.

What, then, is truly meant by "the realism of the mystery of salvation in the actual celebration"? This principle correctly and fully states that the events of salvation history really and truly take place here and now as they are liturgically celebrated. Through the liturgy, we re-enact, so to speak, in the bosom of the Church, the mystery of redemption in its creative totality, spanning from God's first revelation in Old Testament times until Christ's return in glory.

How can this be true? *The events of salvation history are not static or confined to a past date in time, for Jesus, around whom these Mysteries center, is not bound by time.* The events of Jesus's life on earth, though the actions of a man, are also actions of the timeless God. Thus we, here and now, can join in the Great Deeds of salvation he performed while he walked on earth. For whenever we celebrate the liturgy, we step outside of time, joining with the angels in heaven in their ceaseless praise of the great "I AM."

Thus, when we celebrate the liturgy of Palm Sunday, we

---

[25] In 1997, attempting to help the reader more fully understand this topic, I copied parts of the next few paragraphs from the author's other writings I had typed. — Ed.

ourselves truly join with the crowd that waves palms and shouts "Hosanna to the Son of David! Blessed is he who comes in the name of the Lord!" In the Paschal liturgy, we ourselves go to the tomb and discover that "He is not here; he is risen, as he said." And in the liturgy of Pentecost, the Holy Spirit descends anew upon us who have prayerfully awaited the promise of the Father. These actions occur in proportion to our reverence and faith in the realism of God's creative power in the celebrated Mysteries. Thus the sanctification of man and of the world coincides with the glorification of God, within the celebration itself.

This reality has always been lived in the Eastern Churches as the wellspring of their strong liturgical life; it is expressed in all their liturgical books, including in the use of the word "today":

> Today Christ enters the Holy City. . . .
>
> Today the Master of Creation stands before Pilate. . . .
>
> Today He who hung the earth upon the waters is hung upon the Cross. . . .[26]

In the West, this concept, the *Mysterienlehre*, was forgotten over the centuries but "rediscovered" by Dom Odo Casel and Maria Laach Abbey in the decades before the Council, as I mentioned in Chapter 1. It was adopted by Pope Pius XII as one of the supports of his momentous encyclical of 1947, *Mediator Dei*. Thenceforth the understanding of the realism of the Mysteries in the celebration became the thriving inspiration of the whole preconciliar Liturgical Movement. By the time of Vatican II it had become the basis of liturgical life in the West as well as the East. CSL appropriated it and thus organically continued the work of the Liturgical Movement. Indeed, this was one of the Council's main inheritances from the preconciliar renewal.

This first principle set forth in CSL's Article 2, the realism of the Mysteries in the celebration, justified and necessitated five significant applications, all of which we will discuss later in detail: (a) the restoration of sacramental realism, (b) active participation in the celebration, (c) use of the vernacular, (d) cultural adaptation of the liturgy, and (e) the priority of the vertical dimension

---

[26] These verses are taken from *The Lenten Triodion* (London: Faber and Faber, 1978), the Orthodox Lenten service book beautifully translated from the original Greek by Mother Mary and Archimandrite Kallistos Ware. — Ed.

in all true Christian worship. The deeper foundation of this subject is a basic principle of religious anthropology (but that was
beyond the scope of CSL): the function of the ritual expression
of the objective mystery is to transfer the mystery as intimately
as possible into the subjective experience of the participants,
without losing anything of its realism or objective power, or of
the Presence of God's Spirit at work in the celebration.

2. Scripture as the Scenario for Re-enacting Christ's Historical Events of Salvation

A second principle follows from CSL's Article 2: *Holy Scripture
is the scenario for re-enacting Christ's historical events of salvation here
and now.* This principle requires that a richer selection of Bible
readings be set up (see CSL 51), not only for the edification of the
faithful, but also and primarily for its "translation into redeeming
mystery." Hence we see the sacramental importance of a clear
proclamation of Holy Scripture.

Three points follow: (a) most significantly, the sacramental link
between the Word proclaimed and the mystery celebrated; (b)
the importance of the homily as an initiation into the mystery
of that particular celebration — and for the faithful's instruction
into that celebration; and (c) the necessity of restoring the central
meaning of the Paschal mystery and the Paschal dimension of
Sunday, as well as the importance of the restored Holy Triduum,
accomplished by Pope Pius XII in 1955.

3. Restoration of the Church as the Mystery of Redemption

A third principle of CSL is *the restoration of the Church as the
mystery of redemption in Christ and his Holy Spirit*, in the spirit of
Lumen Gentium. Five crucial theological ramifications follow:

a. *The importance of the Real Presence of Christ and his Spirit as the
basis of all efficacy of the liturgy* (as explained in the first principle
of this section), and hence also as the basis of the realism and
necessity of the ordained ministry. This causality of the minister
as the carrier of Jesus's redeeming presence (stressed by both CSL
and *Optatam Totius* on priestly formation) is very real — in virtue
of his ordination, *not* in virtue of delegation by the community
(as some dissenters erroneously teach).

b. *The tremendous realism of the Eucharistic Presence,* which is
repeatedly stressed as the *analogon principale* of all Presence of

Christ in Christian worship and community: Christ in his state of sacrifice and of glory, thus "materializing" these Mysteries in their very celebration.

c. *The necessity of restoring priestly ministry to its fulness* by restoring the permanent diaconate as one of the three essential degrees of the priesthood—the diaconate, the presbyterate, and the episcopate (deacon, priest, and bishop)—according to the Early Church's tradition.[27]

d. *The sacramental importance of the actively participating community.* This principle was always in the mind of the Council, throughout CSL and the later decrees. From it arose the restoration of the Divine Office as the ecclesial prayer of all segments of the people of God. From this principle also arose the priority of community celebration (concelebration) above private celebration (private Mass, private Office, private baptism), without doing away with the latter absolutely. As Father Godfrey Diekmann has rightly brought to the fore,[28] Vatican II has restored full citizenship to the laity, whose main act is their active participation in worship. I hasten to add that this does *not* mean that parish liturgy committees are to "make up Masses": such a practice is a manifest deviation from a well-intentioned endeavor to involve the laity.

e. *The need to restore awareness of the bishop as successor of the witnesses of the Resurrection and hence as the primary presider over the celebration of the Mysteries that stem from the Resurrection.* The bishop's primary role is that of *leitourgos* (celebrant) and dispenser of grace: he is the primary celebrant of his diocese, not primarily an administrator.

The Constitution on the Sacred Liturgy also restores the vertical dimension of this celebration principle in Article 50: "Other parts [of the liturgical rites] . . . are to be restored to the vigor they had *in the days of the holy Fathers . . .*" [emphasis added]. Here it is (1) the vigor of Christian worship of the Early and Patristic Church and (2) the *integrity of Holy Tradition* that are given as the model of all work toward liturgical restoration.

Hence the authority of, and real recourse to, Holy Tradition take precedence over all other considerations, including adaptation, as Pope John XXIII strongly reminded us in his opening address to the Council—even though the wording of worship

---

[27] The permanent diaconate was re-established by Pope Paul VI's Apostolic Letter *Sacrum Diaconatus Ordinem* issued *motu proprio* on June 18, 1967.—Ed.

[28] Diekmann, "Vatican II Fading Away?"

may be adapted. This overarching priority of Holy Tradition is affirmed in Article 23:

> Finally, there must be no innovations unless the good of the Church genuinely and certainly requires them, and care must be taken that any new forms adopted should in some way grow organically from forms already existing.

If all the above criteria are fulfilled, the resulting holy liturgy will indeed be *the fount and summit of all Christian life*, as in CSL 10. Such liturgy is the vital force for making all the people of God of one mind and one heart, centered around the Paschal mystery re-enacted in the Eucharist, so that the sanctification of man and the glorification of God always coincide in the celebration of the Church's worship.

APPLICATIONS: CSL'S ARTICLES 37–40

We now move on to the key problem of *adapting the liturgy to the genius and traditions of the peoples*, the subject matter of CSL's Articles 37–40 and the primary applications of CSL's theological principles.

The first draft of CSL on the subject of liturgical adaptation was drawn up by Fathers Godfrey Diekmann and Johannes Quasten. However, the actual work from which these articles arose was especially entrusted to Bishop Malula and me, because adaptation of worship to the genius of the peoples was our specialty. As these articles and hence the principal teaching of the Council on adaptation were our work—and our main contribution to Vatican II—I humbly presume to know the mind of the Council in these matters.

Here follows the text of these articles:

> 37. Even in the liturgy the Church does not wish to impose a rigid uniformity in matters which do not involve the faith or the good of the whole community. Rather does she respect and foster the qualities and talents of the various races and nations. Anything in these people's way of life which is not indissolubly bound up with superstition and error she studies with sympathy, and, if possible, preserves intact. She sometimes even admits such things into the liturgy itself, provided they harmonize with its true and authentic spirit.

38. Provided that the substantial unity of the Roman rite is preserved, provision shall be made, when revising the liturgical books, for legitimate variations and adaptations to different groups, regions and peoples, especially in mission countries. This should be borne in mind when drawing up the rites and determining rubrics.

39. Within the limits set by the typical editions [*libri typi*] of the liturgical books it shall be for the competent territorial ecclesiastical authority mentioned in Article 22:2 [bishops' conferences], to specify adaptations, especially as regards the administration of the sacraments, sacramentals, processions, liturgical language, sacred music and the arts, according, however, to the fundamental norms laid down in this Constitution.

40. In some places and circumstances, however, an even more radical adaptation of the liturgy is needed, and this entails greater difficulties. For this reason:

(1) The competent territorial ecclesiastical authority mentioned in Article 22:2 must in this matter carefully and prudently consider which elements from the traditions and cultures of individual peoples might appropriately be admitted into divine worship. Adaptations which are considered useful or necessary should then be submitted to the Holy See, by whose consent they may be introduced.

(2) To ensure that adaptations may be made with all the circumspection necessary, the Apostolic See will grant power to this same territorial ecclesiastical authority to permit and to direct, as the case requires, the necessary preliminary experiments over a determined period of time among certain groups suitable for the purpose.

(3) Because liturgical laws usually involve special difficulties with respect to adaptation, especially in mission lands, men who are experts in the matters in question must be employed to formulate them.

Now we come to my insider's insights, which I hope will help clarify a multitude of common misconceptions.

1. The rules of Articles 37–40 apply only to the Western Church or Patriarchate — that is, to the Latin (Roman) liturgy — and not to the Eastern Churches. Further, within the Western Patriarchate, these rules apply especially to the countries of established

Christianity, such as in Europe and North America, with the exception of Article 40, as I will explain shortly. I use the term "Western Patriarchate" purposely, because CSL envisions in the West a situation parallel to that of the Byzantine Patriarchates of the East. In the Byzantine Patriarchates (Churches headed by Patriarchs), small, accidental differences exist in the worship of the various Churches—for instance, the liturgies in the Melkite Church and the Slavic Churches are slightly different from each other—but they all faithfully follow the Byzantine Rite. Worship in each Byzantine Church is clearly discernible as being of the Byzantine Rite, though it is expressed somewhat differently in each Church. CSL has in mind a parallel concept regarding adaptation of the Roman Rite to the different countries of the Western Church.

2. The basic norm and binding authority to which the Church in all the Roman Rite countries must adhere are the Latin *libri typi* (also called *editiones typicae*). These are the Latin model books to which all liturgical texts in all languages must conform. They are not just "sources of inspiration" but are literal and obligatory norms. Nevertheless, as Article 37 says, strict uniformity need not be imposed: these model books provide for variations—*ad libitum* choices—that give sufficient leeway for local or national adaptation, while keeping the substantial unity of the Roman Rite in the Western Patriarchate. But I emphasize that *only* those variations provided for in the *libri typi* may be used.

3. The organic continuity of the Western liturgical tradition from the Fathers to the present takes precedence over all adaptation: any "new form" must grow organically out of the existing ones without a real break or discontinuity, as Article 23 states. A break with true Tradition is always a disaster for the piety of the faithful and often for the liturgy itself. Hence there is no provision for creating a new Mass, a new liturgical year, a new Divine Office, et cetera.

4. It is the role of the bishops to adjudge any adaptations within the limits of the *libri typi*: that is, to judge which variations provided for by the normative *libri typi* should be taken and which should not; this must be done always in accordance with the above-described fundamental principles of CSL. The General Instruction on the Roman Missal (1970) gives this leeway: " . . . Bishops' Conferences are empowered to lay down for those under their jurisdiction norms which accord with traditions and

temperaments of their people . . ." (Chapter 1, no. 6). But this leeway may be used *only* within the parameters of the *ad libitum* choices given in the Mass rite itself.

5. Now we come to CSL's Article 40. (How vividly I remember the sessions of the Preparatory Commission where our work was discussed!) It is of utmost importance to understand this fact: *CSL 40 was written and intended for the mission countries* (such as those of Africa) where Christianity had not yet had the time and opportunity to settle into an adapted "Christian culture." In such countries — and *only* in such countries — the norms of adaptation given in Articles 37–39 do not suffice. Thus Article 40 was written.

It is clearly contrary to the context of Articles 37–39, and indeed to all of CSL, to apply Article 40 to the usual situation in a developed Western country. But, alas, this has been done frequently in Western countries, even without the prescribed conditions: namely that the local bishop must submit his proposals for deeper adaptation to the Holy See, and this may be done only after the necessary experiments, supervised by appropriate experts, have been carried out. Many abuses have arisen from an undue extension of Article 40 to the dioceses of old Christianity, whose believers have been disturbed by manifold unauthorized innovations.

I must add that, although extraordinary ministers of the Eucharist are not mentioned in Article 40, the concept is the same. The provision for extraordinary Eucharistic ministers was created specifically for the mission countries — for churches where there are not sufficient priests to administer the Holy Mysteries — not for the countries in which Christianity was long established. The now-common practice in the West of Eucharistic ministers distributing the Holy Mysteries while the priest rests in his chair is an extraordinary abuse of the intent of CSL.

Unfortunately, improper use of Article 40 has been often supported by erroneous defenses published in technical liturgical magazines. To counteract this trend, in 1994 the Congregation for Divine Worship and Discipline of the Sacraments issued a special decree, *Varietates Legitimae,* "Inculturation and the Roman Liturgy," as commentary and guidance on Articles 37–40.[29] An example of proper and successful implementation of Article 40

---

[29] See *Notitiae* 30 (1994), pp. 80–115. [This document may also be found at https://adoremus.org/1994/03/instruction-inculturation-and-the-roman-liturgy. — Ed.]

was our work in Africa with the *Messe Zaïroise* (the Zaire Rite of
the Mass): carefully following CSL's prescriptions, we performed
several trials, under the supervision of skilled representatives of
different tribes, the constant oversight of myself as liturgist and
anthropologist, and the leadership of Bishop Malula.

6. A further insight into CSL is this: in stating all these principles, CSL avoided using the now-popular term "inculturation,"
because it is ambiguous, incorrect, and one-sided. Adaptation
should not be done one-sidedly, objectively, within the liturgy
only, but also in the culture into which the liturgy must be
adapted subjectively. Crucially, as CSL elaborates in Articles
14–20, *liturgical adaptation is primarily a matter of worshipers being
instructed in the liturgy so they feel "at home" and familiar with it.* The
matter of the liturgy itself being adapted to the common cultural
and anthropological genius of the worshipers is secondary. This
first basic principle of the worshipers' subjective formation was
essentially ignored by the postconciliar liturgical subcommissions,
just as they overlooked the importance of the historical roots and
anthropological continuity at the core of any culture, as I will
explain in Chapter 3.[30]

7. Finally, all the above principles are proposed in CSL in clear
and practical wording, without the ambiguous show of words
used in the man-centered Council documents. Thus, in CSL
there was no (built-in) danger of misunderstanding or deliberate
adulterating, as there was with some other documents.

The Constitution on the Sacred Liturgy was truly committed
to its purpose as stated in the title of its first chapter, "General
Principles for the Restoration and Promotion of the Sacred Liturgy." It did so not by throwing out the baby with the bath water,
nor by creating a new liturgy, nor by making any essential break
with the organic evolution of the liturgy and thus hurting the
piety of simple worshipers—but rather by clearly and firmly
adhering to the Scriptures and Holy Tradition.

---

[30] I highly recommend an address by Cardinal Ratzinger, given in Hong
Kong in March 1993, entitled "In the Encounter of Christianity and Religions, Syncretism is Not the Goal," reproduced in *L'Osservatore Romano*,
April 26, 1995, pp. 5ff. Therein Cardinal Ratzinger showed that the approach
of most current liturgists to inculturation is wrong, because their concept
of culture is lopsided—an extremely serious error.

CHAPTER 3

The Postconciliar
Commissions
and Documents

Revere the LORD, you his saints.
They lack nothing, those who revere him.
—Psalm 33/34:10

ARTICLE 1: CHRONOLOGY AND CLARIFICATIONS

As we noted earlier, this book distinguishes five chronological stages, corresponding generally to the first five chapters of this book:

1. *The preconciliar period*, extending from the beginning of the Liturgical Movement in the 1940s (and earlier) through the work of the Council's Preparatory Commission in 1959–62, with all its hopes and optimistic preparation;

2. *The Council itself*, from 1962 to 1965, when this hopeful renewal was confirmed;

3. *The first postconciliar phase*, from January 1964 to the late 1960s, when the postconciliar commissions aborted this hopeful renewal;

4. *The second postconciliar phase*, from approximately 1968 to 1981, during which a spirit of rebellion arose and spread *within* the Church; and

5. *The third postconciliar phase*, from 1978 to the present,[1] which saw the postconciliar work's wholesale betrayal to rebellion and dissent, in collaboration with secular forces *outside* the Church.

The careful reader will note overlapping dates in this chronology. I have given only general time frames for the three postconciliar phases because they are impossible to delineate perfectly; therefore also in Chapters 3–5 some material will be intermingled.

The reader should also take note that in this book, focused as it is on the Constitution on the Sacred Liturgy, I will speak of

---

[1] The author wrote this in 1997.—Ed.

the "postconciliar" period as beginning with establishment of Pope Paul VI's Consilium in January 1964, although the Council itself continued until December 1965.

For the Council to be truly a success, it was necessary that the blueprint of the preconciliar renewal, taken up by the Council, be further worked out, honestly and completely, by the postconciliar commissions. Unfortunately, this did not occur. I cannot emphasize this point too strongly: *there was perfect continuity between the preconciliar period and the Council itself, but after the Council this crucial continuity was broken by the postconciliar commissions.*

Some historians of the Council assert that the postconciliar liturgical crisis is merely the logical result of a crisis that was in the making before Vatican II; some postconciliar dissenters have used this claim to justify their rebellion. Having been active in both the preconciliar Liturgical Movement and the postconciliar liturgical subcommissions, I have tried in this book to make a nuanced yet truthful assessment of that claim—which I believe to be false.

As I've alluded to before, there are deep differences between these two periods, as follows.

1. Before Vatican II, a deep scientific research into—and love for—the ancient sources and Holy Tradition was shared among the renewers. This study of Scripture, liturgy, and Fathers was done by first-class, pastorally-minded scholars and traditional schools; hence the results of their research were reliable and permanent and in fact formed the undergirding of the Council's work. By comparison, the rebellious theologians after the Council are amateurs who are not conducting serious scholarly study but are merely rehashing each other's errors.

2. Before the Council there was great respect for the Magisterium and the Petrine Ministry, and sincere love for the Church in spite of her flaws. Yes, some rare dissenters existed. But no organized movement of dissent or disrespect for authority was present, as is now the case.

3. The preconciliar renewers were very careful to distinguish between the teachings of the popes who promoted and wisely guided the renewal, and the blunders or reactions of some subalterns—because the movement's leaders constantly emphasized the *sensus Ecclesiae* and her Holy Tradition. In the postconciliar period, however, Pope John Paul II, Cardinal Ratzinger, and other

Church leaders are often rejected and defamed precisely *because* they adhere to orthodoxy and Holy Tradition.

Between the preconciliar and postconciliar times, then, something changed drastically—including in the Council's commissions entrusted with its work. *After the Council they became more and more infected by a new high-handed spirit whereby some commission members put themselves and their opinions above the Council documents on which they were supposed to work in the very spirit of the Council Fathers.* Worship became the primary victim of their high-handedness, but this man-centered viewpoint also deeply affected the problem of religious liberty and the Church in the world. *It was essentially a switch from the objective, vertical ascent toward God to the subjective, horizontal gravitation in man.*

This infection by self-righteous *Hineininterpretierung* (putting one's own subjective interpretation into a text) took place gradually during the *first* postconciliar phase, as the commissions worked on interpreting the Council documents. The *second* postconciliar phase, one of rebellion and dissent, followed after these commissions' work was published. In the *third* phase this spirit of rebellion aligned with secular culture and became so strong that it overwhelmed even the concerns of the Council itself. Henceforth the concern became no longer the working out of the life-giving message of Vatican II, but rather a radical "new church" in the spirit of secular society.

I must note, before we proceed, that two groups of persons were opposed to the Council and its work, but for entirely different reasons: (1) a small group of conservative clergy, as I described above, who acted in the name of the *Church*; and (2) the rebels, who acted in the name of the *world*. The conservatives rejected the Council as too progressive; the rebels rejected it as too conservative. I think the first group, who loved the Church, foresaw the disaster that lay ahead and wanted to spare the Church from it. The latter group seemed to have no love for the Church but rather desired to force their agenda upon her; they and their work will be the object of much of our further analysis.

It is also important to clarify that two groups of documents on the liturgy were published after the Council: (1) *those by the Roman Congregations, which were faithful to CSL*; and (2) *those by subcommissions of the Consilium, many of which deviated from CSL.*

Our critique of documents in the rest of this chapter pertains to those issued by the Consilium's subcommissions.

Now let us briefly look further at the three postconciliar phases as they pertain specifically to the Constitution on the Sacred Liturgy.

1. The members of Pope Paul VI's Consilium and its subcommissions (including myself) began their work of interpreting CSL in January 1964. Thus began the first phase, a time of creative work of fellows: study, meetings, and discussions within the subcommissions. This work was initially good, but it soon became infected by erroneous attitudes. While it went on, the Church outside was initially in peace as the people awaited the subcommissions' documents, especially the Roman Missal with the new Mass rite (the *Novus Ordo*). But as months and then years passed, turmoil began and increased, and some priests and bishops began to take matters into their own hands.

2. This attitude ushered in the second phase, which began in the late 1960s upon the release of the subcommissions' documents, and especially upon the release of Paul VI's *Humanae Vitae* in 1968. More and more the observance of laws and the respect for objective Church rules and authority were undermined, until soon the whole Church began to look like a storm-tossed ship that had thrown away its oars and rudder. Thus the second phase was a time of turmoil, lawlessness, and organized dissent within the Church.

3. The third postconciliar phase involves alliance with the world. The ailments of the second phase caused more than the miscarriage of CSL; they were also the seeds for a further development, in which secularism took over and exerted growing pressure upon weak leaders in the Church to align with its demands. This is the period in which we are living.

Cardinal Ratzinger spoke of the situation thus in 1985:

> I am convinced that the damage we have incurred in these twenty years is due, not to the "true" Council, but to the unleashing *within* the Church of latent polemical and centrifugal forces; and *outside* the Church it is due to the confrontation with a cultural revolution in the West.... [2]

---

[2] Cardinal Joseph Ratzinger with Vittorio Messori, *The Ratzinger Report: An Exclusive Interview on the State of the Church* (San Francisco: Ignatius, 1985), p. 30.

ARTICLE 2: "CAUTION! MEN AT WORK!" (THE EXPERTS)

The *dramatis personae* of the postconciliar period can be divided into four levels of causality: (1) the experts or *periti* who did the work, (2) the bishops who approved their work, (3) the priests who applied it in practice, and (4) the faithful, including the religious and especially the nuns, who enjoyed or suffered from it.

We will begin with the experts. When in daily life we see a sign declaring "Men at Work," we recognize it as a warning of danger. In the life of the Church, such a warning should have been given after the Council, for danger surely lurked in the workrooms of the postconciliar commissions.

The postconciliar Commission on Liturgy, the Consilium, officially called the *Consilium ad Exsequendam Constitutionem de Sacra Liturgia* (Council for the Implementation of the Constitution on the Sacred Liturgy), was established by Pope Paul VI on January 25, 1964, a month after the promulgation of CSL.[3] (It was an heir of the Consilium created by Pope John XXIII in 1962, after the Preparatory Commission for Liturgy was deposed on the Council floor, as I mentioned above.) The rest of this chapter will discuss the work of Pope Paul's Consilium. The reader should note that when I say "subcommissions" I am speaking of the subcommissions (sometimes called "study groups") of this Consilium.[4]

Many participants in Pope Paul VI's Consilium had worked with Pope John's Consilium in 1962–63. The postconciliar group, however, was substantially expanded with new collaborators

---

[3] The website of the Dicastery for Divine Worship and the Discipline of the Sacraments provides this historical description (italics are in the original): "As a parallel institution to the *Sacred Congregation of Rites*, the *Consilium* carried out its mandate autonomously until 8 May 1969, when the *Sacred Congregation of Rites* was suppressed and in its place two new Congregations were created, the *Congregation for Divine Worship* and the *Congregation for the Causes of Saints*. The *Consilium* thus was integrated within the *Sacred Congregation for Divine Worship*, continuing to work on the implementation of the liturgical reform, albeit with limited powers of its own. Finally, the *Consilium* would remain in operation until the end of its mandate to implement the liturgical reform as established by the Second Vatican Council." See www.cultodivino.va/en/chi-siamo/storia/il-consilium-ad-exsequendam-constitutionem-de-sacra-liturgia.html.—Ed.

[4] Father Boniface almost always used the longer term "postconciliar Commission on Liturgy" instead of "Consilium," but I have changed those references to "Consilium" (or occasionally "Paul VI's Consilium") for brevity and because it is the more widely used term.—Ed.

appointed by an *ad hoc* authority in Rome, giving the impression that a large number of widely-recognized liturgical scholars participated in it. According to the official listing,[5] it consisted of forty-eight Members (eleven cardinals, thirty-six bishops, and one abbot); 146 Consultors, mostly priests plus a few lay scholars and musicians; forty-four Advisors, mostly from abbeys and theological faculties; and six Observers. These Observers included five Protestants, apparently the same men whom Pope Paul VI consulted before choosing the *Novus Ordo*; we will return to this.

Father Annibale Bugnini, who had been Secretary of the Preparatory Commission for Liturgy, became Secretary (i.e., active dynamo) of Paul VI's Consilium, responsible for overseeing the schedule and work of all its subcommissions. His influence was crucial, as we shall see. Cardinal Giacomo Lercaro of Bologna was the President but did not actively participate in the meetings.

Within the Consilium, the different areas of liturgy were entrusted to thirty-nine subcommissions (study groups).[6] I was

---

[5] *Elenchus: Membrorum, Consultorum, Consiliariorum, Coetuum a Studiis*, the official listing of the Members, Consultors, Advisors, Observers, and subcommissions of the *Consilium ad Exsequendam Constitutionem de Sacra Liturgia*, is a small booklet, all in Latin, published by the Vatican in 1967. Throughout this chapter I have referred to my copy to fill in details about personnel. [I still have this booklet (which is the second edition; the first was published in 1964) and have also used it extensively, including for the next footnote. — Ed.]

[6] Because this information is not easily available, we include a listing of these subcommissions or Study Groups (*Coetuum a studiis*), copied verbatim from the *Elenchus* booklet described in the previous footnote: 1. *De Calendario*; 2. *De Psalterio recognoscendo*; 3. *De psalmis distribuendis*; 4. *De lectionibus biblicis*; 5. *De lectionibus patristicis*; 6. *De lectionibus historicis*; 7. *De hymnis*; 8. *De cantibus Officii divini*; 9. *De generali structura Officii divini*; 10. *De Ordine Missae*; 11. *De lectionibus biblicis in Missa*; 12. *De oratione communi seu fidelium*; 13. *De Missis votivis*; 14. *De cantibus in Missa*; 15. *De generali structura Missae*; 16. *De Concelebratione et de Communione sub utraque specie*; 17. *De ritibus peculiaribus in anno liturgico*; 18. *De Communibus Breviarii et Missalis recognoscendis*; 18 bis. *De orationibus et praefationibus recognoscendis*; 19. *De rubricis Breviarii et Missalis*; 20. *De libro I Pontificalis*; 20 bis. *De Consecratione Virginum*; 21. *De libris II et III Pontificalis*; 22. *De Rituali I*; 23. *De Rituali II*; 23 bis. *De Rituali III (de Paenitentia)*; 24. *De Martyrologio*; 25. *De libris cantus liturgici revisendis et edendis*; 26. *De Caeremoniali Episcoporum*; 27. *De collatione cum aliis Ritibus*; 28. *De re theologica*; 29. *De re biblica*; 30. *De re iuridica*; 31. *De re historica*; 32. *De re stilistica*; 33. *De re musica*; 34. *De principiis pastoralibus*; 35. *De applicationibus pastoralibus*; 36. *De aptatione ingenio et traditionibus populorum*; 37. *De arte et liturgia*; 38. *De Codice iuris liturgici conficiendo*; 39. *De Ritibus Cappellae Papalis*. — Ed.

assigned to Subcommission no. 22, *De Rituali I*, on the Sacraments, in which we worked on the initiation sacraments: baptism, confirmation, and Holy Communion. I was also assigned to Subcommission no. 23, *De Rituali II*, on the general nonsacramental rites. In addition, I had the privilege of assisting at several other subcommissions, especially in the final stage, when the bishops approved the subcommissions' work. My participation in the final stage gave me firsthand knowledge of a primary way in which the Council's work was sidetracked by the postconciliar commissions, as I will describe later in this chapter.

Even now I can see the experts in my mind, operating first around the green table of the Preparatory Commission, then Pope John's Consilium, then Pope Paul's Consilium. In the beginning of our postconciliar work, the spirit of excitement and brotherhood was strong and generated good results, as long as the experts stuck to the text and spirit of CSL. I would like to remember the experts primarily as scholars who wanted to serve the Church.

But after working with them for some time, I came to see how their personal differences began to dominate: their belonging to this particular school or order or country, their view on the importance or unimportance of history and Church Tradition, their past scholarly work, their personal likings. Many of these men were in-depth research scholars, lopsided toward their own field of study. Secretary Bugnini, who was rather a horizontal "overview scholar," often gently overcame these experts' tyrannical misgrowth and brought them to agreement beyond their specialty. But personal differences quickly came to claim the status of absolute values which the more aggressive experts imposed upon others.

So gradually a rift grew among the experts. Two factors were involved. First, the ambitions, characters, and idiosyncrasies of both persons and groups became more and more blatant and difficult to handle; the situation was especially difficult between some Germans and French. Second, some experts broke more and more away from fidelity to CSL, valuing their own opinions above the Church and the Holy Spirit. These men became highly aggressive and often prevailed in the final decision-making process, as we will see. Some of my most painful memories of this period are of certain experts' reckless tyranny, which had harmful consequences for the whole Western Church.

Thus infighting and politics grew in the bosom of several sub-commissions, mostly between different schools and individual experts who wanted, at almost any price, to have their views accepted as the only valid ones. One example is the relentless ostracism practiced by the *relator* (president) of Subcommission no. 9 on the Divine Office.[7] This subcommission's work began well, in genuine collaboration. But gradually the domineering of the *relator* became so unbearable that the experts who disagreed with him were forced to leave—until only he and his secretary remained, to do all the work and to push his views all the way through as an *opus unius hominis*!

BUGNINI'S ROLE

The trend away from adherence to CSL spread to the top, to Secretary Annibale Bugnini. Throughout the Liturgical Movement, the Preparatory Commission for Liturgy, and Pope John's Consilium, Father Bugnini had been faithful to Tradition and the Magisterium. But after the Council he changed. Based on my personal friendship with him, I believe that this change arose not from purposeful malice, but rather from weakness. He seemed to me very impressionable: if someone pushed him one way, he went that way; if someone pushed him the other way, he went there instead.

But Father Bugnini was also a politician, and one who wanted power. In order to gain power he had to appear successful, so he went along with those who were the most vocal and apparently powerful. He was heavily influenced by the modernists who broke from fidelity to CSL, the most outspoken of whom was Johannes Wagner from the Trier Institut in Germany. Before long, Bugnini stopped inviting to the meetings those "reactionary" members who dared to adhere to the text of CSL or to sound principles of religious anthropology. I know this as fact, because Bishop Malula and I were among those who fell out of his favor.

What role did Bishop Malula and I play in the midst of this growing tension and polarization? After a short time, Bishop Malula lost all desire to participate in the subcommissions. The revolutionary boutique of scholars made him feel useless; they

---

[7] The author did not identify this person.—Ed.

treated him as an ignoramus and even insulted him. In addition, the subcommissions' entire work was going counter to CSL and was useless for the mission countries, especially those of Africa. Bishop Malula stated this fact more than once to Secretary Bugnini. On such occasions Bugnini answered the good bishop with remarks so atrocious they are forever etched in my memory:

> *Bugnini*: If you cannot agree, set up your own commission in Africa.

> *Malula*: Where will our Church, poor as a beggar, get the funds to do such a thing, while you here avail yourselves of the money of the whole rich West?

> *Bugnini*: *N'importe*. We here work from the assumption that the modern Western man is *the* man *tout court*, the model of all true humanity, for all countries and cultures, and for all ages to come.

That was the straw that broke the camel's back. Furious over such an arrogant and absurd insult, Bishop Malula vowed never to return. He authorized me to replace him and instructed me accordingly. I suppose Father Bugnini and his people were happy to be rid of an "enemy," according to the emerging policy of excluding those who were faithful to CSL.

We will return later to Father Bugnini's revealing response to Bishop Malula, for it became apparent that his opinion about the supremacy and normative value of modern Western man was part of his agenda—and consequently part of the agenda of the Consilium's subcommissions he oversaw.

At this point, one might ask the obvious and serious question: from whence does one man, or group, get the right to impose his way of praying or celebrating upon the whole Western Church? This question goes to the heart of the dubious validity, or at least the liceity, of much of the work of the Consilium's subcommissions, for they often worked in defiance of CSL, the only authoritative norm given by the Council.

MY REJECTION

I did not fare much better than Bishop Malula, and in the end I met the same fate. Here I will relate three personal experiences, among many that could be told.

One of the last general meetings of the Consilium was dedicated to liturgical language. I was to give a paper on how the new Christian cultures (such as Africa's) saw this problem. Bishop Malula and I spent several hours in deliberation and study to bring together all our experience, for the profit of the Church. The bishop, a highly-cultured man and outstanding linguist, had worked his entire adult life on building up a Christian language, in the vernacular, fitting for Holy Scripture and worship in Africa. His strong conclusion was this: worship requires a holy language, permeated with reverence and awe of God and thus lifting up the worshipers to truly meet with God and the divine world.

So I gave my talk, opening with a description of Bishop Malula's experience and continuing with my own anthropological research. But my presentation was generally rejected. The experts had already made up their minds: they had no intention of learning from these half-wild Africans! They had already decided that the new liturgy was meant for the poorly-educated, secularized, modern Western man (the model of future culture, as Father Bugnini had said). They reasoned therefore that its language should be on this same under-civilized level—not street language *per se*, but close to it—so there would be no break between the liturgical services and man's usual language outside of them. I strongly protested. In revenge, they decided not to mention my talk in the index of the proceedings.

A second unhappy experience occurred in a meeting of Subcommission no. 22 on the sacraments, *De Rituali*. Each of the eleven members took turns leading the meetings. It was my turn, and the topic was the sequence of the sacraments of Christian initiation and the age of confirmation, a subject on which I had just written a book, *La Confirmation: doctrine et pastorale*.[8]

The teaching of CSL on this subject is not outspoken, but its spirit is clear. Article 71 says that the original sequence of the sacramental stages—baptism, then confirmation, *then* first Eucharist—should be restored as it was instituted by Christ,

---

[8] With Daniel Scheyven, *La Confirmation: doctrine et pastorale* (Bruges: Apostolat Liturgique, Abbaye de Saint-André, 1958). I also wrote several other studies on the topic: see, e.g., *Worship*, 1959, pp. 332–48. [See also the author's article "On Confirmation," in *Homiletic and Pastoral Review*, November 1972, pp. 59–67, archived at https://www.catholicculture.org/culture/library/view.cfm?recnum=522.—Ed.]

for these are successive stages of one unbreakable unity in the organic initiation process. Hence, CSL's instruction is that no sacramental act may be inserted between baptism in water and baptism in the Spirit (confirmation).

So I stated that baptism and confirmation belong unbreakably together, for confirmation *enables* us to celebrate the action of fully belonging to the Church, namely the Eucharist. Thus, it makes no sense to have first communion before confirmation. Further, it makes no sense to delay confirmation until the teenage years or even adulthood, under the pretext that confirmation is the sacrament of Christian maturity, which is falsely put on a par with physical maturity.[9]

At that time in Germany, the theological error prevailed of postponing confirmation even to the time of preparation for marriage, which the Germans saw as the main act of two persons' adulthood. Our subcommission's two German members, Monsignor Balthasar Fischer (the *relator*) and his younger friend, Alois Stenzel, SJ, held this view. They would not give in one inch to the rest of the members, nor did they want to vote and decide by majority, for in that case they would have lost.

My final resource, as leader of the meeting, was the ecumenical argument. I pointed out that if we perpetuated the Western abuse of splitting confirmation from its co-sacrament of baptism and from its fullness of finality in the Eucharist, we would be perpetuating one of the major roadblocks to union with the Eastern Churches — for one of the East's significant criticisms against the West is the West's violation of divinely-instituted Holy Tradition in cases such as this. Most of the subcommission's members were sensitive to this argument. They allowed me to call in Father Aloysius Ligier, the great Jesuit scholar of Eastern theology, who was that very day teaching in the college where we were meeting. And in our afternoon session he strongly confirmed the Eastern argument.

Did our German friends give in? Rather the opposite. After this day's events were over, they performed such maneuvers in Rome that this whole subject was taken away from our subcommission

---

[9] For a more recent discussion of this topic (which cites this author's work) see Joshua Madden, "*Circa Aetatem Discretionis*: A Proposal in Favor of Restored Order Confirmation," *Antiphon* 21.3 (2017): 228–51. *Antiphon* is the journal of the Society for Catholic Liturgy. — Ed.

and transferred to the commission of the bishops, under the pretext that confirmation is an episcopal rite. In fact, however, confirmation should *not* be an episcopal rite but the work of the priest, who initiates the whole person into the Church, but that is a discussion for another time.

The commission of the bishops later came out with the mongrelized combination that has become the Western Rite of Confirmation. In taking this action, the bishops unfortunately tried to satisfy all sides. Rather than straightforwardly working out what the Council and CSL had decided, they went against it, and in the process they missed a unique chance for progress toward unity with our Eastern brethren.

Thus to this day the Western Church's initial sacraments remain out of sync with the divinely-established order of baptism, then confirmation, and then first communion. As a result, for decades millions of young people in the Western Church have been deprived of the great spiritual benefits of being confirmed at an early age. By their mid-teen years many decide not to be confirmed at all, and vast numbers of them stray from the Church—perhaps even to their eternal detriment. In addition, the Church has been deprived of the priestly and religious vocations that may have resulted from youthful years being lived in the grace which the Holy Spirit bestows in the sacrament of confirmation.

A third example of how I fared in the Consilium's subcommissions pertains to my last official task (in 1974–75): I was asked to offer suggestions for improving the *Benedictionale*, which was meant to be a book of blessings for lay people. The draft given to me was written almost entirely from a clerical perspective: lay people assisting clerics in the clerics' blessings. This perspective was quite counter to my personal experience. Where I grew up in Belgium, the whole culture was permeated with Christianity and its age-old ritual. There, blessings given by lay people in their homes and at work were as common as the air we breathed. For instance, parents blessed their children at bedtime, the father blessed the meat before cutting and serving it, the mother or daughters blessed their fresh-baked bread before slicing it, and many other home and social customs were followed throughout the year.

In my response to the commission, therefore, I insisted on the restoration of such customs as a true liturgy for the faithful, as they indeed were before the clericalization of the Council of Trent degraded them to mere folklore. I never received a response to my remarks but learned indirectly that they fell on "bad soil." Was it because that particular subcommission felt my views to be an attack against clericalism? This would have been an ironic twist, for clericalism was the opposite of the subcommissions' general tendency toward secularism. Whatever occurred then, I was pleasantly surprised, when the *Benedictionale* came out years later, to see that some of my suggestions had been accepted.

Reading about these personal clashes, one might conclude that it was impossible for the *periti* to work together. But I enjoyed working with most of them. Some spiritual giants like Father Josef Jungmann exercised a soothing influence, although he was firmly opposed to some iconoclastic novelties being proposed, including the altar facing the people, an issue we will discuss later.

I shared the disappointment of Father Jungmann and many other dear friends in the Consilium at the iconoclasm of our rebellious colleagues. Most of these holy men went to their reward before seeing the tragedy of this demolition unfolding in the Western Church. But they are certainly now the Church's powerful intercessors: Cardinal Malula, Josef Loew, Bernard Botte, Johannes Hofinger, François Vandenbroucke, Emil Longeling of Cologne, Deacon Cornelius Bouman of Nijmegen, and many others who have gone before us marked with the sign of faith and are now celebrating the heavenly liturgy.

THE BISHOPS SILENCED

In addition to my regular tasks, I assisted several subcommissions during their final stages, when the bishops were present to approve their work. The bishops were significantly disadvantaged in these meetings, for two critical reasons: (1) they had not participated in the experts' discussions on the matters, and (2) the experts presented the material to the bishops, most of whom were neither theologians nor liturgists, in a highly technical way.

Sometimes the bishops asked for more explanation, but they were generally very accommodating toward the experts and rarely rejected or substantially changed the experts' propositions. At most of these sessions, I felt I was assisting at a joke, for the bishops were often manifestly manipulated by the *relators*—some of whom dared even to silence the bishops for their "incompetence"!

In the aftermath, some bishops told me they felt obliged to approve "the wonderful work of these all-competent experts." Indeed, more than once in subcommission meetings I had heard bishops say, "You experts are appointed by the Church to work all these things out; the Church trusts you because you are experts. It makes no sense that we, who are not specialists, would presume to correct your work, on which you have labored so long and assiduously." Other bishops later expressed privately to me how much they regretted the course those events took, knowing it was because they themselves "let things go," feeling unable to change them in the face of the impenetrable wall of the experts' perceived competence. The experts' aggression and the bishops' lack of real intervention explain the tenor of the documents and why many are so lacking in the pastoral dimension.[10]

I have been a professor of theology and liturgy at several colleges and universities for almost fifty years. During that time I have gathered broad experience of the tragic inbreeding and incompetence of many who are called "experts" and "scholars." Sadly, many of them, especially the most aggressive ones, do not deserve the confidence placed in them. As I will discuss later, the secular media, and the rebellious Catholic media, are largely responsible for these persons' unduly-inflated public reputations of competence.

Unfortunately, the deferential attitude of bishops toward experts has been inherited in America and other countries: replacing Church documents with the private authority of experts has become a common practice in many chanceries. Although bishops are the only *true* "men of the Spirit," they frequently allow themselves to be overwhelmed by the supposed superior technical capacity of their advisers.

This example of the experts overwhelming the bishops shows again how the human factor played a huge role in the great drama of postconciliar reform. Although the whole battle appeared to

---

[10] In 1996 Dom Alcuin Reid contacted the still-living Council Fathers who had voted to approve *Sacrosanctum Concilium*, asking for "their recollections of the conciliar debate on the sacred liturgy and whether *Sacrosanctum Concilium* was seen as a fundamental plan of how the sacred liturgy was to be reformed, or whether they saw themselves as delegating authority to reform the liturgy to the experts." For the revealing survey results, see Alcuin Reid, "The Fathers of Vatican II and the Revised Mass: Results of a Survey," *Antiphon* 10.2 (2006): 70–90.—Ed.

revolve around *documents*, the real confrontation revolved—and still revolves—around *persons*, with their differing backgrounds and idiosyncrasies.

ARTICLE 3: THE POSTCONCILIAR
LITURGICAL DOCUMENTS

We noted briefly in Article 1 that two kinds of documents were published after the Council, from two sources. It is important here to distinguish between them: (1) those by the *Roman Congregations* as commentaries on, or applications of, a particular Council *document*; and (2) those composed by *postconciliar commissions* as further clarifications of a *topic* in the Council's sixteen primary documents.

Such documents pertaining to the Constitution on the Sacred Liturgy fall into these two groups:

1. *Twenty-four documents issued between 1964 and 1974 by Pope Paul VI and the Sacred Congregation of Rites.*[11] These deal with, for example, concelebration, Communion under both species, the worship of the Eucharist, distribution of Holy Communion and eucharistic ministers, music in the liturgy, and liturgical translations. They were faithful to CSL and the intentions of the Council Fathers.

2. *Further documents issued by the Consilium's subcommissions, which set up the new rites and books proposed or prescribed by CSL.* All the new liturgical books were fruits of these subcommissions. They became official and binding documents because they were promulgated by the Sacred Congregation for Divine Worship, supported by an Apostolic Constitution of Pope Paul VI.

The subcommissions' documents pertaining to the liturgy, and the liturgical books themselves, can be further divided into two categories: (1) those that adhered faithfully to CSL and aimed primarily at restoration of the ancient Tradition; and (2) those that essentially created a new liturgy. Here I will list a few topics, with brief comments.[12]

---

[11] Here, for simplicity's sake, I refer to these as emanating from the Sacred Congregation of Rites because it and its successor, the Sacred Congregation for Divine Worship, issued a large percentage of them. [All of these documents, with notations of their precise sources, are included in Flannery's *Vatican Council II: The Conciliar and Post Conciliar Documents*, cited above.—Ed.]

[12] Most of the documentation and my reasoning here come from my book, *Culte chrétien en Afrique après Vatican II* (Immensee, Switzerland:

1. Documents Faithful to Tradition and CSL

a. *The rite for reception of adult catechumens (Rite of Christian Initiation of Adults or RCIA).* This rite *per se* is generally a fortunate adaptation of the old Roman rite to our modern sensitivity and its reception has been excellent. However, it leaves too much leeway for modernistic instructions either added to the rite or requested by it; thus in many locations the rite has become polluted with heresy.

b. *The anointing of the sick.* This updated rite closely follows the prescription of CSL 73; thus it is no longer the "last sacrament" or "extreme unction" administered only to the dying, but is correctly a sacrament for the spiritual or physical healing of any seriously sick persons. However, a lack of proper catechesis has resulted in it sometimes being applied too broadly, even to include just old age.[13] This is a clear example of the way in which the uprooting of an age-old tradition upsets the entire sacramental theology if it is not well prepared.

c. *The rite of ordinations,* from bishop to minor orders. Most of this work was very good; however, the suppression of the subdiaconate was inconsistent with a return to the ancient sources as intended by the Council Fathers. Fortunately, in the restored Tridentine Mass in the West, the subdeacon has fully recovered his rightful place.

d. *The consecration of churches.* This rite, too, contained excellent elements. I regret, though, that the dropping of some valuable Carolingian elements deprived the rite of symbolism that had given it the mystery-filled dramatics so beloved by the faithful — and which had been an element of ecumenical *rapprochement* with the East.[14]

Nouvelle Revue de science missionnaire, 1974). Although I originally wrote it after my eleven years in Africa as an application of the postconciliar liturgical documents for the Church in Africa, it is primarily an evaluation of the documents themselves and hence is still practical for the Western Church today.

[13] Eastern Churches make a clear distinction between the anointing of the sick in general and the Mystery (Sacrament) of the Sanctification by the Holy Oil, which is celebrated very solemnly over the grievously sick by seven priests, assisted by the whole congregation of the faithful in prayer.

[14] Michel Andrieu, *Les Ordines Romani du haut Moyen-Âge* (Louvain: Spicilegium sacrum lovaniense bureau, 1931ff.), is a basic resource on the normative formation of the Roman Liturgy, including the Carolingian development.

e. *The funeral rite.* This is a good adaptation to the practical needs of the local Church. The desire of the Council to restore a resurrection perspective, however, is often applied in the rite with such cold radicalism that no room is left for grieving—a need previously met through details such as Gregorian music and the *Dies irae.*

f. *Scripture Readings.* The restored order of readings was a good endeavor to present a richer share of the Word of God in the liturgy. However, the choices were not always fortunate and pastoral, and some mistakes were made due to faulty scholarship.[15]

2. Documents that Created a New Liturgy

The *Novus Ordo* certainly belongs in the category of documents that created a new liturgy, but I will treat it at length in Article 5 and discuss only two examples here.

a. *The new Church calendar.* The new calendar has some good qualities, but overall it looks much like an abstract exercise for a class in Western heortology. The element of popular devotion was systematically removed, in disregard of its role as one of the basic ingredients of a living liturgy. For instance, the authors adopted mostly recent saints and dropped many earlier ones who still enjoyed popular veneration. They filled the calendar with Italian and French saints, substantially excluding the Eastern Churches and those of the Third World. Further, they selected saints who were outspokenly active and excluded a multitude of saints who lived hidden lives of prayer and asceticism. All these actions amounted, in effect, to imposing the pattern of the West, narrowly seen, upon the whole Church, as though Christianity had not existed, for instance, for fifteen centuries in Ethiopia, or for nearly twenty centuries in the Christian Near East and India.

b. *The Liturgy of the Hours (Divine Office).* The fact that the Divine Office was restored as the prayer of not only monks and clergy but also the faithful was excellent. However, the postconciliar writers essentially *created a new Office*, contrary to the instruction of CSL 23, which bears repeating:

---

[15] Professor Gerard Rouwhorst, in his article "De Lezing van de Schrift in de Romiense Liturgie" in *Tijdschrift voor liturgie* 80 (June 1996), pp. 202ff., evaluates the entire work of subcommissions no. 4, *De lectionibus biblicis*, and no. 11, *De lectionibus biblicis in Missa*, including suggestions on how to correct their mistakes.

Finally, there must be no innovations unless the good of
the Church genuinely and certainly requires them, and
care must be taken that any new forms adopted should
in some way grow organically from forms already existing.

The flaws in this new Office are many; here I will emphasize
just one. If the Divine Office is to be truly the "prayer of the
Church," it must be provided a *dual* structure and ethos — one
for private prayer and one for recitation or singing in common.
Some patterns for ease of singing, such as the Gregorian or Byzantine systems of eight tones, should have been built in. But the
president of this subcommission refused to allow a dual structure,
and the Office was treated as a text to be merely read or silently
meditated upon, not celebrated.[16]

The necessity of a dual structure arises from the specific difference between celebration and prayer (although the latter ought
to fully penetrate the former). Celebration and prayer are not
just quantitatively different; each has its own irreducible laws.
This subcommission's experts took as their paradigm "praying a
private text" instead of "celebrating a liturgy of prayer"; hence
they failed to provide actions or rubrics or gestures (except eventually incense at the Magnificat in Vespers), which would have
been of great benefit.

These shortcomings correspond with the Western culture that
has lost the art of *singing* one's prayer, as the Psalms invite us to
do. So the new Liturgy of the Hours is well suited for the West's
religious culture, but the other cultures' thirst for true "celebration
of prayer" is not quenched by this sterile model. This situation
urges us to again ask the question: Who in the Church has the
right to impose his way of praying upon the whole Church? And
who has the right to interrupt the centuries-old organic flow of
prayer tradition in the Western Church and also to ignore the
ancient tradition of her sister Churches in the East?

ARTICLE 4: RECEPTION OF THE ROMAN MISSAL

In the first few years after the Council, the new Roman Missal was awaited with eager expectation as the most important

---

[16] The author did not specify whether this was Subcommission no. 8. *De
cantibus Officii divini* or no. 9. *De generali structura Officii divini*, but it likely
was no. 9, whose *relator* he mentioned above. — Ed.

postconciliar document, for the Eucharist is the central act of every Catholic's religion. Finally, on March 26, 1970, six long years after the Constitution on the Sacred Liturgy was approved, the new Roman Missal was promulgated by Decree of the Sacred Congregation for Divine Worship.

Reactions to the new Missal, especially the *Novus Ordo*, were mixed. The first came from a group of conservative Roman theologians, under the leadership of Cardinals Alfredo Ottaviani and Antonio Bacci. They utterly rejected the new Missal, and even accused it and the *Novus Ordo* of heresy, because of the almost total omission of the sacrificial character of the Eucharist and other serious reproaches, some of which we will discuss later.

In the United States, the priests, laity, and religious had not been involved in the documents' preparation; thus they were largely unaware of what was to come. Hence, during this first postconciliar phase the Church in America was mostly at peace; one would have even thought that she was still in the creative preconciliar period. All this drastically changed the moment the Roman Missal and other postconciliar documents were dropped upon the people, as highly explosive material. The change was sudden, widespread, and deep. Clergy and laity alike were completely unprepared for the new liturgical books. It is absolutely necessary to realize the drastic and unprepared nature of this change, because it was the cause of, and marked the beginning of, the deep crisis that has upset and unsettled the Western Church ever since, like convulsions of cosmic proportion.

Most priests in the United States, to my observation, generally accepted the postconciliar changes. But often they did so for erroneous reasons. Some welcomed the changes because the liturgical documents seemed to give them leeway to create their own celebrations. Soon, unfortunately, this apparent freedom took on a life of its own, and seminaries were falsely teaching that the Council had given priests a new "right" of liturgical experimentation.

Other priests (such as in Holland) actually felt the *Novus Ordo* was *backward* because, during the long wait for the Missal, the Mass rite had in some places already been developed, without authorization, much beyond this point. As Dom Lambert Beauduin would have said, "*Le ver était déjà dans la pomme*" — the worm was already in the apple. Due to the wait, many bishops, priests, and faithful were already so accustomed to celebrating without definite rules that they were not going to return (and, alas, they have not to this day).

Loyal and orthodox liturgists were perhaps the most disappointed by the new Missal. They knew that perfection and unanimity are impossible, but they also knew there is quite a distance between a particular option and a mediocre result which comes from constantly compromising on essentials. They immediately recognized that the *Novus Ordo* exceeded all measure of compromise. Moreover, they were critically aware of this fact: *the Novus Ordo is not faithful to CSL but goes substantially beyond the parameters which CSL set for the reform of the Mass rite.*

LACK OF PREPARATION

Most countries suffered from a serious lack of preparation for the postconciliar liturgical documents. The Sacred Congregation of Rites issued several decrees for the faithful to prepare the terrain for promulgation of the Missal, but they were woefully inadequate. Bishops, priests, religious, and faithful alike were not duly prepared and instructed by adapted catechesis and dialogue; thus they were not ready to become respected partners responsible for putting the documents into practice. The documents were just dropped on them, to be accepted willy-nilly.

This was especially unfortunate in America, which already suffered from a longstanding lack of liturgical education for the clergy and religious. Apart from some blessed exceptions, most U. S. bishops of that time were not much interested in liturgy. They were rather poor celebrators and teachers of liturgical theology and practice: to them liturgy was mainly a set of rubrics. For them, therefore, the liturgical renewal demanded by the Council consisted of simply switching over from one set of rubrics to another. It did not matter much if the new rubrics were wrong or unfit for their people; their chief concern was to "just do it." Consequently, the bishops did not implement in advance the long, careful instruction that their clergy and faithful needed.

A notable exception to this problem occurred in Africa, where Bishop Malula wisely instituted an obligatory six-month plan of catechesis and formation for clergy and laity to prepare them for the Council's changes. During that period I gave intensive workshops and retreats in Zaire and other Central African countries, in order to interest the whole people. Because of this preparation, the people of Central Africa accepted the Council's changes—and the proper theology behind them—to their great benefit.

If proper formation and catechesis such as this had been done in America, the whole postconciliar scenario would have been quite different. *I am convinced that this lack of preparation was a primary cause of the deep crisis that has upset the Western Church ever since.*

THE ROLE OF POPE PAUL VI

Not all the clergy and faithful were eagerly awaiting the Roman Missal; some were actually dreading it. Why? In part because they had heard that Pope Paul VI had asked the collaboration of five Protestant theologians, including even some who did not believe in the sacrificial character of the Eucharist or the Real Presence.[17] One of Pope Paul's queries of these Protestants had been whether or not the planned Mass rite, the *Novus Ordo*, would bring the Catholic Church closer to her Protestant brethren. It is asserted that the Protestants' unanimous "yes" tipped the scale toward its final introduction.

I personally asked Father Louis Bouyer, who was close to Paul VI, what influenced the pope to choose the *Novus Ordo*. He said in essence that the pope was instructed and convinced by the subcommissions' rebels that the Church, and the Protestants, wanted this Mass. So the pope said, in essence, if that is so, I give in. The *Novus Ordo* was indeed favorable toward ecumenical efforts with Protestants—but it gravely hurt those efforts with the Eastern Churches, contrary to the Council's intent.

In approving the Roman Missal, Pope Paul VI bypassed the *Missa Normativa*, which had sat on his desk since 1967. I remember well how Father Josef Jungmann led the meetings of the

---

[17] These appear to be the Observers listed on page 42 of the Vatican's *Elenchus* booklet of Consilium personnel (cited above): Professor Raymond George of Wesley College in England; Canon Ronald Jasper, an Anglican, also from England; Dr. Massey Hamilton Shepherd, Jr., an Anglican at the Church Divinity School of the Pacific in Berkeley, California; Friedrich-Wilhelm Künneth, a Lutheran from Geneva; and Brother Max Thurian from the ecumenical Taizé community in France, who later converted and became a Catholic priest.—Ed.

subcommission on the Eucharist, where the whole rite of the new Mass was played out before our eyes as we made our corrections. It was a delicate task, making decisions on the Holy of Holies of the entire liturgy, but Father Jungmann led the meetings with such care as if he were dealing with Jesus himself. Our work resulted in the *Missa Normativa*, a well-composed Mass Rite which was proposed to the Synod of Bishops in 1967 but never adopted, to our sincere regret, as it had many advantages over the later-imposed *Novus Ordo*.[18]

THE LAITY'S RESPONSE

What was the laity's reaction to the new Roman Missal? For the most part, like many priests, they initially welcomed the changes, though based on incomplete reasons. For example, some were happy merely that the services were shorter and simpler. More important, they were glad that the services were now in the vernacular. For many people, the vernacular was the great "savior" that overshadowed and justified all the other changes; unfortunately, however, it became a sort of narcotic that dispensed them from further critical thinking.

Opinion polls during this period regularly created erroneous perceptions of this situation. When the laity were asked about the liturgical changes after the Council, their response was overwhelmingly favorable. The pollsters misread this to mean that the majority approved of *all* the secular novelties, and the liturgical rebels publicized this false reading to promote their own agenda. But what the laity *en bloc* voted for was *the vernacular*. They did *not* vote for the secularism and banality that increasingly crept into the liturgy.

This truth becomes obvious when we look more closely at the laity's response. While the dissenters worked to manipulate Church authorities and public opinion, as we will describe later, the truly faithful laity began to awaken. They came to realize that they had been fooled and cheated by negligent Church leaders who had acquiesced to aggressive theologians. This increasing awareness became the seed for marvelous new growth. The faithful

---

[18] Unfortunately, the author, who is not listed in the 1967 *Elenchus* as a participant in Subcommission no. 10, *De Ordine Missae*, gave no further details about this situation or his involvement with the *Missa Normativa*. The history of these developments is available elsewhere. — Ed.

began to discern the sharp discrepancy between the primary Council documents, which gave the genuine teaching of the Church, and what the postconciliar commissions and rebellious theologians had made out of them. Then, as the rebels became so openly opposed to the Magisterium and the Holy Father as to be in a state of schism, honest believers came to see clearly which side they should support in this sad competition.

One result of this awakening was the rising up of orthodox, intellectual laypersons who founded excellent schools and colleges as well as superb lay magazines and other media. Courageous publications such as *Homiletic and Pastoral Review*, *National Catholic Register*, *The Wanderer*, *Crisis*, *First Things*, and later *30 Days*, *The Catholic World Report*, *Inside the Vatican*, *Caelum et Terra*, *Forefront*, *New Covenant*, and *Sursum Corda* chronicled the abuses and encouraged the faithful to persevere in the truth. Over the years the positions have become gradually more polarized, the rebels versus the truly faithful. The apostasy has become more general, but it has triggered a healthy reaction and renewal that promises great things for the future.

Alongside the growth of orthodox faithful, a wonderful new Pentecost, announced and prayed for by Pope John XXIII and his successors, began to blow into faithful Catholics. This occurred in the arising of two new movements in the Church: the *charismatic movement* and the *Marian movement*. Both movements were begun and carried on primarily by the "little ones" who were suffering the most from the crises. They were quite different from each other but inspired and led by the same Spirit, who still governs his Church and who, through these movements, is awakening her. Significantly, in the 1990s these movements are converging, as the Holy Spirit prompts the faithful to a deeper appreciation of the crucial role of the Mother of God in our times.

The charismatic and Marian movements are precisely the opposite of the movement of rebellion and secularism. They are like a living commentary on *Lumen Gentium*, the Dogmatic Constitution on the Church, the Council's principal document. They are also like a return to the Early Church, where the gifts of the Spirit — such as healings, prophecies, and manifest answers to prayer — freely bloom, to delight the poor and little ones and to confound the haughty rebels (as in the Magnificat, Lk 1:51–53).

The charismatic movement in the Catholic Church began in 1967. Its intent was for every Catholic to live the gospel to its fullest, on all levels of life. Because the movement was more open to the pneumatic dimension of the Church than to her institutional expression, it took some time for the gloom of suspicion against it to be dispelled. But soon its marvelous fruits became a powerful witness to the Holy Spirit's working in its members: deep prayerfulness, love for the Church and her leaders, great brotherly love for insiders and outsiders, various initiatives for in-depth Church renewal in the true sense of Vatican II — and a deep devotion to the Holy Spirit and his work in souls and in the Church. For it is he, after all, as Lord of the Church, who animates her and all true renewal from within. In short, in the charismatic movement a new but authentic sound was heard in the Church that boded well for the future.

A short while later the Marian movement arose and became the proper "movement of the Mother of God." After the Council, rebellious theologians had tried to obliterate all Marian devotion, intending to make the Church appear more like a Protestant denomination. But they failed to reckon with the Hostess! Just as they had failed to reckon with the Holy Spirit, so they also failed to acknowledge the power of the Mother of God, the life-giving symbol of the Church.

In recent years Mary has taken revenge, so to speak, against those who would deny her exalted role in the plan of salvation. Through countless authentic apparitions and prophecies all over the world, on every continent and in almost every country, she has proven and nurtured her movement. To her apparition sites she has attracted her little ones — those in need, young and old, sick and healthy — who have flocked there by the millions. Through her messages the Mother of God has created and fostered the basic element of all renewal, the backbone of all worship: prayerfulness and living the gospel — without which, I would add, even the best postconciliar document is only a noisy gong (1 Cor 13:1). What Pope John Paul II is doing through the worldwide outreach of his encyclicals, his book *Crossing the Threshold of Hope*, the new *Catechism of the Catholic Church*, and especially his pastoral travels — to all this Mary is giving a soul and root in prayer and the spirit of the gospel. In essence, *the Mother of God is mobilizing the whole world for the coming of the kingdom.*

THE RELIGIOUS SISTERS

Here I must interject some thoughts about the crisis of the religious sisters, a subject on which I feel qualified to speak due to many years of contact with their situation.

After the Council, the sisters tackled the reform of their communities with eagerness and honesty, as the Council had invited them. Some congregations entered well into the intentions of Vatican II, by updating some external and institutional expressions of their evangelical commitment without losing their fervor and substance. Some, especially new congregations founded upon the Council's principles — such as Mother Teresa's Sisters of Charity — have enjoyed prodigious growth. These congregations are like a living commentary on the Decree *Perfectae Caritatis* on the Adaptation and Renewal of Religious Life (1965), and its complement, *Ecclesiae Sanctae*, Pope Paul VI's Apostolic Letter of 1966. The *National Catholic Register* published a revealing survey in 1995 showing that sisters who live in obedience to the true teachings of the Church are happy precisely because they are living out their consecration to Christ.

Other congregations of sisters suffered a grave crisis after the Council and have not yet recovered. They were ill-advised by untrustworthy counselors, mostly theologians among the male religious who seemed to find morbid satisfaction in infecting these good sisters with their own rebellion against Church authorities and even the most common-sense traditions. Under this influence, many sisters opened themselves to secularism and pagan feminism, to the great detriment of themselves and their congregations.

These congregations' destruction was aided by corrupt psychologists. This tragedy was brought into the open by the confession and apology, published in 1995, of Dr. William Coulson, a psychologist, about his work with Dr. Carl Rogers, famous for his "nondirective therapy."[19] Dr. Coulson has recounted how, for several years beginning in the mid-1960s, he and Rogers contaminated several religious orders with humanistic psychology. (His confession, made with agonized regret, is one of the most important testimonies in support of the thesis of this chapter.) Realizing the depth of this situation, the Vatican intervened in 1983 with the marvelous decree *Essential Elements in the Church's*

---

[19] See the 1995 Special Edition of *The Latin Mass*, pp. 12–17.

Teaching on Religious Life but many religious, both male and female, rejected it, to their own tragic undoing.

ARTICLE 5: THE EUCHARIST AND THE *NOVUS ORDO*

Having discussed other liturgical documents and the fallout from the unprepared release of the Roman Missal, now we turn to the *Novus Ordo* itself.

The steamroller of man-centered horizontalism (as opposed to God-centered verticalism) has flattened all liturgical forms after Vatican II, but its main victim is the *Novus Ordo*. Its creators made a grievous mistake by pushing a "return to simplicity" to the point of impoverishing the ritual and destroying the sense of celebration and mystery. In modern Western thought and practice, the horizontal dimension of celebration seems to exclude the vertical dimension of reverence. Yet true liturgy and true celebration are exactly the reconciliation of both: the active involvement of the faithful sharing in common in *their ascent to God*, and in integrating *God's descent to men* in faith.

The element of true celebration has essentially departed from the *Novus Ordo*. The main reason for this bookish (and talkative) removal of the soul from the Mass is what Norbert Höslinger rightly referred to as "man putting himself forward as the prime mover instead of God."[20] The main loser in this process is *the mystery*, which should be, on the contrary, the main object and content of the celebration. Our primary attitude *vis-à-vis* the mystery must be reverence and awe, its fitting milieu. When these are lacking, the celebration, or what is left of it, speeds on to its undoing.

Only when given a reverent setting and a sufficient amount of time can the worshipper gradually penetrate into the hidden meaning of the mystery, by a religious acceptance and not just a mental understanding. In total neglect of this fact, the authors of the *Novus Ordo*, who had no interest whatsoever in the field of religious anthropology, stripped the new Mass almost as much as possible of all anthropological patterns proper to true ritual. They apparently considered rituals to be gratuitous and useless activities because they are not utilitarian and productive. We will return to this topic.

---

[20] Norbert Höslinger, *Bibel und Liturgie*, 1970, no. 2, p. 1.

DETERIORATION OF THE EUCHARIST

Perhaps the worst result of ignoring the principles of religious anthropology, as evidenced in the *Novus Ordo*, is the deterioration of the Eucharist. Here I will discuss four areas that must be corrected.

a. *The duration of the Mass* must be sufficient. Anthropologists emphasize that religious activities of great importance—and the Eucharist is the center of all Christianity—need, first of all, a certain duration, to show their full advantage. So the element of time must be considered here. In his *mind*, man can jump from one concept to another, just as the body can change quickly from one movement to another. But in his *spirit*—in his heart—man, in his God-filled ritual, needs the slow rhythm of reverence, in which each ritual complex moves unhurriedly to the next and each ritual flows organically out of the one preceding it, as it was from ages past. The whole eucharistic rite of the *Novus Ordo*, however, is deeply distorted by rattling off the Word service, smuggling away the preparation of the gifts, and rushing through the Anaphora and Holy Communion. The duration of twenty minutes or even less for daily Mass is but a parody of the divine and sacred. Hasty modern Western man needs calm and respect to respond from his self-centered ego to the holiness and otherness of God. We must finally begin to make the Eucharist very precious, for It is, indeed!

b. *The entrance and exit rites* of the Eucharist must be given sufficient time and explicitness. The anthropological law of discontinuity between "the world" and the sacred action requires a certain amount of time for worshippers to step over from our secular lives to the Sacred at the beginning of the liturgy (in the entrance rite). Similarly, at the end of the liturgy, we need sufficient time to return, "fully charged," from the intensely sacred back to the secular world (in the exit rite).[21] In the *Novus Ordo* these rites are largely inadequate. Of course, elaboration on the entrance and exit rites would make the celebration longer—but that would be one of its good results!

c. *The Word service*, of God truly speaking to his people called

---

[21] Elsewhere the author has described the human need for about fifteen minutes at both the beginning and the end of liturgical services for this transition between the profane and the Sacred to take place. I asked the author in 1996 to explain the subject here, but he replied, "Too long!"—Ed.

together to hear his Word, should be worked out, ritually, by texts
and actions. A longer dialogue before and after the readings is
necessary, as is surrounding the gospel reading with more solemnity as the real presence of the Word (meaning Jesus) speaking
to his people.

d. *The Anaphora* (the Eucharistic Prayers or canons) especially
needs a totally new approach or, rather, a return to the pre-Vatican
II arrangement. The second canon should be abandoned altogether
as much too schematic: it was originally meant as a schema for
free elaboration by the bishop; we will return to this topic shortly.
The omission of gestures is a more important flaw. Gestures were
introduced during the Carolingian reform, precisely to make it
easier for the faithful to follow this long solitary prayer. As soon
as the Roman Canon spread from Rome to become the rite of
the Western Patriarchate under the Carolingians, one of the
first documents on liturgical and pastoral accommodation was
the *Ordo qualiter cruces*, containing extensive gestures. This *Ordo*
was followed all over the West — until, ironically, after Vatican
II, the Council of active participation!

Psychologically seen, such a long prayer as the Anaphora, even
in the vernacular, can be helpful as an expression of mystical
ecstasy. But as soon as it becomes ritual and has to express the
theological content of the words, ritual acts must be added. Thus
the sacred gestures and blessings of the celebrant express, on
the one hand, the personal involvement of the minister in the
sacramental action. But on the other hand they express in rites
the often abstract or figurative contents of the Anaphora prayer
in order to bring this sublime content over into the mostly-silent,
but nevertheless active, participation of the faithful.

A LOPSIDED HISTORICAL APPROACH

Another major error of the Consilium's subcommissions was
their narrow and lopsided historical approach. I must be very
brave indeed to dare disagree with their prestigious historians
and their inventions in the postconciliar documents! Yet I am
qualified to comment in some of these fields, for I specialized in
them and made a lifelong study of the original liturgical sources,
under the aegis of great scholars, in the most distinguished European academic centers. Here I will limit my comments to those
matters of my expertise.

My main disagreement is not with the scholarly ability of the subcommission members, but with their mistaken starting points and norms. In their efforts to reform the Mass, these scholars, to their credit, wanted to return to the correct sources. The sources they chose were those of the oldest Roman liturgy: for example, Justin (d. 165), Hippolytus (d. 235 or 236), and other very primitive liturgical or patristic witnesses. To a casual observer this might seem a logical selection.

The subcommissions, however, overlooked a fundamental fact. These second- and third-century authors describe only a very schematic and rudimentary rite, one celebrated for a small group of people in a small space (mostly the catacombs), during or under threat of persecution. These circumstances forcibly reduced the celebration element of the liturgy to a minimum, that is, to an austere framework; examples are Justin's schematic description of the Eucharist and Hippolytus's Anaphora (the second canon of the present Roman liturgy). Neither of these was meant for a full-fledged celebration, nor is either one suitable for such a celebration in our day. Yet the liturgical experts took these abbreviated texts as the model for the new Roman Mass rite.

An even more serious error is this: by limiting themselves to this rudimentary early pattern, the subcommissions excluded consideration of all further development and growth of this primitive nucleus from the catacombs all the way into its massive style suitable for the basilicas. They especially discarded the later Carolingian maturity: a fully-grown, adult liturgy. Yet it was this mature liturgy—not the primitive so-called Roman model of the Early Church—that was at the basis of the Roman liturgy until Trent and beyond. All these facts have been irrefutably proven in Father Josef Jungmann's *Missarum Sollemnia* and the works of Antoine Chavasse, Theodor Klauser, myself, and especially Michel Andrieu.[22] Klauser's findings are absolutely fundamental, yet they were apparently ignored by the authors of the new Mass rite.

---

[22] Josef A. Jungmann, *The Mass of the Roman Rite: Its Origins and Development (Missarum Sollemnia)*, 2 vols. (New York: Benziger, 1951). See also Antoine Chavasse, "Les plus anciens types du lectionnaire et de l'antiphonaire de la messe," *Revue Bénédictine* 62 (1952): pp. 3–94; Theodor Klauser, "Die liturgischen Austauschbeziehungen zwischen der römischen und der fränkish-deutschen Kirche vom 8. bis 11. Jahrhundert," *Historisches Jahrbuch* 53 (1930): pp. 169–89; Boniface Luykx, *Der Ursprung der gleichbleibenden Teile der heiligen Messe*, cited above; and Michel Andrieu, *Les Ordines Romani*, cited above.

Necessary to understanding this subject are further facts regarding the history of the Roman liturgy. When thinking of the "Roman rite," we should keep in mind that the "primitive Roman liturgy" was a small, insignificant rite limited to one city that was subject to constant abuse and attacks by Germanic warlords. The rite was divided into three branches, one of which, the Gelasian tradition, was under strong Gallican (Syrian: i.e., Eastern) influence. Had not the Carolingian imperial liturgists saved the Roman liturgy at the moment of its otherwise fatal crisis (as Theodor Klauser has shown), it would have been swallowed into either the Byzantine or the Syrian liturgy during the time of the "Eastern" popes. Let me explain.

It was Carolingian liturgists who, in the eighth century, preserved the Roman documents, both the different *Ordines Romani* and the books for readings, singing, ordinations, et cetera. With this material, in the eighth to ninth centuries the Carolingian liturgists of the Aachen School, aided by a worldwide network of monasteries, rebuilt the Roman liturgy. But as this material was quite incomplete, they had to use many elements, especially prayers, from the pre-existing Gallican (Eastern) liturgy from Gaul and Spain, with which they filled out the Roman framework that was too poor and schematic.

Thus grew a new type of liturgy, composed of three key elements. It was an organic blending of the old *Roman* framework, enlivened with numerous wonderful devotional prayers for celebrant and faithful from the *Gallican* liturgy, and structured according to the model of the *Eastern* liturgies (especially for their support of the gestures and postures by private or common prayers).[23]

This new Carolingian liturgy was introduced into Rome by the reform of the Germanic emperors in AD 962–65 and reached its acme in the eleventh century. I coined the term "Rhenish liturgy" for this mature Carolingian liturgy of the eleventh century because it reached its adulthood in the great monastic and cultural centers of the Rhineland.[24] (Recall from Chapter 1 that

---

[23] See Henri Leclercq and Fernand Cabrol, *Dictionnaire d'archéologie chrétienne et de liturgie* (Paris: Letouzey & Ané, 1907 and many eds.), s.v. "Apologies" and "Flaccius Illyricus." See also André Wilmart, *Auteurs spirituels et textes dévôts du Moyen-Âge latin* (Paris: Bloud et Gay, 1932).

[24] See *Der Ursprung der gleichbleibenden Teile der heiligen Messe*, cited above.

Father Josef Jungmann accepted my scholarship on this topic and revised his *Missarum Sollemnia* accordingly.) This new type of Mass liturgy was accepted in Rome in the twelfth century as the true Roman liturgy, as the manuscripts show.[25]

The same process took place with the whole Carolingian liturgy: calendar, Divine Office, sacraments, "Great Rites" (rites of the liturgical year and ordinations), and music. The Rome-oriented Franciscans spread this liturgy throughout the West in the thirteenth century. Finally, it was this further-developed Carolingian liturgy that the Council of Trent promulgated as the official Roman liturgy in the sixteenth century.

This noble and rich pedigree was destroyed by the new liturgy after Vatican II. Its authors had a special aversion to the second and third elements of the Carolingian liturgy: the devotional prayers and the "private" prayers supporting the ritual gestures. That they should have such an aversion was very strange, because it was exactly these two elements that made the cerebral celebration flow over into the total active participation, body and soul, of the faithful, and thus made the objective celebration an event of prayer. Was this not precisely the deeper purpose of the liturgical reform of Vatican II? And must not elements that foster the worshippers' total involvement be especially important for any promoters of active participation?

I have discussed this point at length because it is perhaps the best proof of how the postconciliar reform "missed the boat" by a mistaken historical approach. Such a mistake draws in its wake of incompetency and exclusivism some other flaws. The lack of appreciation for the devotional and prayerful side of the liturgy resulted in a cold and horizontal loosening-up of ritual without expressed and prayed-out connections in the very rhythm of celebrations. This was a lack which the Carolingian liturgy had remedied quite fortunately and successfully, producing an enormous monument of Christian religious culture for all ages. The recent reformers dared to destroy this monument because they mistook the particular ancient Roman liturgy to be a model of "noble simplicity." And they made of it a pedestrian, marketplace liturgy, where nobility has been banished.

---

[25] Adalbert Ebner, *Quellen und Forschungen zur Geschichte . . . des Missale romanum* (Freiburg: Herder, 1896 and later eds.).

PLACEMENT OF THE ALTAR

I mentioned earlier that Father Josef Jungmann vigorously opposed the priest and altar facing the people. His reasons were many, and the West would do well to consider them anew; I will mention five.

1. First, the great importance of "easting": that everyone—faithful *and* priest—celebrate facing the east, whence the Risen Lord returns among his people-at-worship. This had been the general practice in all the liturgies of East and West from the very beginning of the Church.[26]

2. The highly important theology of both the ministerial priesthood and the general priesthood of the faithful, joined together in a common vertical ascent to God under the leadership of the ordained minister.

3. The distraction (and horror) of celebrant and people constantly looking into each other's eyes.

4. The impropriety of the people watching every detail of priestly rubrics that are not meant to be watched or vivisected.

5. The danger of horizontalizing a most holy (vertical) celebration, destroying reverence and awe and turning the Holy Mass into a social party.

Until the end of his life, Father Jungmann desperately battled against the growing monopoly of the altar facing the people and the destructive consequences that were already becoming generalized. He died in 1975 in deep sadness, powerlessly witnessing the systematic demolition of his realistic dream, the main work of his long and saintly life: a real liturgical renewal and restoration based upon the authentic sources, as opposed to some passing novelty. When his last letter to me arrived, a few days before his death, I wept as I read of his great disappointment—it seemed it sent him to his grave—which would gradually become the great disappointment of so many of us in the Church.

We need to put this problem of the altar facing the people in a broader perspective. This current, almost universal custom is one of two main paradigms of the new liturgy. It has been imposed with radical intransigence as though it were prescribed by the Council, and thus has been generally accepted by priests and

---

[26] Exceptions are four Roman basilicas that were oriented differently for non-liturgical reasons.

faithful as a great step forward. It is treated on the same plane as the second main paradigm of the new liturgy: the vernacular. Yet there is a great difference between these two. The vernacular is overall a blessing—though it must be used in accord with the Council's necessary restrictions, and translations must be accurate. The altar facing the people, however, is perhaps the most serious flaw and expression of the incorrect approach to true worship so common in the changes after the Council.

First, nowhere in the liturgical documents of Vatican II is the altar facing the people prescribed or presupposed as the common norm. The *only* prescription is that, at the incensation of the altar, the priest or deacon must be able to incense all around the altar; thus the altar should stand free from the wall. Yet many have taken this to the extreme, with the result that hundreds of beautiful and age-old church interiors have been irreparably destroyed by pushing the altar forward into the middle of the people. This has been done under the auspices of a false or exaggerated theology that the people are the real and main priesthood and the ordained priest is just a minister.

A theological flaw is at the base of this change and of the whole new liturgy: the notion that liturgy is the "work *of* the people" and hence horizontal. (In the next chapter we will see that, in fact, the true meaning of the Greek word *leitourgía* is a vertical "work *for* the people," an entirely different meaning.) In this notion, celebration is a horizontal gathering of the people around the altar; hence "eye contact" between priest and faithful is essential. Prayer to God, and an attitude of being totally oriented toward God in adoration and praise, is considered outdated and boring. This weakening or even destruction of the vertical dimension has become perhaps the basic counterfeit of the new liturgy as well as the undoing of the true Church. One might say that therein lies the original sin of the new liturgy and the corruption of what the Council had intended.

The great German liturgist, Monsignor Klaus Gamber, has clearly shown what I have experienced and written here: the *Novus Ordo* is manifestly contrary to the intent of CSL and *would not have been approved by the Council Fathers*. Rather, it was forced upon the Western Church by the order of Pope Paul VI, to assure the goodwill of our Protestant brethren. As Gamber wrote:

> ... Much more radical than any liturgical changes intro-
> duced by Luther... was the reorganization of our own
> liturgy—above all the fundamental changes which were
> made in the liturgy of the Mass. It also demonstrated
> much less understanding for the emotional ties which
> the faithful had to the traditional liturgical rite.[27]

Notwithstanding my statements about its failures, the *Novus Ordo* does have points in its favor, discoverable by any impartial participant. I have already mentioned that the vernacular, which it utilizes, aids true active participation of the faithful. In addition, the *Novus Ordo* can provide an intense vehicle of sharing between celebrant and faithful, for the simple reason that this rite is conceived and set up on a chiefly horizontal level. *If* the celebrant knows how to truly celebrate and how to preside humbly and prayerfully, and *if* he is a "vertical" man of God in prayerful oneness with God as well as with the people, he will be able to use the *Novus Ordo*'s leeway to bring about more meaningful participation.

If also, from the other side, the congregation is a true community, vibrant in faith and attuned to the celebrant, both priest and faithful will be able to use this leeway for mutual sharing-in-prayer and celebration. But it is absolutely necessary that the overly-horizontal dimension be always and thoroughly broken through, by the vertical fire of faith and fervor which both sides contribute to the celebration. This is extremely difficult, and therefore occurs very infrequently—yet it is possible. Unfortunately, most liturgical training in seminaries, workshops, and magazines has recourse mainly to diversions or pacifiers, thus skirting the real solution: to resolutely break through the horizontalism of the *Novus Ordo* by a strong vertical dimension.

Much more could be said about the *Novus Ordo*, but new specialized magazines such as *The Latin Mass* cover the subject well. Overall, I am convinced that the *Novus Ordo* is generally a failure: it suffers from a manifold inherent infirmity. The Consilium's subcommission that created it faced a very difficult task, in which it failed. So we must accept the consequence: the Western Church needs a new rite of the Mass.

---

[27] Klaus Gamber, "The Reform of the *Ordo Missae*," *The Latin Mass* (May–June 1993): p. 40. See also Msgr. Gamber's study "Altar of the People" in the same issue, pp. 29–36. [These articles were published in English after Gamber's death in 1989.—Ed.]

A POSSIBLE SOLUTION: PLURIFORMITY

What is the solution to this massive problem? I submit that *pluriformity*—that is, the coexistence of different forms of liturgical celebration while maintaining the essential core—could be a great aid to the Western Church. Some people are horrified by the very thought, and that is understandable, because since Trent the Western Church had only one rite. Yet before Trent this was not the situation. In the fifth to eighth centuries, the city of Rome was home to three different Mass rites represented by different Sacramentaries: the usual parish rite, the monastic use, and the curial texts, all of which coexisted peacefully.

It was only under the later Carolingian polity, beginning in the late eighth century, that the idea of a single model gradually emerged. But even then there was no uniformity, as the different offshoots of the *Ordo Romanus Primus* clearly show.[28] The same may be said for the description of the Mass rite in the later *Ordines Romani*: the imperial rite of the papal liturgy of *Ordo I* (from around AD 720) was soon simplified down to the subsequent *Ordines*, all the way to *Ordo X* in the eleventh century. Further, in the Middle Ages each religious order had its own rite, as did each major diocese.[29] There was only one canon, the so-called Roman Canon; it was the rites surrounding the canon that were different.

Pope John Paul II in fact adopted the principle of pluriformity when he restored the Tridentine Mass in 1988. So the Tridentine Mass could be one of several forms of celebration. Another could be a thoroughly revamped, reverent version of the *Novus Ordo*. Another could be either the *Missa Normativa* of Father Jungmann, or a new project Monsignor Klaus Gamber described in his 1993 book, *The Reform of the Roman Liturgy*.[30] These three Mass rites could beneficially exist simultaneously in the Latin Church. All of these, however, will need a thorough reform, in the *true* spirit of Vatican II, giving due respect for Holy Tradition, majesty

---

[28] See the editions of Michel Andrieu, *Les Ordines Romani*, cited above.

[29] The author's doctoral dissertation at Louvain, directed by Dom Bernard Capelle, was on the Premonstratensian rite of the Mass: *Essai sur les sources de l' "Ordo Missae" prémontré* (Tongerloo, Belgium: Sint Norbertus-drukkerij, 1947).—Ed.

[30] Klaus Gamber, *The Reform of the Roman Liturgy: Its Problems and Background* (San Juan Capistrano, CA: Foundation for Catholic Reform, 1993).

and reverence, and the principles given here or in Monsignor
Gamber's book.

Pluriformity would especially allow the restoration of some
originally private prayers that have deeply influenced Western
spirituality, such as, for example, the Psalm *Judica* (Ps 42:1, "Vin-
dicate me, O God ... ") at the beginning of the Mass, and the
very idea of the "prayers at the foot of the altar." It could also
restore the old Offertory prayers as alternatives, and put the kiss of
peace at the Offertory where it belongs. Many other propositions
regarding pluriformity could be made, but they must always be
sanctioned by the Church authority.

Strictly speaking, the principle of pluriformity is not foreseen
in CSL. Its introduction can thus be seen as *praeter legem* (outside
of the law), but it is not *contra legem*. Indeed, pluriformity may
well prove a necessity or advantage for the Church, because we
now live in an open society where everyone is accustomed to
deciding for himself. My feeling is that someday pluriformity
will indeed return in the West, with like-minded people bonding
together to worship according to various rites.

ARTICLE 6: THE TRIDENTINE MASS,
REVERENCE, AND HOLINESS

The historical existence of simultaneous multiple rites underlies
the decision by Pope John Paul II, set forth in the Apostolic Letter
Ecclesia Dei (July 2, 1988), to make the Tridentine rite—in either
Latin *or* the vernacular—again available for common use. The
pope's decision was not a questionable concession to the pressure
of traditionalists, but rather a wise decision perfectly fitting the
Roman liturgical tradition and the real needs of the Church. In
Ecclesia Dei, John Paul endorsed the "rightful aspirations" of those
who prefer the ancient liturgy, in a vision of the world's bishops
allowing it widely and generously:

> To all those Catholic faithful who feel attached to some
> previous liturgical and disciplinary forms of the Latin
> tradition I wish to manifest my will to facilitate their
> ecclesial communion by means of the necessary measures
> to guarantee respect for their rightful aspirations. In this
> matter I ask for the support of the bishops and of all
> those engaged in the pastoral ministry in the Church....

> . . . Respect must everywhere be shown for the feelings of all those who are attached to the Latin liturgical tradition, by a wide and generous application of the directives already issued some time ago by the Apostolic See for the use of the Roman Missal according to the typical edition of 1962.

Cardinal Ratzinger has also given his support, declaring that the old Mass is a living and, indeed, "integral" part of Catholic worship and tradition, and predicting that it will make "its own characteristic contribution to the liturgical renewal called for by the Second Vatican Council."[31]

Just what is this contribution to the renewal, in the mind of these two great men of the Church? Let us begin our discussion with an argument *ad captandam benevolentiam* (to win the goodwill) of those who object to the Tridentine Mass. This Mass has been restored to use in the Western Church by her highest authority and for serious reasons. The most important reasons are, I believe, restoration of the faithful's eucharistic devotion and their sense of reverence and the holiness of the eucharistic mystery — and hence the enhancement of their true active participation, one of the primary goals of CSL. Moreover, the Tridentine Mass may be introduced only under the guidance of the local ordinary (bishop) as the high priest of the local Church. Thus it is a lawfully-permitted way of celebrating the Mass, in full accord with the Church's objective rules. *Ecclesia Dei* therefore recommends that the bishops be very lenient in granting permission for celebration of the Tridentine Mass when a sizeable number of faithful ask for it and a priest is willing to celebrate it. Bishops should not require repeated beseeching as though being asked for a harmful privilege; in fact, episcopal refusal to permit celebration of the Tridentine Mass would be a painful abuse of power.

LATIN AND THE VERNACULAR

This brings us to the issue of language. What did the Council Fathers intend regarding Latin and the vernacular in the liturgy? As an eyewitness, I can state with certainty that a wholesale

---

[31] From his introduction to a French missal. See *The Latin Mass*, Special Edition 1995, pp. 19–23, for more on Cardinal Ratzinger's position in the dispute about the Tridentine Mass.

abandonment of Latin as the liturgical language of the Western Patriarchate is against both the true spirit of Vatican II and the prescriptions of CSL and Rome's later decrees.[32] Both CSL and the decrees wanted to keep Latin, as stated in CSL 36:

> (1) The use of the Latin language, with due respect to particular law, is to be preserved in the Latin Rites.

Note that it says the "use," not just the abstract principle, of the Latin language. Article 36 goes on to state:

> (2) But since the use of the vernacular, whether in the Mass, the administration of the sacraments, or in other parts of the liturgy, may frequently be of great advantage to the people, a wider use may be made of it, especially in readings, directives and in some prayers and chants....

> (3) These norms being observed, it is for the competent territorial ecclesiastical authority mentioned in Article 22:2 [bishops' conferences], to decide whether, and to what extent, the vernacular language is to be used....

So the Council envisioned a balance between Latin and the vernacular. Let's unpack this further.

A main concern of the entire renewal movement both before and during Vatican II was to bring the people of God back to active participation in the liturgy. The common conclusion of this divinely-inspired movement was that *fidelity to the primitive tradition of all the Churches requires a return to use of the vernacular.* (Many people forget that in the third to fifth centuries Latin was the vernacular, the common language of the people!) However, this return to the vernacular need not be total: the vernacular should be used only as much as the people need it and to the extent that their religious culture can absorb the loss of a liturgical language. Therefore the Council and related papal documents struck a wise balance between Latin and the vernacular, and allowed for local adaptation by the bishops.

All official statements on use of the vernacular in the Western Church make clear that a distinction must be made between the *principles* regarding its use and their *applications*. There are two

---

[32] See Avery Dulles, "Revive Latin," *The Catholic World Report* (September–October, 1992): pp. 29ff.

principles: (1) the right to use the vernacular, with all this entails (including the Pandora's box of troubles inherent in translations, which we will discuss later); and on the other hand (2) the need to keep Latin as the "mother tongue" of the Roman rite — of the *libri typi (editiones typicae)*, the Latin norms that serve as models for all translations into the vernacular.

The *applications* of these principles must maintain a balance between the two; they must also balance them with the Tradition of the Roman rite and the authorities of the Church. Consequently, for example, use of the vernacular does not mean building up a whole new worship (e.g., an "American rite"); the rite must always remain the genuine Roman rite of the *libri typi*. Even if some alternative forms are allowed in the vernacular, they should still be the *ad libitum* choices made available in the *libri typi*. Introduction of the vernacular was certainly never intended to allow the invasion of banality and liturgical abuses we have seen in recent years.

Since the vernacular is meant to make the faithful's participation easier and fuller, Article 36 gives the areas where it can be used: "... especially in readings, directives and in some prayers and chants." Hence, again, there is no question of a wholesale abandonment of Latin, although keeping Latin should not obstruct real active participation. Perhaps the best solution would be to keep in Latin the Eucharistic Prayers and the Ordinary of the Mass — the Gloria, Sanctus, and Agnus Dei (plus the Kyrie, which is Greek) — because people know, or can easily be taught, their meaning and melody.[33]

REVERENCE AND HOLINESS

A primary reason the faithful flock to the Tridentine Mass is *their need for the reverence, holiness, and prayerfulness* that emanate from the Presence of God in its very celebration. This Mass is a prayerful, true, and sacred ritual, a holy acting out of a mystery before the face of God, in holy language, and directly facing him. One feels in the Tridentine Mass a reaching out to the Holy One

---

[33] I am aware that some faithful request the Tridentine Mass from a desire to preserve Latin as a sacred language. We may regret that Latin has practically disappeared from the schools, for it had been to a great extent the tutor of Western civilization. However, the most sacred rite of the liturgy should not be seen as a means for keeping Latin alive.

and a living contact with him, an opening-up to the unspeakably Sacred, expressed in symbols and rituals (of which the *Novus Ordo* was purposefully "cleansed"). This Mass has become so popular in America and Europe because it restores reverence as the primary "element" of celebration. The need for reverence explains the phenomenal success of recordings of Gregorian chant, such as the one from Santo Domingo de Silos in 1991, wherein millions of people all over the world, especially young people, have rediscovered the God of beauty who was still singing in their hearts.

Gregorian chant is the musical expression of the age-old reaching out to the transcendent and is thus the main creator of the Tridentine Mass's atmosphere of reverence and awe. This chant was a wonderful inheritance from the Eastern Church that developed fully in the West, thus becoming one of the most precious treasures of Western religious culture. The hunger for the Tridentine Mass and Gregorian chant shows the great necessity of good music for good worship.[34] Yet in our day countless celebrants, music directors, and "liturgy commissions" continue to impose banal, low-quality music on faithful souls Sunday after Sunday.[35]

The typical Western celebration has so thoroughly abandoned reverence and beauty that most clergy and laity no longer even realize what they are missing. In the present crisis it is easy to understand why the promoters of the Tridentine Mass overlook the loss of the active participation insisted upon by CSL in order to win back the treasure of great price: the nobility and reverence which the Western Church desperately needs.

Reverence, the mother of all virtues, is greatly extolled by Dietrich von Hildebrand, who has profoundly stated: "*The depth*

---

[34] Of course, my statements praising Gregorian chant do not intend in the least to depreciate the wonderful Flemish and Italian polyphonic church music, the glorious traditional Catholic hymns, or the beautiful music (mostly in harmony) of the Eastern Churches, which CSL itself encourages. [The *Adoremus Hymnal*, published by Ignatius Press in conjunction with the Adoremus Society for the Renewal of the Sacred Liturgy, is an excellent resource. —Ed.]

[35] Abbot Boniface did not categorically reject all recently-composed church music. For instance, we sang some of the more tasteful Marian and praise songs in a weekly informal prayer meeting in the monastery's refectory (dining hall). But such music was never used in liturgical services. —Ed.

and plenitude of being and, above all, its mysteries will never reveal themselves except to the reverent mind."[36] This general principle of daily experience applies especially to worship, which is the channel for reaching out to God as he is and as he reveals himself. Hence, the faithful's common-sense demands for the Eucharist in the form of the Tridentine Mass, and for reverence in general, reveal the overall flaw of the postconciliar "renewal" endeavor, as opposed to the genuine renewal proposed by the Council itself. The present lack of reverence in the Western Church — and the need for it — is the main reason why the entire postconciliar "renewal" must be overhauled.

The destruction of the Sacred is the deepest assault on man's dignity in his thinking and living.[37] This is true because the Sacred is the highest value and reference in human thinking and living, which in turn is true because the Sacred is God's direct impact upon his creation. The consequences of this assault are enormous and all-pervading. For instance, it imposes upon man, who is made for the Beyond, the naturalization of the supernatural and the supernaturalization of the natural, by making the *Diesseits*-man[38] the norm of all values. With this comes the total *relativism* of these values, which is at the basis of our inextricable modern crisis.

With the waning or destruction of the Sacred, *Beauty* is also starved. Beauty is the reflection of the Divine, as is *Truth*, the guarantee of the *Reality* of this impact of God upon his creation; and it is through *Ritual* that man celebrates the Sacred as source of *Grace* and life. This means that, when the Sacred is thrown out by lack of reverence, the ultimate reference to the *principale analogon* and norm is thrown out, so the whole fabric of values of knowing and living disintegrates. As a result, worship as the primary source and guarantee of the Sacred in our lives turns into the ridiculous, the great enemy of the Sacred; and social life is built on lies.

From this death of the Sacred in worship flows the death of respect for authority, truth, and beauty, and the resultant breakup

---

[36] Dietrich von Hildebrand, *The New Tower of Babel: Modern Man's Flight from God* (Manchester, NH: Sophia Institute, 1994), Chapter 5.
[37] The rest of this chapter was a late (1997) unedited addition to the manuscript. — Ed.
[38] The meaning is generally "the man of this present world." — Ed.

of families and a proliferation of evils in society. In general, the respect for life dies, as is seen in the acceptance of abortion and euthanasia and all kinds of violence. These evils originate, ultimately, from the death of reverence, especially in its origins in worship. When reverence is gone, all worship becomes only horizontal entertainment, a social party. Here again the poor, the little ones, are the victims, since the obvious reality of life as flowing out of God in worship is taken away from them by "experts" and dissenters. This is very serious indeed.

And so we come to the next chapter, on the second postconciliar phase.

> Tears stream from my eyes
> because your law is disobeyed.
> My part, I have resolved, O LORD,
> is to obey your word.
> —Psalm 118/119:136,57

CHAPTER 4

"What Have We Done with Vatican II?"

The LORD turns his eyes to the just
and his ears to their appeal.
The LORD is close to the broken-hearted;
those whose spirit is crushed he will save.
— Psalm 33/34:17,19

ARTICLE 1: SEEDS OF (R)EVOLUTION

In 1987 the late Peter Hebblethwaite gave a summer course at the University of Notre Dame entitled, "What have we done with Vatican II?" Coming from him, it was an ironic question, because he and many of his friends contributed to the question's negative answer. But concerned people from all ranks of the Church have asked the same question. Although of course this book cannot answer it fully, examination of a few elements is necessary to our discussion of the postconciliar evolution.

This chapter will give more detail of the Council's aftermath inside the Church. The next chapter will step into the wider circle of secular crises and trends with which the postconciliar dissenters identified. But to comprehend fully that deep undoing of Christianity we must first realize how the inner crisis of postconciliar dissent scattered the seeds of revolution wherever it went.

The aftermath of the Council was characterized by two main agents. First was the postconciliar commissions. These operated privately, in the office and in meetings around the green table, away from the eyes of the public; I have given some examples above.

The second agent was a number of men, especially theologians backed by magazines, who operated in the open, both inside and outside the Church. These men desired the Council to be, above all else, the instrument of a thorough alignment with secular culture. To promote their agenda they openly ventilated varying opinions about the problems of the Council. They also exaggerated and distorted the need for change and updating in the Church. Of course, such a need had been suggested by the Council's man-centered documents such as *Gaudium et Spes*. But the Council documents were motivated by pastoral concerns, whereas these dissenters and their supporters in Catholic and secular media were obsessed with an impatient desire for speedy and thorough inculturation.

The media have been highly influential in the postconciliar revolution in general, but their influence was especially significant on the new liturgical books and rites. Pope Paul VI had prescribed but one task for the Consilium: the proper implementation of CSL. But public pressure from the dissenters and their media contributed to the subcommissions drifting farther and farther from that task. The media also exacerbated the overall polarization that began to develop immediately after the Council: within only five years, around 1970, they began speaking about "the liberal flank of the Church" and "the Catholic progressives who won the victory over the conservatives."[1]

This polarization became even more dramatic in the delicate area of contraception, after the release in 1968 of Pope Paul VI's encyclical *Humanae Vitae*. Whole groups of theologians (e.g., in the United States and Canada) and even entire episcopates (e.g., in Germany) publicly rejected the pope's teaching on this crucial issue. After 1968, *Humanae Vitae* became both the origin and the litmus test of the growing dissent in the Western Church.

Pope Paul's delay in promulgating *Humanae Vitae* added to this crisis.[2] In the mid-1960s, some theologians were already publishing arguments in favor of allowing contraception. Sensing the danger, orthodox bishops and priests were asking Pope Paul to set forth the Church's teaching on the subject. Yet he delayed. By the time he did act, the majority of the commission advising him was in favor of contraception. Had he acted promptly, such a majority would not have arisen, and *Humanae Vitae* would not have caused such a reaction.

---

[1] Promoting dissent is, of course, the main purpose of the *National Catholic Reporter* (not to be confused with the faithful *National Catholic Register*). It has been rightly said that when the *National Catholic Reporter* is no longer found in chanceries and rectories, the crisis of the Church in America will be over and she will be saved.
[2] The material in this paragraph was added from a recorded interview with the author in 1996; see Appendix B, Further Reading. — Ed.

From this situation the dissenters drew a dramatic conclusion, so typical of the second postconciliar phase: "Now you see that we can't trust all that comes from Rome, especially from the popes, especially in their directions on implementing the Council." At the outset this opinion was only whispered among like-minded brothers and sisters, but as time passed the dissenters became more bold, with theologians and liturgists bonding together in a systematic bypassing of CSL and the whole of Vatican II. At first they at least paid lip service to invoking "the spirit of Vatican II." But gradually they elevated themselves above both Council and CSL, as if the only norm that mattered was the secular culture into which henceforth the "new liturgy" had to fit.

In the beginning, such inner dissent was more a general practical attitude than an *ex professo* teaching. I believe that at first this attitude was inspired chiefly by disappointment of the optimism carried over from the preconciliar hopes. But gradually, especially after 1968, it was triggered by the strong reaction against *Humanae Vitae* and was systematically organized by a highly efficient circle of Church politicians.[3]

THE DESTRUCTION OF CATHOLIC EDUCATION

These politicians' infiltration began with the seminaries, many of which were turned into hotbeds of rebellion, forming priests who would popularize this new "faith." An unbelievable but true tragedy is that good seminary candidates have been refused entrance precisely because they were not imbued with the spirit of rebellion against the pope and Magisterium in matters of liturgy, morality, and social and priestly life. Such discrimination has been practiced — incredible though it may seem — for the purpose of *preventing rather than fostering vocations*, to ultimately bring the Church down to a horizontal organization consisting only of laity, without ordained ministers.

Catholic universities, some of them quite prestigious, were also secularized, under the pretext of academic freedom, as if the gospel meant the destruction of human freedom and dignity! This took place supposedly under the pressure of losing governmental subsidies, although it has been proven that the government

---

[3] See the important study of James V. Schall, SJ, "What if Catholics Weren't So Wimpy? Our Culture's Fear of a Robust Catholicism," *New Oxford Review* (June 1996): pp. 17ff.

never required such secularization. This process was especially tragic because most of the dissenting theologians were attached to "Catholic" universities and colleges, and thus felt backed by their prestige or indebted to their support.

Movements also arose which worked to destroy true Catholic education on the grade and high school levels. This was mainly the work of religious sisters who had become secularized and subsequently gave up all Catholic catechetics. Here the "little ones" were defenseless victims: the youngsters did not learn the true faith but rather were indoctrinated into falsehoods. The victims were *also* the parents who put their trust (and hard-earned money) in these schools, completely unaware of the sisters' new agenda and that their children's faith was being systematically stripped from them. Such reckless discarding of all Catholic instruction has created a whole generation of religious and spiritual illiterates.

This *trahison des clercs*, treason by the "white-collar church," is deplorable for multiple reasons.[4] First, victimization of the poor and little ones of the gospel is counted by the old catechism among the sins calling for revenge from heaven — even if for only the bad example (*scandalum pusillorum*, scandal of the little ones) given by the leaders. Second, this rebellion is built upon false bases, which we will discuss in the next article. Third, this betrayal is fed mainly by a rejection of Church authority, especially the pope, and a practical discarding of the Council in favor of a haughty conceit. "Haughty conceit" may seem a severe judgment, but certainly those will agree who have witnessed the irreparable damage done to the little ones — and the pain caused to faithful priests and to holy nuns suffering at the hands of their rebellious sisters.

Yet despite all this negativism, the Holy Spirit is still at work. Thus we see a growing stream of conversions into the Church, a wonderful flowering of vocations to new religious orders, a renewed fervor among many young clergy, and the blessed faithfulness of older clergy. In short, among those who truly love the Church, a new adult Christianity is taking over, now strongly aided by the dynamism and documents of Pope John Paul II.

---

[4] Among the rich literature on this topic special mention goes to the late Christopher Lasch's last book, *The Revolt of the Elites and the Betrayal of Democracy* (New York: W. W. Norton, 1996).

ARTICLE 2: DIAGNOSIS OF DISSENT

Let us now look more closely at the inner operation of this rebellion during the second postconciliar phase. I do not pretend to have an explanation for everything, because in such currents there are as many imponderables as the human psyche has inscrutables. But I can bring to light some elements that deserve our attention and cry out for correction.

The liturgical rebellion is but one of the forms of dissent in the Church. In this article I will identify two *general* directions of dissent, to give the background of the liturgical revolution, both from a distance and close up.

VIEW FROM A DISTANCE

The dissenters in the Church for the most part are taken seriously and enjoy much recognition. Here are a few reasons for this odd phenomenon of injustice.

1. Sociology shows us that people like to applaud those in opposition to authority, because humans have a deep need to make someone or something responsible for the failures and unhappiness in our own lives, families, or society. The dissenters provide a rallying point for those who feel such a need to oppose authority.

2. The dissenters are mostly priests, nuns, or bishops. The average person assumes that these leaders have an essential message, have thought through what they are promoting, and act with wisdom. *Thus the dissenters are abusing the charism with which they have been invested by the Holy Spirit and the Church.*

3. The mass media relentlessly play up the disagreements between dissenters and those loyal to the Magisterium. They inflate the importance and authority of the dissenters—and the supposed evil of the dissenters' opponents. Their present enemies are, of course, Pope John Paul II and Cardinal Ratzinger, representing "Rome, the oppressive system that must be abolished."

4. Some bishops and superiors continue to invite dissenting priests and nuns, even those who have been silenced by Rome, to lead talks and workshops, run chanceries, teach at Catholic colleges and universities, and publish heretical articles. For instance, many bishops have for years included the weekly column of destructive dissenter Richard McBrien in their diocesan newspapers, where it corrupts the minds and hearts of the unsuspecting

faithful. Thus they aggravate the situation by making the dissenters indispensable and even purported norms of orthodoxy.

I cannot give a complete diagnosis of dissent in the Church without briefly discussing the aforementioned Richard McBrien and another paradigm of dissent, Hans Küng. What I write here about these men is accompanied by my sincere respect and sympathy for their *persons*; it is their *theology and attitudes* I reject.

Swiss theologian Hans Küng was a professor at the University of Tübingen in Germany until his retirement in 1996. Though not a leader in the liturgical revolution, he is the standard-bearer of their dissent, expressed in the theological field. For instance, his 1994 book *Great Christian Thinkers* takes every possible opportunity to denigrate all Church authority. After treating seven thinkers from Saint Paul to Karl Barth, Küng concludes his book with an eighth chapter entitled "What Theology is Desirable Today?" Standing as judge above the others, he proposes his own thinking: that theology and theologians should be free from all interference or oversight by Church authorities, and that scholarly rigor should be the only norm of theological (and all) authority. Hence, for Küng, the hierarchy has no role in the future of theology (or liturgy) or even in the future of the "new church." With great sorrow I see that Küng's rejection of Church authority has evolved for him into a rejection of Christianity itself and essentially an alignment with its enemies.

Richard McBrien is professor of theology at Notre Dame University and the darling of the U. S. rebels. He stepped into the open in 1985, when the U. S. Bishops condemned his book, *Catholicism*, as inaccurate and misleading. The bishops re-issued their warning after a revised (1994) edition appeared;[5] yet McBrien continues to defiantly spread his errors via all sorts of media. I have before me a list of 113 errors in his book, many of them major deviations from Church teaching.

McBrien's case is not about the right to hold his own opinions; it is about the bishops' obligation to safeguard the integrity of Catholic doctrine. Crucially, it is also about *the faithful's right to receive that doctrine unadulterated*. In this postconciliar confusion, many of the faithful do not know whether theologians, priests, and directors of religious education are teaching them from the

---

[5] See *The Catholic World Report*, May 1996, p. 21.

authentic Magisterium — or from heretical books such as that of McBrien. The faithful have the right to receive the truth, and dissenters such as Küng and McBrien must be prevented from spreading their lies.

A CLOSER LOOK

When one looks at the dissenters' message and especially at their inner disposition in the light of the gospel and Holy Tradition, quite a different picture comes to the fore, one especially noticeable to persons such as myself who knew several of them before their open rebellion. (I would like to clarify here again that I do not intend to attack anyone personally.)

The desire and need for reform in the Church is as old as the Church in Corinth; see Saint Paul's second letter to the Corinthians.[6] Therefore I want to express my approval of the *principle* of inevitable (yet respectful) dissent in the Church. But by this I refer only to disagreement coming from those who suffer under real abuses and air them respectfully. In this sense the number of true dissenters in the Church is actually quite small. Let me explain.

There is quite a difference between disagreement and disobedience; between differences of opinion kept to oneself and dissent blazed abroad; between humble disagreement among scholars and proud public proclamations of one's attacks on authority; and, of course, between respectful acceptance of the Church's God-given teaching charism and blunt disparagement of it. Unfortunately, the second half of each of these alternatives is usually the case in the dissent we are discussing here.

What are the chief causes of this negative attitude? We must be delicate in answering this question, because here we enter into personal areas and could easily give the impression of lacking respect for the inner psyche of those involved. But this forces us to ask another question: how can healing ever come when these problems keep being swept under the carpet and are not addressed? So here I will be honest, but with much compassion and forgiveness.

---

[6] See also the summary of Professor Lorenzo Albacete's address, "The Praxis of Resistance," *National Catholic Register* (August 13, 1995): p. 5; and his article of the same title in *Communio*, Winter 1994, pp. 612–30. Albacete spoke of the theological *and psychological* involvement in resistance within and through the Church, for it is always *persons* that practice resistance or dissent.

The most easily recognizable category of dissenters consists of those who have ever clashed, supposedly or actually, with those in authority, and who, after that clash, broke off communication that could have saved and restored their relationship. (I will speak here in the past tense, but such situations continue in the present.) Instead of seeking reconciliation, they nursed feelings of rejection and hatred, either openly like Küng and McBrien or, more commonly, in a coldly calculated manner — until they reached the point of speaking about "the monstrous hierarchy" (Küng's very words). While licking their wounds, such dissenters began rejecting, and hating or combating, all that is related to the persons in authority: the Church authority as teaching body, her teaching itself, and the whole "patriarchal system."

Next they began courting like-minded "soul brothers and sisters." These partners were not only fellow theologians but, appallingly, also outsiders they had previously avoided as enemies of the Church. These outsiders were secularists who rejected miracles and the whole supernatural faith dimension of Scripture, such as the infancy narratives, the Resurrection, and Christ's healing miracles. They also rejected God's impact upon the events of history and its Christological dimension.

In short, the dissenters came to align themselves with a wholesale attack on Christian spirituality, which of course resulted in a loss of prayer and prayerful worship. They attacked the spirit of the Beatitudes and the Magnificat and, indeed, all the events in which God vertically breaks through man's horizontal, self-centered behavior.

Meanwhile, the dissenters' own inner insecurity was shown by their need for affirmation, which they pursued by joining together with other dissenters, in meetings and workshops, in attacking Church authority. They also worked to gain influence in chanceries and with the (hated!) authority. Their fervor in these destructive endeavors accounts for the imposing numbers of their publications and their ruthless use of the media.

What is the source of such a need for affirmation in so many priests and religious? The great Dutch specialists in this field, Catholic psychiatrists Conrad Baars and Anna Terruwe, have written much to elucidate the phenomenon. This need is rooted in an often-deep-seated residue of suffering, arising not only from childhood experiences but also perhaps from hurts at the hands of a sometimes-tyrannical, pre-Vatican II Church authority, from which they have never recovered. Their dissent is a cry for love and understanding from the despised authority; yet their willful lack of gentle humility takes away the condition necessary for healing.

Hence, for many dissenters, it is a question not so much of dealing with the theological problems of others as of dealing with the psychological problems in themselves. So much could be resolved, and so soon, if they would accept these premises — and if they would turn away from their own rebellious minds, the applause of the media, and their fallacious success with unthinking followers, and rather take humble refuge in a true devotion to the Mother of God.

SCANDAL OF THE LITTLE ONES

I feel compelled yet again to warn all those involved — especially the hierarchy, priests, and nuns — of the tremendous and exceedingly real problem of the scandal of the little ones. Who are these "little ones"? In addition to children, young people, and parents as mentioned above, they are millions of adults who have not the time, money, opportunity, educational background, or critical thinking abilities to make their own academic studies and find or discern the truth — and who consequently must rely (or feel they must rely) on theologians, priests, and religious. If these theologians and others pump into the little ones' lives the litter of their own unresolved problems, how will the little ones ever recover and learn the truth? Having grown up in the "old Church," I am deeply scandalized that almost no attention is paid to this problem. Indeed, Rome under Pope John Paul II is almost the only authority that still has the "guts" to silence or depose those who have long continued in deeply misleading teaching or erroneous pastoral attitudes.

A further group of little ones are deeply hurt by dissent and false teaching: those outside the Catholic faith, especially the multitudes honestly searching for the true Church. Some of these, though desiring to become Catholic, are rebuked, discouraged, or scandalized by the constant criticisms of the dissenters. Others fall prey to priests who, imbued with the heretical notion of indifferentism, counsel them that Catholicism offers no advantages over their current religion. What a terrible responsibility these dissenters bear in the eyes of Christ, Lord of the Church!

Also injured are those who leave the Church. As the reader has surely experienced, millions of once-faithful Catholics have abandoned the Western Church amidst the postconciliar turmoil. Some have joined Protestant churches where they no longer receive the benefit of the sacraments, adhere to Holy Tradition, or honor the Mother of God and the saints. Hundreds, possibly thousands, of prayerful, truth-seeking Catholics each year join the Orthodox Churches. For them this may be a blessing, because in the Orthodox Churches they will find what had been stolen from them but they so eagerly desired: beauty, reverence, and the sense of majesty. Others discover the Eastern Catholic Churches where they find the deep reverence and beauty of Orthodox worship while gratefully remaining in union with Rome (see Appendix C).[7] Tragically, however, vast numbers of those who leave the Church abandon their Christian faith entirely. May the Lord have mercy on them and draw them back to the truth in the bosom of his Church.

The problems are painful and rampant. But the dissenters do not make up a large part of the Church. A majority of bishops, priests, religious, and lay people — although the leaders often remain silent when they should speak out against errors — are nevertheless essentially faithful. God is still at work in his Church, and a healthy reaction of gospel-minded "friends of the Church" has set in, on all levels of life. These comprise a worldwide movement under the discrete leadership of Pope John Paul II, manifestly guided by the Holy Spirit.

ARTICLE 3: PRINCIPLES OF OPERATION

Having seen "men at work" (the experts) and the results of their work, we must now take a closer look at the principles that inspired or guided their work on the liturgy. These principles are, first and chiefly, the "theology" behind their work, and second, the forms and logics into which they translated this "theology," as the ritual expression of the new liturgy. Problems could have arisen — and indeed did arise — from both of these sources. I will tackle them in order.

---

[7] Many faithful Catholics who wish to attend the Latin Mass but cannot are finding solace and nourishment in these Eastern Catholic Churches, where they experience in the Divine Liturgy (the Mass) the same profound beauty and reverence as in the High Mass, but sung in the vernacular. — Ed.

ERRONEOUS THEOLOGICAL FOUNDATIONS OF THE NEW LITURGY

Most members of the Consilium were chosen by the *ad hoc* authority in Rome because of their sound theology and practical liturgical knowledge and experience. I am convinced that, at the outset, sound theology was indeed at work. A highly significant example is that almost all the members accepted the concept of the real presence of the mystery at work in its very liturgical celebration (the *Mysterienlehre*), which Pope Pius XII had adopted as a support of *Mediator Dei* and which had become the basis of liturgical life. The intent of CSL, as of the Liturgical Movement, was precisely to bring the Mysteries closer into the participation of the faithful, but with full respect for Holy Tradition and in continuity with it, in a wise balance of all the elements of worship.

Soon, however, I saw this sound theological foundation become sidetracked, first by individual pressures within the subcommissions and later by secular contaminants. A certain radical impatience took hold, resulting in a misinterpretation and a "forcing" of some truly sound principles of CSL. For example, the principle of the vernacular called for its use in the parts of the liturgy meant for the people's understanding—not for doing away with Latin or using street language or free translations. And the principle of utilizing a more popular style of music called only for inserting the very best of such music into a dignified worship; it did not mean eliminating Gregorian chant altogether and replacing it with cheap tunes.

Behind these revolutionary exaggerations were hidden three typically Western but false principles: (1) the concept (à la Bugnini) of the superiority and normative value of modern Western man and his culture for all other cultures; (2) the inevitable and tyrannical law of constant change that some theologians applied to the liturgy, Church teaching, exegesis, and theology; and (3) the primacy of the horizontal. Let us look closely at each one.

THE "SUPERIORITY" OF MODERN WESTERN CULTURE

Father Annibale Bugnini's assertion about the superiority of modern Western man is symptomatic. The reader will recall that when Bishop Malula objected that the Consilium's work was of no use to the African people, Bugnini dismissed him, replying in essence, "We here work from the assumption that the modern

Western man is the perfect man, the model of all true humanity, for all countries and cultures, for all ages to come."

Father Bugnini's statement, made twice in my presence, is important for two reasons. First is the persons involved. Bugnini was Secretary of the Consilium and thus had enormous influence over the subcommissions' operation and results. Bishop Malula was the only representative of the African continent,[8] and he henceforth boycotted the meetings in protest. Second is that Bugnini's arrogant statement in fact rendered well the policy of the Consilium. Thus we see that *the subjective, not the objective,* theological standpoint of the Consilium's Secretary (and its members) was a strong factor in decisions regarding the postconciliar liturgical documents.

The terrain for this switch from the objective to the subjective had been gradually prepared by theologians such as Karl Rahner. His work gives a typical example of how an almost imperceptible deviation toward subjective (and secular) thinking gradually grew into an entire thought system of a wholesale aberration, transposing God as Being into God as mystery — that is, going from objective Being to our subjective *perception* of It, and from there to our subjective *experience* of It, which is then falsely promoted as the main and absolutely reliable means of "knowing."

Thus has the objective been supplanted, to the extent that now, as psychiatrist Robert Coles has stated: "We live in an age of applauded subjectivism."[9] We touch here the origins and foundation of the pagan New Age religion — in which man becomes his own god — which aims to replace Christianity as the religion of the future.[10] It is for the postconciliar dissenters a dubious honor that they have prepared the way for this new paganism by destroying Catholic theology and liturgy.

---

[8] The *Elenchus* does list three other Consilium participants from Africa, but perhaps they were less active or influential; this is not clear. — Ed.

[9] See the solid study by a young Episcopal priest, Charles W. James: "Karl Rahner's Baneful Impact on Theology," *New Oxford Review* (Sept. 1995): pp. 9–13.

[10] Multiple forms of New Age paganism, including overt witchcraft, were rampant in the area where the author's monastery is located. In more subtle forms it has invaded many Catholic Churches to their detriment. For a recent brief article on the topic, see Deacon Derrick Johnson, "Have Nothing to do with the Dragon" at https://denvercatholic.org/have-nothing-to-do-with-the-dragon-part-i-new-age-practices. — Ed.

THE TYRANNICAL LAW OF CONSTANT CHANGE

The second erroneous principle of the postconciliar reform is the tyrannical law of constant change in Christian moral and theological teaching, biblical exegesis, and worship. Not long after the Council this concept was shouted from the rooftops. Books on the subject flooded the market; it was also a primary topic for pastoral workshops and diocesan newspapers. All this was orchestrated by leaders of the dissent, while the hierarchy negligently stood by. The dissenters proclaimed that the only certainty we have is "how we *feel* in the midst of all these changes," since to them man's *feelings* are normative for truth and life. Theirs was a totally man-centered approach to life and hence, inevitably, to worship. They believed that worship should catch people's attention by constant change, and be shaped by how people feel.[11]

Here the anthropological law of Jean Cazeneuve steps in.[12] This law correctly observes that one of the fundamental requirements for good and true worship is its unchanged continuity, its familiarity. Worshippers need to know what to expect and should not be subjected to unprepared surprises. If this law is violated, worship will suffer, as will the spiritual life of the believers. The law of Cazeneuve helps to explain the havoc after the Council: the failure of Church leaders to provide instruction about the coming changes greatly disoriented the faithful and harmed the cause of the liturgy. As I noted above, I am convinced that this lack of preparation and instruction was a primary cause of the deep crisis that has upset the Western Church ever since.

One might ask, "Then must the liturgy always stay the same in every detail in order not to upset the people?" Not at all. Some changes may be introduced; indeed, good liturgy is seasoned

[11] One of my nephews was head of a pediatric hospital in Africa. In the 1970s he moved back to Europe, where his whole family went to Mass on Sundays and weekdays. After many weeks, the pastor visited him and asked, "What do you think of *my* Masses, Doctor?" Roger replied, "I thought the priest *has* no Mass. It is the Mass of the Lord Jesus Christ and of the Church." "All that nonsense!" retorted the priest. "If you don't like what I make out of the Mass, I don't want you there." And that was it.
[12] Jean Cazeneuve's *Les rites et la condition humaine* (Paris: Presses universitaires de France, 1958) is perhaps the most important book on the topic of religious anthropology.

with incidental changes, but they should be few and the people should be prepared well for them. They should not be novelties, but ways to express more explicitly the divine mystery, made within the boundaries of the permissions given by the *libri typi*. These changes should not affect the essence of the celebration, the substance of its structure, and the spirit and wording of its expression. So we see that the idea of attracting people by constant novelties is exactly contrary to true and good worship; yet it is encouraged by most liturgical magazines and workshops.

In addition, one must guard against exaggerations and switching over to relativism or absolute change without any stable core. The liturgical rebels have made both mistakes, and, unfortunately, those who hold absolute relativism tend to make their wishes into reality. Contrary to their theory, at good worship even children attentively follow the service, though the services are essentially the same Sunday after Sunday. We witness this in our monastery church, half full of little children, deeply interested in the wonders of Byzantine worship.

I must add that the law of Cazeneuve applies mainly to worship, not to ordinary practical life. Variation and change are needed in daily life, to counteract the boredom that sets in when the same pattern is repeated without change. The Aristotelian principle *vita est in motu* (life is in movement) is often — and for good reasons — invoked in the context of daily life, but this principle cannot be applied to the liturgy.

The law of Cazeneuve rests on the deeper anthropological *law of continuity and discontinuity*. In all cultures, true worship, as an expression of the holy, lies essentially in discontinuity with the profane (meaning here the secular or unsanctified).[13] That is why worshippers keenly feel the need that the priest dress in liturgical vestments and use dignified language and gestures. Yet worship forms the deeper meaning and normal climax of the

---

[13] Most modern studies on this topic are built upon the foundational work of Mircea Eliade, especially his *The Sacred and the Profane: The Nature of Religion* (New York: Harcourt, 1959 and many eds.), which is the most easily approachable source on religious anthropology. See also James Hitchcock, *Recovery of the Sacred: Reforming the Reformed Liturgy* (San Francisco: Ignatius, 1995), which amply shows that CSL did not intend the desacralization of the liturgy but rather the opposite. See also Thomas Day, *Where Have You Gone, Michelangelo? The Loss of Soul in Catholic Culture* (New York: Crossroad, 1993).

profane; hence, there is also a certain continuity between them. But the movement of "adaptation" in this process of continuity is determined by worship and *not* by the profane. It is through worship that the profane is sanctified; worship must not be taken over by the profane.

The profane is sanctified by sacramentalizing it: for example, bread becomes the Body of Christ, changed from the most usual profane thing into the highest divine Reality. By giving this divine dimension to the profane, worship is *per se* the creator of beauty. This explains why the inner tendency of the new liturgy — despite its claiming the opposite — is actually the *destruction* of the divine beauty which Holy Tradition had accumulated in the Church's worship, and why cosmetic corrections cannot solve the new liturgy's problem.

THE PRIMACY OF THE HORIZONTAL

Important in all the above is a third, even deeper, erroneous principle of the postconciliar "reformers": the primacy of the horizontal. Father Bugnini and the proponents of change believed that the first and real foundation of "good worship" was its horizontal (i.e., man-oriented) dimension, and that its vertical (God-oriented) dimension was secondary, following from the other. I have already given examples of this dislocation of priorities, but it is good to repeat the subject here, for this is perhaps the primary cause of the demolition of the postconciliar Roman liturgy.

The primacy of the horizontal is the basic principle of the agenda of the second postconciliar phase. In this principle, liturgy's first dimension is horizontal, as a social action of the people to create a down-to-earth sharing among the participants. The result of horizontalizing worship is the almost totally socialized and man-centered dimension of the liturgy now found in most parishes. But this destroys the most basic meaning of all worship. It is a tragic desacralization of Christian worship, where man, not God, is central, and the liturgy becomes a fireside affair, a civil performance intended to make everyone feel happy, as in some Protestant groups. I would add that healthy church life consists (as good Pope John said) of a people of believers thronging around the laden table of the Word and the Eucharist, as one big, vibrant "we" composed of many egos. In our day, however, the individual ego is told to prevail and become the norm.

APPLICATIONS OF ERRONEOUS THEOLOGY

The postconciliar liturgical reformers erroneously held that, since constant change is "the law" for worship, the people (faithful and priests) are the ones qualified both to make this law and to judge it. This improper appropriation of power is now followed in almost all levels of the Church, mostly by means of liturgy commissions. Yet it manifestly runs counter to the oft-repeated rule of the Council. CSL's Articles 22, 26, and 40, for example, state that authority in matters liturgical is invested only in the Apostolic See of Rome and others "as laws may determine." For the reader's reference, here is the full text of Article 22:

> (1) Regulation of the sacred liturgy depends solely on the authority of the Church, that is, on the Apostolic See, and, as laws may determine, on the bishop.
>
> (2) In virtue of power conceded by law, the regulation of the liturgy within certain defined limits belongs also to various kinds of bishops' conferences, legitimately established, with competence in given territories.
>
> (3) *Therefore no other person, not even a priest, may add, remove, or change anything in the liturgy on his own authority* [emphasis added].

Many object to such limitations, saying, "But doesn't the term 'liturgy' itself mean 'work of and by the people?'" No, the primary meaning of the word liturgy (*leitourgía*) is "work *for* the people" (from the Greek *leiton ergon*) *by* the public authority.[14] The subjective involvement of people and ministers is crucial in liturgy. Indeed, it includes the whole area of active participation. But the objective (vertical) dimension — the "work [of God and the Church] *for* the people" — is the first and proper characteristic of true Christian worship.

This constant teaching of the Church has not changed but rather was confirmed by CSL and its twenty-four satellite documents. The liturgy's aim is not primarily the horizontal "gathering of people," and certainly not their *social* gathering; there are other occasions for that. The liturgy's aim is our reaching out (vertically) to God in homage and supplication, and God's (equally vertical)

---

[14] See G. W. H. Lampe, *A Patristic Greek Lexicon* (Oxford: Clarendon, 1987), pp. 795–96, s.v. *leitourgía*.

reaching out to us in the form of his Word and his Mysteries. In other words, *worship is essentially our vertical ascent to God and the equally vertical descent of God to us*; both of these actions occur in sacramental forms, that is, ontologically. The goal of worship and of all religion is to bring the Sacred into the profane (the secular arena) of human life as its irreplaceable channel to God.

Under the influence of theologians like Edward Schillebeeckx, however, horizontalism sank to even lower depths. They sought to streamline the liturgy so in line with Protestantism that only the general priesthood of the faithful, and not the ordained priesthood, is considered valid or necessary. The Constitution on the Sacred Liturgy espoused the basic, correct *theologoumenon* of the universal priesthood of the faithful (1 Pet 2:9). But the dissenters, in their subjective interpretation, pulled the ordained, ministerial priesthood down to the level of the general, unordained priesthood, and lifted up the latter to the level of the former. Thus ordained priesthood became to the dissenters a superfluous luxury; they began to ask questions such as: "Why bother with the ministerial priesthood any longer?" Further: "If there must be ordained ministers, why can't we ordain women?" And ultimately: "Why should we have to listen to bishops or to Rome? Let the bishops make the Church visible in public affairs, but let us 'do our own thing' without interference."

THE CRUCIAL ROLE OF RELIGIOUS ANTHROPOLOGY

From this flattening of the Sacred by horizontalism follows an important question: What in Scripture justifies our (correct) appeal to the dimension of the Sacred as an irreplaceable opposite of the profane? The same text from 1 Peter (2:9–10) gives the answer: being built up (by worship) upon Christ, we become a *holy* nation, after the *profane* status we had before we belonged to the worshipping community.

This biblical answer is strongly confirmed by *religious anthropology*. This was perhaps the scholarly field most overlooked by the postconciliar liturgical renewal. Yet it is crucial. Mircea Eliade has shown in several of his books, including *The Sacred and the Profane: The Nature of Religion*,[15] that the Sacred is not only a basic and

---

[15] Cited above. See also Hitchcock, *Recovery of the Sacred*, cited above. Damian Fedoryka's *Abortion and the Ransom of the Sacred* (Front Royal: Christendom, 1991) shows the true dimension of the Sacred in relation to life and death.

primary ingredient of human life; it is also the particular object and "element" of worship, as water is for fish. As Father Josef Jungmann often warned the subcommission leaders (but alas! he was unheeded), the *Novus Ordo* was essentially built up outside the perspective of the Sacred and its demands. Proof of this is that the two "lungs" of the Sacred—reverence and symbolism—have practically disappeared from worship. And "worship" without symbolism and reverence (holiness) is a contradiction in terms.

This point is important for another reason: *holiness* is the bridge between worship and practical life, the bridge from the vertical to the horizontal dimensions of life, the bridge from our relation to God the Creator and Redeemer to our relation with his creatures and the Church of the redeemed. Thus finally the whole of life may be permeated and transformed by holiness. This interpenetration of holiness with our relation to God is shown in good worship, where beauty is the great proof of holiness-at-work, as if it were the splendor of God's glory.[16]

The deeper reason for the necessity of holiness is that our personalities are very consistent: if our worship has been a truly sacred action and not just a civil social party, holiness will flow over into our whole lives as our outreach to God and his outreach to us. Therefore, the usual argument that "life is sacred by itself without any need for all these pietistic frills" is utterly wrong. Every honest person experiences from his daily sins that this argument is a great lie.

The same reasons apply to *symbolism*, the other "lung" of the Sacred, which has been discarded from the new liturgy as much as possible, under the pretext that modern man has no feeling for symbols but goes directly to the "reality." This is another lie: look, for instance, at the logos on our modern youngsters' T-shirts, their use of incense, their expressions of love. Symbols are finally and essentially vertical and climb up to a hidden meaning beyond their materially-graspable elements. So, for example, referring to Holy Communion as "sitting down at the table of the Lord" is not a pietistic curiosity or an empty formula from a bygone culture, but is perfectly understandable within our hearts and dreams of happiness.

---

[16] See Ernest Skublics, "The Holiness of Beauty," *The Canadian Catholic Review* (December 1992): pp. 34ff. See also the entire Spring 1991 issue of *Epiphany* on the sense of the Sacred.

TRESPASSES AGAINST ANTHROPOLOGICAL LAWS

The new liturgy contains several trespasses against true anthropological laws, as follows.

1. *The dropping or abbreviating of all repetitions of ritual formulas and gestures.* The repeating of ritual formulas and gestures is a basic anthropological principle in worship. From it stem important forms of prayer in all religions: for example, the Hail Mary prayed on the rosary beads in the West, the Jesus Prayer prayed on the Jesus knots in the East, and repeated ejaculatory prayers in private devotions. But someone in our subcommission gave the typical objection: "These old customs make no sense anymore. If you need God's mercy, just tell him once; that will do. Did not Jesus himself enjoin us to make prayer short?" This comment blatantly misinterprets Christ's words: recall that Jesus praised the widow for her persevering, repeated prayer (Lk 18:1–8).

2. *Simplified vestments.* The loss of symbolism resulting from any essential simplification of vestments is to be regretted. Simplification can be justified to some extent, as long as the celebrant wears both chasuble and stole over the cassock. But never should only a stole, with or without an alb, be allowed, even for concelebrants. The objection I have heard that chasubles on each concelebrating priest would mean a variety of colors is a very weak excuse.

3. *The destruction of sacred space.* Modern liturgical dissenters categorically reject the holiness principle we discussed above in reference to church buildings and other sacred spaces. In their thinking, sacred space does not exist: it is the *person* who makes space holy, because (they say) the person is holy in whatever he does, unless it is manifestly sinful. Thus for dissenters there is no longer any difference between the Sacred and the profane. Yet throughout history the consecration of the church building has always been one of the major Christian rites. It is the solemn occasion in which the bishop "hands over" to God this space exclusively for his worship, just as a neophyte is handed over to God in baptism in water and the Spirit.

The failure to understand sacred space is an extension of the failure to understand the liturgy's vertical dimension, the orientation toward God, compared to which all else is secondary. For modern liturgists a church is a horizontal gathering place of the people; hence they encourage talking before and after services in order to build up "church" by socializing, which radical horizontalism considers just as sanctifying as worship. Thus too the sanctuary is no longer preserved as a sacred space; it has even become a place for secular performances, some of them outright blasphemous. I believe this was a "selling point" for the introduction of altar girls, a subject to which we will return.

This erroneous attitude has tragically caused some pastors to invite architects of a secular mindset to "renew" their old, wonderful churches, turning them into empty, dead shells, devoid of devotional items or statues (are the saints no longer our friends?), and putting the tabernacle somewhere in a corner. Thus they have made the church a show hall rather than a home for prayerful worship or a place to "hide away in God." I remember Professor Émile Lousse, the famous historian of Louvain University, saying repeatedly that the main witness of a culture is its public buildings. What poor witnesses these new churches are! This heart-rending destruction has been accomplished with the money of the poor, in witness to the poverty of our spiritual culture, withered away at the hands of ministers who no longer seem to know to whom the House of God belongs.[17]

4. *The poor state of liturgical music* is another result of neglecting the laws of religious anthropology. Thomas Day treated the subject very well in his book, *Why Catholics Can't Sing: The Culture of Catholicism and the Triumph of Bad Taste*,[18] which I recommend to every bishop, priest, seminarian, liturgist, and music director in the United States and elsewhere. Day's book traces the passage from the former largely-silent American parish church that had no music director (an absence that was then wrongly taken for granted) to the present church where the music director and musicians with their microphones overpower the people at such deafening levels they cannot hear themselves sing. Although parishioners are by now accustomed to the overwhelming PA

---

[17] A parish not far from the author's monastery abandoned its beautiful old building with stained-glass windows and high marble altar, and built instead an extravagant new structure akin to a hotel lobby. It was funded in part by pressuring unsuspecting poor farm workers to allow deductions from their paychecks. — Ed.

[18] Thomas Day, *Why Catholics Can't Sing: The Culture of Catholicism and the Triumph of Bad Taste* (New York: Crossroad, 1990). Day comments about the postconciliar liturgists that "Roman Catholicism, which survived the Dark Ages and the bubonic plague, may not be so lucky with this menace." [A revised and updated version of Day's book came out in 2013. — Ed.]

system, this phenomenon has destroyed the very anthropological function of liturgical music.

Liturgical music must, first of all, express the unspeakable values of the heart, and, second, gather up the individual believers into a common ascent to the unseen God and draw down his grace into the world of common faith and individual emotion. Good liturgy needs beautiful music that stirs the heart and is easy to sing and easy to remember. Unfortunately, the "liturgical renewal" has almost globally produced the opposite.[19] The new liturgy has suffered much, after the practical disappearance of Gregorian chant, because a great deal of the music that replaced it is poorly composed, with insipid lyrics and melodies that are difficult to sing. This is a great pity, because, superficially seen, it is often through the singing (along with the homily and the sharing) that people are drawn to, and stay in, a particular church. Unfortunately, most pastors do not realize this.

5. Pedestrian language is a further example of the new liturgy's violations of anthropological principles. We will return to this later. But here I must repeat that, as the brilliant linguist Bishop Malula emphasized, worship requires a holy language, permeated with reverence and awe of God, thus lifting up the worshipers to truly meet with God and the divine world.

THE RELIGION OF INCULTURATION

In Chapter 5 we will step from the second into the third post-conciliar phase, from the situation inside the Church into the wider circle of the modern crises of the West. But first I will attempt to bridge these chapters, discussing the main elements of the evolution from dissent against the Second Vatican Council's documents into open rebellion. In this transition between phases, inner-Church quarrels over the liturgy became the battlefield onto which the larger weaponry of the post-Christian culture was brought. Thus dissent within the Church became a part of the general political climate and problematics of this culture, and

---

[19] Rev. George Rutler, in a lengthy review of *Why Catholics Can't Sing* (see *Homiletic and Pastoral Review*, August–September 1991, pp. 75–79), has given the same causes I've presented here, including the horizontal "ego renewal" wherein the joy of the redeemed is crowded out by the ego of the celebrant and all sorts of commissions. See also Peter Kreeft's article "Snakebite on Music," *National Catholic Register* (October 1989): pp. 1, 7.

thus the postconciliar dissenters entered into the new "religion" of inculturation, which made Christianity (and its primary representative, the Catholic Church) its willing handmaid.

What matters primarily in this new religion is "political correctness" in order to make the Church fit into the post-Christian culture. The difference between the true Catholic faith and this new religion of inculturation may be seen by comparing two similar documents: (a) the beautiful 1988 Apostolic Letter of Pope John Paul II, *Mulieris Dignitatem* (On the Dignity and Vocation of Women), and (b) the politically correct "Pastoral Reflection on Women in the Church and in Society" approved by the U. S. Bishops in 1994. The latter, which succumbs to pressure from the media and secular culture, has already been swept into oblivion, whereas the former continues to grow in importance and relevance because it is the expression of the ever-fresh gospel and Holy Tradition of an ever-young Church.[20]

Let us now consider some principles of this politicized atmosphere wherein the dissenters operate in almost total freedom, while only the Holy See offers correct leadership to the contrary.

First, because this politicized atmosphere penetrates and determines all areas of life, its expression in public opinion *makes* (creates) morality or ethics, *makes* "theology" or lack of it, *makes* social relationships and government politics. In this atmosphere, life is only *Diesseits*: it consists only of the here and now, of what happens on this side of death. Thus instant happiness, success, power, "having," and "doing" take precedence over "being" and over the *Jenseits* (the beyond) of absolute truth and lasting values. In short, in this view absolute relativism is the only norm of life and being. This relativism is also proposed as the only interpretation of reality, even to the extent that this seemingly tolerant relativism ultimately turns rather into the most intolerant tyranny and obtrusiveness.

This relativism and all its accompaniments are the antipodes, the exact opposites, of the gospel and two millennia of the wisdom of Holy Tradition in the Church.[21] I repeat this point:

---

[20] On this subject I strongly recommend the rich study of K. D. Whitehead, "To Appease the Unappeasable," *The Catholic World Report* (March 1995): pp. 52–58.

[21] See Thomas Molnar, *The Church: Pilgrim of Centuries* (Grand Rapids: Eerdmans, 1990).

present-day relativism is totally at odds with the truth of the gospel and the Church. A battle is being waged between these two camps. And the battle will increase, demanding vigilant courage of any true spiritual leaders in this post-Christian world, because, in our secular culture, truth, holiness, virtue, and spiritual values of personal and social life are no longer of any account. Bishop Fabian Bruskewitz of Lincoln, Nebraska, gave a heartening example of such courage in March 1996 when he issued a warning to Catholics of his diocese forbidding them to belong to certain immoral and anti-Catholic organizations.[22]

The powerful salesmen of this destructive relativism, as I have said before, are the media. For them what matters most, as anyone can see, is sensational reporting, which draws people away from prayer, the core of life. They thus build up a tyranny of public opinion, imposing their will even on the Church and leaving no room for the Christian message. They proclaim man to be the highest norm of truth and values, and psychology, power, and progress to be the new religion. So all-penetrating is the media's empire that almost all the weak and vulnerable have succumbed and aligned themselves with their agenda. Our Catholic universities — with a few blessed exceptions — have also given in to this pressure, even against the clear teaching of Rome and the bishops. The only remaining incorruptible witnesses of the truth contained in Revelation are the pope, his bitterly-attacked Curia, and the (Eastern) Orthodox Churches. Pope John Paul II, Cardinal Ratzinger, and the Curia are relentlessly and unjustly rejected by the media; the Orthodox Church witnesses are simply ignored.

Let us simplify the picture once again. The core of this crisis consists in moving the center of being from God to man, from the vertical to the horizontal. Yet in reality the essential dimension of all liturgy is a vertical orientation toward God in praise and sacrament; therein it meets with the ontological structure of human soul and society. This orientation toward God is, anthropologically seen, the strongest and most indestructible motivation for relationships (such as love between persons); it calls for ritual to build up personality and society.[23]

---

[22] See "Excommunications in the Heartland," *The Catholic World Report* (May 1996).
[23] See Tom Driver, *The Magic of Ritual: Our Need for Liberating Rites that Transform Our Lives and Our Communities* (San Francisco: Harper, 1991).

The whole thrust of our post-Christian crisis, then, is the destruction of this liturgical undergirding of human life. Here is the key point: *as liturgy is the first victim of the crisis, working to restore true worship must be one of the first tasks in any effort to overcome the crisis and restore true culture — and such work will produce the first benefits.* If one understands this fact, he will understand the importance of my in-depth coverage of the postconciliar liturgical crisis in this book.[24]

A CRISIS OF GRACE

One last question must be addressed before we move on. Why is the Christian reaction — especially that of the bishops — so weak and cowardly in the face of this wholesale sellout of Christian culture? It is because we are witnessing, above all, a crisis of grace. We are in dire need of a renewed outpouring of the Holy Spirit, which Pope John XXIII meant the Council to be. Grace is the soul of organized religion, the soul of the Church that is too much seen only as an institution. Sacrifice and prayer — especially contemplation and mysticism — are forgotten items in the postconciliar "new church" and new world.

As Father Benedict Groeschel says in his book *The Reform of Renewal*,[25] which I highly recommend, the personal reform of the individual Christian is the active core of all authentic renewal of society, of the Church, and of her worship. For that reason the real problem goes much beyond issues such as the Tridentine Mass, the vernacular, or Gregorian chant. *We need a renewed return to the gospel, especially to the whole Sermon on the Mount, so ignored in the present culture.* We need a renewed return to Holy Tradition, as was called for by the preconciliar movement. We need a return to the Council itself. This does not mean turning the clock back, but returning to the wellspring of all truth and life in the Blessed Trinity and Revelation.

All this requires a true conversion. Conversion contains two movements: a turning *away* and a turning *toward*. We must turn

---

[24] Then-Cardinal Ratzinger made precisely this point in his 1997 statement captured in Dom Alcuin Reid, ed., *Looking Again at the Question of the Liturgy with Cardinal Ratzinger* (Farnborough: St. Michael's Abbey Press, 2003), p. 141: "[T]he true celebration of the Sacred Liturgy is the centre of any renewal of the Church whatsoever." Abbot Boniface would surely have included this quote had he known about it. — Ed.

[25] Benedict Groeschel, *The Reform of Renewal* (San Francisco: Ignatius, 1990).

away from all forms of self-conceit and ego-centeredness which have denatured true worship and true Holy Tradition, including seeing the Church as an institution and the liturgy as its entertainment. We must turn *toward* clear teaching by the Magisterium instead of blurring all the issues, as the postconciliar decay did to the Council documents. We must turn *toward* the priority of prayer and holiness and reverence in the liturgy, in order to enter, body and soul, into the life-giving mystery that is celebrated. Hence arises the equally important eschatological dimension of worship as the manifestation of Christ in glory and majesty, giving the worshippers a deep, humble piety that places them under the Holy Spirit, the Word, and Holy Tradition.

If only the Consilium's subcommissions had been humbly obedient and stuck to the task allotted to them by CSL and the Council at large, many of the problems I describe in this book would never have arisen. Dietrich von Hildebrand rightly summarized the problem in *The Devastated Vineyard*:

> The basic error of most of the [postconciliar] innovations is to imagine that the new liturgy brings the holy sacrifice of the Mass nearer to the faithful, that shorn of its own rituals the Mass now enters into the substance of our lives. For the question is whether we better meet Christ in the Mass by soaring up to Him [the vertical dimension], or by dragging Him down into our own pedestrian, workaday world. The innovators would replace intimacy with Christ by an unbecoming familiarity. The new liturgy actually threatens to frustrate the confrontation with Christ, for it discourages reverence in the face of mystery, precludes awe, and all but extinguishes a sense of sacredness. What really matters, surely, is not whether the faithful feel at home at Mass, but whether they are drawn out of their ordinary lives into the world of Christ—whether their attitude is the response of ultimate reverence, whether they are imbued with the reality of Christ.[26]

---

[26] Dietrich von Hildebrand, *The Devastated Vineyard* (Chicago: Franciscan Herald Press, 1985). See also the interview of Robert Moynihan with Cardinal Ratzinger, "Restore the Sacred," *Inside the Vatican* (August–September 1995): pp. 16–19.

The situation is bleak; indeed, it may seem that Peter's barque has lost its moorings in this terrible storm. But even now golden rays are breaking through the clouds, as faithful laity and clergy rise up. In our last chapter we will offer suggestions and hope for a new dawn.

> O Cross, you are the royal scepter of Christ,
> the victory of the Christian people, and the glory of
>   the true faith.
> Protect those who prostrate before you,
> so that the false teachings may not triumph over us.
>   (*Exapostilarion* for Friday, Tone 2, from the
>   Byzantine Divine Office)

CHAPTER 5

From Dissent to Organized Hatred

Who is he who longs for life
and many days, to enjoy his prosperity?
Then keep your tongue from evil
and your lips from speaking deceit.
Turn aside from evil and do good;
seek and strive after peace.
——Psalm 33/34:13–15

IN THE PREVIOUS TWO CHAPTERS, WE SAW
how the Consilium's subcommissions grossly overstepped the
prescriptions of the Constitution on the Sacred Liturgy and
made up a new liturgy according to their own interpretations.
During the first postconciliar phase (Chapter 3), the subcommissions created new principles of operation that inevitably
evolved into an attitude of disobedience and rebellion; this
attitude soon further evolved into one of open attack against
the Church and her authority. During the second postconciliar
phase (Chapter 4), the matter still remained chiefly within the
Church and revolved mostly around the liturgy. But as the years
progressed the tension grew until it finally burst open into the
larger domain of the secular world and thus into general apostasy. This degeneration of the rebellion into an all-out embracing
of secularism characterizes the third (and present) phase of the
postconciliar period.

The distinctive feature of this third phase is that we have now
entered a post-Christian era and culture. The conflict between
the heritage of Vatican II and its postconciliar deformations
has broken into the public forum and become part of the dramatic clash between the two kingdoms mentioned in the Gospels (Mt 13:38; Jn 1:10–13, 7:7, 14:30–31). These clashes no longer
occur behind closed doors or within the due discretion of usual
Church affairs and diplomacy; now they take place openly, with
virulent attacks of hatred and bitterness, as in the times of the

most fatal persecutions. It is as Jesus foretold in John 15:18: "If the world hates you, know that it hated Me first." Thus hatred, with a destructive radicalism, has become the new tonality in which this third phase operates, as the Mother of God predicted at Fatima in 1917, and as she continues to warn in her many apparitions.

Since the two main leaders of the Church, Pope John Paul II and Cardinal Ratzinger, are aware of the third secret of Fatima, they are not afraid of "naming the demons" in their response to these concerted attacks, nor of telling things as they are, nor of vindicating the revealed truth in spite of all the ridicule heaped upon them. We have seen this in their many excellent recent documents, especially the new *Catechism of the Catholic Church* and Pope John Paul's interventions on all the current problems of mankind. The "demons" they name are, above all, the various media which are working out a systematic agenda, masterminded by a combination of secularism and the organized powers of evil.

In this chapter we will look at all these elements of the third postconciliar phase. We will not only treat the liturgy but also give witness to the gradual decomposition of the entire Christian heritage to the rhythm of the decomposition of human culture. We will see that this happened mainly because of the betrayal of Vatican II by the sidetracking of truth into secular, absolute, man-centered relativism. Because the topic is so extensive, we will follow this decomposition through its various "paradigm shifts."

This chapter contains many descriptions of problems in Church and society. But let the reader take heart—Chapter 6 will offer a beautiful and uplifting antidote to these ills.

ARTICLE 1: FROM HORIZONTALISM TO SECULARISM

As we discussed above, egocentric horizontalism has been perhaps the seminal principle of the postconciliar crisis. Such horizontalism has gradually sapped Christianity of its life, as a tragic revenge of Father Bugnini's haughty rebuke of Bishop Malula. Once this man-centeredness was entrenched, it was easy to throw God out altogether. Into this vacuum moved the egalitarian relativism of strident feminism; then came pagan inculturation that adapted everything to the measure of man, not God. Finally the New Age entered, as the new religion in which man becomes his own god. Only one element remained to follow: anger and hatred, with accompanying bitterness and spiritual violence.

To begin this aspect of our discussion on horizontalism, we must go back to its context early after the Council. *Lumen Gentium*, the Council's document on the Church, in its second chapter, restored the basic notion of the Church as "the people of God." Many persons prone to exclusive thinking erroneously latched onto this phrase, concluding that the (vertical) theology of the Mystical Body of Christ had been replaced by the (horizontal) notion of "the people," analogous in every way to its secular parallel on the civil and political level. In their zeal for the phrase's horizontal aspect, they forgot its equally important, vertical aspect: we are the people "*of God.*"

We are all a (horizontal) "people of God" because we are, *first*, "all in Christ," forming one (vertical) person in Christ; we are called together (horizontally) in order to celebrate his Mysteries and *thus* be saved (vertically). Saint Paul uses the theological statement "*in Christ*" 164 times in his letters, showing that the emphasis is not on radical equality of members but on "life in Christ," in all its mystical, liturgical, and social dimensions. (Sadly, these days life in Christ is almost never the topic of sermons, catechesis, or pastoral letters; in my experience, bishops and priests speak about all kinds of expediencies, but almost never about life in Christ, about holiness.)

One of the first applications of life in Christ is that the Church is not governed as a democracy; it is not a horizontal organization. The authority in her bosom is sacramental (i.e., ontological): it is the expression of a mystery of salvation. This foundation is rejected by almost all the dissenters. For them, authority is seen as an evil (a necessary evil, some allow), something that does not belong to the inherent "baggage" of the Christian. They say, therefore, that the pope or bishops or religious superiors have no right to lead.

Hence we see the sprouting up of tyrannical parish councils, "ruling teams" for religious, and nun-chancellors who overpower the bishops, all of which serve to level down differences of authority. In such a framework the Holy Spirit has become largely unemployed — or allowed to work only in the individual person and then only according to a self-centered agenda. The rejection of authentic Church authority is the basis also for rebellious theologians' demand that they, "who really know the business," should be a hierarchy parallel to the Church hierarchy. That the Church hierarchy was instituted by Christ nearly 2,000 years ago means nothing to them; they ridicule it as ancient, outdated, and founded on wrongly-interpreted sources.

This horizontal image of man embraces the attitude that the model for man is the *science-man* that Father Bugnini had in mind: the human being who stands totally free from all depth-dimension, all religion, history, and tradition, and is rather geared totally toward the present reality.[1] Although history is truly and essentially a vertical dimension of life and events, the rebellious theologians say that history too is subject to horizontalism and relativism. For them the past has no importance or meaning, because man lives only in the here and now. Tradition, which gathers and preserves past experiences, is to them pure fiction created by those who want to exploit others.

Hence these theologians place no value on continuity and normative values, such as those of the gospel and the Early Church, for they hold that man's inborn, emerging evolution is constantly lifting man up from a lower stage to a higher one. It is like babies becoming children, becoming teenagers, becoming adults, becoming citizens of a country — and all countries coalescing into one Nation, with no transcendent outlook or escape, where all striving is bent inward, unto the evolution of the Self, in a worldwide egalitarian horizontalism.

BLACKOUT OF TRUTH

The horizontalizing movement wreaks havoc not only in the area of emotions and feelings, but especially on the level of *truth*. This is obvious when one looks at the movement from the vista point of worship and Bible research. In the third phase of post-conciliar decomposition, various horizontal streams of thinking

---

[1] Fortunately, this image of the "science-man" is now being abandoned even by many scientists, some of whom are religious persons who know that what matters first is not science but life-values, which are deeply rooted in the "myth and story" category. This category, the deepest category of truth and meaning, is the framework God used for his Revelation, completed in Jesus Christ and handed down in the Holy Tradition of the Church — all of which are vertical values.

are beginning to coalesce. Take as an example liberation theology and radical feminist theology. Proponents of these identify themselves as victims of patriarchal monotheism. They see God the Father as an abusive father sending his Son to die on the Cross. Hence, they say that we must get rid of the Cross, for it is a sign of torture, humiliation, and abuse. They especially reject the Trinity, because the Trinity defies the human mind, and for them the mind is the norm of all truth and reality.

God is Truth, revealed in Jesus Christ (Jn 14:6), and hence Truth is absolutely primary, as God Himself is primary Reality, that is, absolutely vertical. Consequently, for man Truth is equal to God's absolute Realism, as Saint Thomas Aquinas wrote. But God as Truth must be known. As Pope Leo the Great (d. 461) said, "*No one draws closer to a knowledge of the truth than he who has advanced in the knowledge of divine things.*" Hence, the Bible is the truth *about* the Truth; it is therefore reliable, as is the Church's proposition of Truth, lived and worshipped by her. Thus those who doubt or undermine truth — or man's thirst for truth — become traitors. (Significantly, the Hebrew Bible contains no word for "doubt.") Yet the main intent of the rebels is to create doubts in order to strengthen their own agenda.

We must quench our thirst for truth at the correct wellsprings, given by the Church and her Spirit-fed Holy Tradition. As Peter said to Jesus, when most of his disciples had left him: "Lord, to whom shall we go? You [alone] have the words of eternal life" (Jn 6:68). Jesus gave them not only his words but also his Body and Blood as food, for true worship can occur only when we fully accept Jesus as he is, the Son of God made man for our salvation — which is the essence of the liturgy.

The wise Dietrich von Hildebrand expressed it well in Chapter 5 of *The New Tower of Babel*, cited above: "The mark of the present crisis is man's attempt to free himself from his condition as a created being... and to disengage himself from all bonds with anything greater than himself." He gives examples of the fallacies of our anti-Christian age: the individualistic self-sufficiency that cuts us off from any authority, the one-sided worship of science, the rejection of objective truth, the notion that the contemporary educational system brings about wisdom, the installation of false objectivity, and the pursuit of instant happiness and fulfillment as ends in themselves.

The first great victim of all these deviations is truth. And when man throws out truth, he himself becomes the real victim, for he perishes from the ensuing destruction of morality. Those most victimized of all—let me emphasize it again—are the poor and the weak, who lack the means or the leisure to investigate these things for themselves. A further victim is community among persons, for individualistic self-sufficiency precludes true brotherly sharing.

The above reveals how some trends that are apparently harmless at the outset grow by their own inner dynamism and degenerate into breeding nests of evil where the prince of this world can work, to the ruin of souls (1 Pet 5:8–9). This is the power that creates secularism, on the foundations of horizontalism, as I wrote in the beginning of this chapter.

What can counteract such destruction? Faith—and so we come to the last point of this article.

THE ROLE OF FAITH

Faith is precisely the opposite of all the negative features of the postconciliar crisis, which is basically a crisis of faith. Faith is the acceptance of the Reality that transcends our senses and understanding; it therefore also transcends empirical science and the natural means of knowledge. Because it cannot be known by the usual sensory and rational means, this Reality must be revealed to us. And indeed it is, by the invisible Father in heaven who lives in unapproachable light (1 Tim 6:16), by his Son, and by his messengers, the prophets—and guaranteed through Holy Tradition by the Church built as the mainstay of truth upon the rock of Peter (Mt 16:15–19).

If acceptance of any one of these basic components—the Trinity, the Scriptures, Holy Tradition, or the papacy—is lacking in a person due to dissent or rejection of authority, that person's faith is lopsided or even destroyed. This lack has an immediate repercussion upon worship, the objective carrier and expression of the Mysteries of revelation and salvation. If worship is stripped of its symbolism and beauty, and especially of its continuity with Holy Tradition, the channels of revelation and salvation are blocked. This has often happened in the new liturgy, where the faith element is weakened or destroyed by secularism. The new liturgy is often so stripped to a skeleton that it loses not only its ritual nourishment but also its appeal to the faith of both minister and faithful. Such an impoverished liturgy perfectly fits into a secular context, but not into the continuity of Christian Tradition.

There is more. When the foundations of true Christian worship are destroyed by throwing out Christ, his precious Cross, the Holy Trinity, the Mother of God, and the angels and saints, a vacuum is created, and something else must replace them. This explains the great attraction of the New Age as *the* worship of these rebels: they think New Age principles will give them everything they need—significantly, without the morals that true Christianity requires of them, for example, in matters of sexual discipline.

Obedience is the main means of overcoming the power of Satan in the whole realm of rebellion. As Jesus said to Saint Margaret Mary Alacoque:

> But listen, my daughter, believe not lightly nor trust every spirit, for Satan is enraged and will seek to deceive you. Therefore, do nothing without the approval of those who guide you; being thus under the authority of obedience, his efforts against you will be in vain, for he has no power over those who obey.

Obedience requires seeing Christ in our true spiritual superiors, which is an act of vertical turning to him in faith. *Those who, in their lack of faith, reject the authority of the pope, and of the superiors in union with him, thus cut themselves off from the spiritual protection afforded to the obedient.*

ARTICLE 2: THE FEMINIST AGENDA

This article on the feminist agenda follows directly from the previous one on horizontal secularism, as applications follow from principles. Its three sections are closely linked: after stating some *general concerns*, I will look at one of the agenda's immediate expressions, *inclusive language*, which is promoted largely by the International Commission on English in the Liturgy (ICEL) and groups whose ultimate goal is *women's ordination*.

GENERAL CONCERNS

The principal firebrands, as it were, that spread the flames of revolt and hatred in the Church are radical feminists. They do so with an irredentist ardor that apparently makes them refuse all reasoning and attempts at mutual understanding. Journalist Donna Steichen, who unmasked this destructive and un-feminine ardor, aptly named this attitude in the title of her valuable book, *Ungodly Rage: The Hidden Face of Catholic Feminism.*[2] Let us look more closely at feminism's origins.

Columnist Suzanne Fields, in her study, "Founding Feminists Beware: A New Generation is in Charge,"[3] gives a clear overview of the feminist situation, as follows. When Betty Friedan published her seminal work *The Feminine Mystique* in 1963, she kindled a true feminine revolution. Her book was a positive and constructive "wake-up call" to women that they could expand creatively and seize greater control of their lives. Friedan and the first feminists wanted not to drive off men and children but to foster the liberating ties that God had put in nature. Very soon, however, "feminism was stolen by a coterie of angry women who only wanted to get even with the men in — and not in — their lives," writes Fields, and radicals such as Bella Abzug and Rosemary Ruether rose to prominence.

In the 1990s, however, says Fields, a new, thoughtful generation of positive feminists has arisen, picking up where Friedan began. Led by Helen Hull Hitchcock, editor of *Voices*, the journal of Women for Faith and Family,[4] they find enthusiastic support in John Paul II's wise teaching and his wholehearted love for the role and person of women. This pope's official addresses on women, printed in *L'Osservatore Romano*, are splendid, especially those on the eminent dignity of motherhood.[5] His "Letter to Women," released in June 1995, prior to the United Nations' Fourth World Conference on Women in Beijing, is a beautiful symphony of praise and appreciation. His writings constantly emphasize the exemplary role of the Mother of God, the true model Woman in her double function of Virgin and Mother, personifying the Church as the virginal and yet fruitful Bride of Christ.

---

[2] San Francisco: Ignatius, 1991.
[3] *Insight*, December 12, 1994, p. 40.
[4] For a history of Women for Faith and Family and its founder, see, e.g., https://www.catholicworldreport.com/2014/11/07/helen-hull-hitchcock-a-light-in-the-darkness. — Ed.
[5] See especially *Evangelium Vitae*, and *L'Osservatore Romano*, August 23, 1995, p. 6.

Recently I have read several moving conversion stories of former radical feminists in the Church. All of them say that the reason they first joined the destructive counterforce, and the reason they stayed with it so long, was a deep feeling of anger: anger at everything, resulting from their unhappy youth, broken marriage, failed religious life, or other circumstances. The anger grew as they began sharing with "sisters-in-anger," adding fuel to the oft-hidden fire of resentment, until anger soon came to underlie everything they did. And so their rebellious attitudes of life developed: to them the very concept of obedience became offensive, enraging, and opposed to human dignity.

These stories reveal that conversion dawns for such persons when they realize the presence and extent of anger in their lives. As they become more honest with themselves, they gradually come to see that their rebellious arguments were merely clichés or pacifiers that did not truly address the issues. Then they begin to follow the path proposed by Pope John Paul II's theology of male and female. They discover that, indeed, God has created all males and females equal in personal dignity (rendered by the term "man"). But this equal dignity is affirmed and expressed in each one's proper task in creation and society according to the different sexes (the differences rendered by the term "man and woman"); only *thus* does each person reach his or her human perfection.

The many people who overlook the differences between the roles of the sexes, blinded by the issue of equal dignity, commit a common mistake in their thinking. The distinction between equal dignity and its expression in sexual differences is a very datum of nature, ordained by God the Creator. Hence, men and women can achieve emotional and physical happiness only when they fully accept this vertical plan of God for the human race, with humility and obedience, and then work it out on the horizontal plane of life.

All the above applies to the crisis of the third postconciliar phase, not only on the level of personal emotion and feeling, but also in the area of worship. How can a person truly be a member of a Church that he or she is working to destroy from within or from without? How can a person truly worship with a Church that she hates because its "patriarchy" has supposedly suppressed women's rights? How can a person still participate in Catholic worship if he or she is also working to build up a false horizontal liturgy or is even worshipping "goddesses"?

I will add here one of my own experiences. In 1982 I attended the annual meeting of the Conference of Major Superiors of Men (CMSM) and the Leadership Conference of Women Religious (LCWR). One of the speakers, the radical Sandra Schneiders, made such bitter and blasphemous attacks on the Holy Father and Church authority, supported by applause from the audience, that it was an unprecedented scandal. I rose to protest, but was unable to get the microphone until the evening of the next day. When I finally succeeded, "conspirators" were posted on either side of me, and when I began my protest, they grabbed the microphone from my hand. Afterward I went to the president of the meeting to protest, but with no success. Then I went to the two hierarchs who were honorary presidents. Cardinal Paul Augustin Mayer, then Prefect of the Congregation of Religious, was very angry and fully agreed with me: "It is a scandal that must be corrected; I will tell the pope." The other hierarch, the Apostolic Delegate, said he was only a diplomat and could not intervene in internal Church problems. The "eucharistic" celebration that evening was the worst sacrilegious manifestation I have ever witnessed. A Trappist abbot and I left halfway through, for we could no longer bear it. I am glad to say that the attitude of the CMSM's leadership has changed very much for the better in the last few years.

Another eyewitness story about disdain for authority comes to mind here. When Pope John Paul II came to San Francisco in 1987, I was invited to concelebrate the solemn liturgy. The preceding evening, the pope led a large meeting of bishops, priests, religious, and laypeople. After he left, some of the bishops relaxing in the hotel spoke among themselves the most bitter, unjust disparagements of a pope that I have ever heard. Yet the next morning these "fathers of souls," seeming to sense no incongruity in their actions, concelebrated with the pope in the brotherly Divine Banquet of the Lord of the Church!

Such spiritual dishonesty shows how the dichotomy between the dissenters' faith and practice has destroyed the Christian ethos and the perspective of the gospel. It is a very real problem: dissent not only morally kills the person of the Holy Father; it first kills the faith in the dissenters and their followers. That such scandals are perpetrated in the highest echelons of spiritual leadership in America makes the ensuing decomposition of the Church quite understandable.

ICEL AND INCLUSIVE LANGUAGE

A second major component of the feminist agenda is inclusive language, in which words (such as "man") formerly accepted as pertaining to both men and women are replaced. In the Church this problem is posed especially by the work of the International Commission on English in the Liturgy (ICEL), which was conceived in 1964 and first met in 1965.[6] ICEL's initial task was to translate into English, for all the English-speaking countries, the *libri typi* of the *Novus Ordo* and the other new liturgical texts as they were released by the Consilium's subcommissions. Recall that the *libri typi*, also called *editiones typicae*, are the normative Latin texts upon which all translations must be based.[7]

It is understandable that ICEL's translations were not perfect. Its translators were required to produce them *in angustia dierum* (in a situation of urgency), because the people were impatient to switch to the vernacular. From the very beginning, however, one could sense that ICEL's work was headed in the wrong direction, for their translators overlooked some basic requirements for any work with religious cultural language: the right balance between tradition and modernity, continuity with the scriptural tongue, expression of the "unspeakable mystery," healthy poetic and emotional expression, and respect for the past—not to mention theological orthodoxy.

Even in ICEL's early days, the eminent language philosopher Ludwig Wittgenstein warned ICEL's translators against manipulating the texts in favor of inclusive language (and other problems we will address shortly). He explained that religious language has an important impact upon a philosophical understanding of religion, because faulty religious language brings

---

[6] The origins of ICEL are recounted by Sister Kathleen Hughes in *The Monk's Tale*, cited above, pp. 259ff. [Sister Hughes was a longtime member of the ICEL Advisory Committee.—Ed.]

[7] CSL 36 names the responsible authority: "(4) Translations from the Latin for use in the liturgy must be approved by the competent territorial ecclesiastical authority already mentioned," i.e., bishops' conferences; see CSL 22:2.—Ed.

impoverishment and wrong doctrine. Yet for years ICEL continued in its errors.

In 1994 and 1995 the United States Conference of Catholic Bishops (USCCB) voted, by large margins, in favor of ICEL's inclusive-language translations. Shortly thereafter, Father William McNamara, founder of the Spiritual Life Institute, rendered well the *sensus Ecclesiae* on inclusive language:

> The final linguistic catastrophe is the American Catholic Bishops' approval of inclusive language in the ancient, sacred texts of the liturgy. The bishops came to this disastrous decision not out of theological reflection, religious experience or episcopal wisdom but out of fear of the loudest lobby in today's Church. Many of the most deplorable mutations in human history were due to this same fear.... Every single bishop I have spoken to deplores this decision and many other decisions as well. But their attachment to and resonance of the Word, the Gospel Truth, has been drowned out by the dull drone of "position papers," by conferences and committees.[8]

The U.S. Bishops' capitulation to ICEL's demands is a serious situation, indeed, because ICEL's work exhibits two trends of an unspoken agenda governing much of the postconciliar work. These principles, deeply hidden in ICEL's work, would have escaped the attention of the unsuspecting Church community, and even most bishops, had not CREDO, an organization of young orthodox priests, unmasked ICEL's hidden agenda in 1994.[9] The two trends are these:

1. ICEL's translators adhere to many principles of the new liturgical and theological thinking that is foreign to both Holy Tradition and Vatican II. They express these principles in their translations, thus smuggling this thinking into the common teaching of the Church through the channel of the liturgy, according to the adage of Vincent of Lérins: "The law of prayer must establish

---

[8] Rev. William McNamara, "Verbal Pollution (Part 3)," *Forefront* (Summer 1995): pp. 25ff.

[9] For a history of CREDO, a society of priests dedicated to the faithful translation of the liturgy, see Father Jerry J. Pokorsky, "ICEL's Failed Legacy," September 28, 2001, accessed at https://www.catholicculture.org/news/features/index.cfm?recnum=20498. Abbot Boniface worked with CREDO for many years. — Ed.

the law of worship" (and vice versa).[10] The evil of such an agenda is that a handful of ICEL translators are unduly appropriating to themselves one of the most sacred functions of the Church, a function strictly reserved to the Magisterium: that of interpreting and passing on the truth.

2. Behind this intent is ICEL's unspoken plan to create an entirely new liturgy closer to Protestant worship and secular thinking, in order to eliminate the differences between Catholics and Protestants. Thus ICEL stresses the horizontal dimension of the Mass and makes the Sacred Liturgy man-centered rather than God-centered. It uses various means, such as (a) doing away with words like "sacrifice," "priest," "angels," and "intercession," as well as "man" as a generic term; (b) decreasing and even abolishing reverence for the Real Presence; and (c) introducing "presiders" empowered not by God but by the congregation. Through these means ICEL is working to clear the way for a more horizontal, democratic Church, which is, of course, the agenda of the whole postconciliar dissent.[11]

ICEL claims as authority for its actions the "Instruction on Translation of Liturgical Texts," an English translation of *"Comme le prévoit,"* a document published in French (not Latin) by the Consilium on January 25, 1969. CREDO (the organization of orthodox priests), in its "Comments and Commentaries" on this Instruction and in its own scholarly "Proposed Liturgical Translation Standards," has shown that ICEL has misinterpreted the Instruction in many places.[12] Further, Father Joseph Fessio, SJ, publisher of *The Catholic World Report*, has discovered that (a) *"Comme le prévoit"* was translated into the English-language Instruction *by ICEL itself;* (b) ICEL's translation of the document differs significantly from the original French; and (c) the differences favor ICEL's agenda![13]

---

[10] This was actually said by Prosper of Aquitaine. — Ed.

[11] For a thorough discussion with examples of ICEL's distorted translations, see Erasmo Leiva-Merikakis, "The catechetical role of the liturgy and the quality of liturgical texts: The current ICEL translation," *Communio* 20 (Spring 1993), pp. 63–83, accessible at https://www.communio-icr.com/files/leiva20-1.pdf. — Ed.

[12] This work of CREDO is published in *The Catholic World Report*, July 1994, pp. 26–40. See also Rev. Vincent Twomey's thoughtful letter in response in the same publication: "Care in Liturgical Translation," January 1995, p. 4.

[13] Joseph Fessio, SJ, "One Bad Translation Begets Another," *The Catholic World Report* (November 1993): pp. 29–33.

In ICEL's work, therefore, we see yet another example of high-handed postconciliar overstepping of the Council's bounds. Just as the Consilium's subcommissions went far beyond their entrusted task and created another liturgy against the clear directives of CSL, so has ICEL gone wrong. Its translations, variants, and *ad libitum* choices do not merely sidestep CSL; they go completely against it.[14] I urge all those involved in liturgical decision-making—and especially the members of ICEL—to ponder CREDO's Comment no. 5, which accurately summarizes the problem:

> The task of the translator is to render the approved Latin text of the liturgy into another language.... It is not the business of the translator, for whom the *editio typica* has the textual authority of an autograph, to perform a secondary effort of critical scholarship....[15]

One of the main issues of the inclusive language debate is use of the term "man." The new positive feminism we mentioned above has no qualms at all about using the generic term "man" to denote male and female persons alike, as the English language has always done. Why then should we give in to the feminist demands? Why not instead simply give our people correct catechesis about the word's generic meaning?

Since we have proof that inclusive language is part of an agenda against Christianity, we may be sure that the inclusiveness will be extended—indeed, it already has been in some places—from the *horizontal* level of human relationships to the *vertical* level of our relationship with God and the Holy Trinity. The preposterous wordings used in reference to God in some parishes are outright sacrilegious.

ICEL's use of inclusive language, therefore, is particularly reprehensible, for by doing so they use their weight as an official organ of the English-speaking Churches to promote the radical feminist agenda. How long will our Church leaders tolerate and even foster such abuses? How long will the U. S. Bishops be afraid to curb those like ICEL who treat the liturgy of the Church as

---

[14] The scholars of CREDO have created translations that are worlds above ICEL's poor work. [A new and far more faithful English translation of the new missal, by an ICEL staffed by scholars who held views akin to Abbot Boniface, was finally issued in 2011.—Ed.]
[15] *The Catholic World Report*, July 1994, p. 27.

their own private domain in which they improvise and experiment in an unholy manner upon this most holy heritage of Christ? Will it take another drastic wake-up call such as that of Archbishop Lefebvre to arouse us from our unholy sleep?

I would add here that from the very first publication of the alternative Anaphoras (Eucharistic Prayers) after the Council, I have defended the apparently Lefebvrist thesis that no one has the right to "compose" new Anaphoras. These prayers belong to the most important patristic documents of the Early Church as *testes Traditionis*, a quality that no later author can appropriate. Adapting existing canons may be allowed, but composing new ones is not an option. This principle applies *a fortiori* to the doubtful liberties ICEL has taken for itself.

TRANSLATION AND INCULTURATION

The use of inclusive language in Bible translations is especially problematic. Ultimately it is a problem of priority between two types of translation: the *literal* and the *conceptual*. Literal translation is concerned above all with fidelity in the very language; conceptual translation aims to render the idea in more contemporary terms, in a "dynamically equivalent" translation. Which approach should be followed? A full discussion of the topic is beyond the scope of this book, but I will touch on some related elements.[16]

First is the importance of culturally accepted language—that *established by long and positive experience of popular use.* We deal here with a significant phenomenon emphasized by Ludwig Wittgenstein, the philosopher of language mentioned above. Language has a double function: it incarnates concepts, feelings, and especially emotions into a culture and, as such, it serves as a vehicle and keeper of this culture in the heart and exchange of a nation or people.[17]

---

[16] Abbot Boniface's analysis here was structured around a lengthy interview (by Dutch media host Joop Koopman) of Bishop Richard J. Sklba of Milwaukee, published in the *National Catholic Register*, August 6, 1995, pp. 1ff. I have condensed it to its key points.—Ed.
[17] When I use the term "language" anthropologically, I do not mean a particular idiom such as Dutch or Ukrainian, but its manner of expression. For example, as *idiom*, Hollandish and Flemish are exactly the same language, but their *genius* and *feeling* are quite different. A good translation renders well the *feeling* of the original, whereas a lesser translation may be totally foreign to it.

Social anthropology shows us that this double function is extremely important in the social, artistic, and spiritual heritage of a people. It makes language take root in the age-old accumulated tradition, the very cultural heritage of a community. This applies especially to religion and its privileged expression: its established worship. If, at a certain moment, especially under pressure of a "paradigm shift," an alienation intrudes into worship and especially into its sacred language, not only are worship and sacred Writ grievously jeopardized, but the creative continuity of a culture as flowing from its mysterious wellsprings of anthropology also suffers an irreparable break. Such alienations are precisely what inclusive language and, in general, street language, are doing to worship. Their proponents invoke the good principle of active participation, but with erroneous intent; *Mediator Dei* (1947) and especially Vatican II gave early warnings against such erroneous applications.

We also could have learned from the Anglican experience. At a certain point they gave in to the pressure for a "proletarianization" of their wonderful *Book of Common Prayer*, that unique treasure of perfectly adequate sacred language. (It was such a treasure because Cromwell had the wisdom to stick to the literal equivalent of the Latin *Vorlage* in the Sarum Sacramentary.) This liturgical clearance sale of the foremost carrier of their liturgical tradition not only devalued their entire worship but also opened the gate for a gradual deterioration of the moral and theological pillars of their church.

The key issue in good translation is fidelity to the original text and how to express that text liturgically, catechetically, and academically. Unfortunately, almost all the ICEL liturgical translations I have reviewed over the years (including in my work with CREDO) have been marked by gross infidelity to the original text. I will never forget one text of a Eucharistic Prayer that was so different from the original Latin *typus* that the *typus* was completely unrecognizable in the insipid "translation." The same infidelity is displayed in recent ICEL translations of the liturgical texts for Advent and Christmas, and those of the *Ordo Missae*: they were undoubtedly influenced by aggressive feminism and secular horizontalism and went far beyond the limits that Vatican II set for the national translators of the Latin *libri typi*. Yet, instead of denouncing the deception that ICEL was forcing upon unsuspecting English-speaking faithful, the U. S. Bishops approved ICEL's work.

Adherence to the Fathers of the Church is essential to building up a truly liturgical and theological language. As I have stated repeatedly, the Eastern Churches have always kept the continuity between the apostolic heritage and further Church Tradition, through the medium of the Fathers. In the West, Thomas Aquinas and the early Scholastics retained the Patristics untouched, together with Holy Scripture, as the Christian source of Holy Tradition. They never tried to replace the Fathers' language with Aristotelianism or Neoplatonism, but rather created the *philosophia perennis* as the new means to express Christian thinking.[18] This patristic concern of continuity in expressing the apostolic heritage in Holy Tradition is almost entirely absent from the dissenters' whole process of "renewing" worship, theology, and catechesis.

The dissenters say that modern man needs change — constant and absolute change — and that we must destroy all that represents going back, conserving, keeping tradition. They think the Fathers represent the *opposite* of the needs of modern man and the Church; thus they reject the Fathers and Holy Tradition as the core of all culture and hence of all inculturation. Ultimately all the dissenters' inculturation suffers from their assumption that their mania for change is legitimate dynamism, when in truth the two are extreme opposites. The postconciliar "reform" would never have taken such an aggressively negative turn had the theologians, liturgists, and ICEL translators remained the humble pupils of the Fathers and Holy Tradition.

As I have lamented before, all these abuses occur to the growing vexation and offense of simple, believing faithful, religious, priests, and even bishops — truly the "poor in spirit" of our time — who want only to follow the Church as Vatican II proposed, but who are instead cornered by ruthless rebels. *The rebels' hateful, disobedient, faithless, and worldly actions betray them — for the hallmarks of true followers of Christ are brotherly love, obedience, faith, and holiness.*

ALTAR GIRLS

The push for women's ordination is a topic much discussed elsewhere,[19] so I will not focus on it here — except to say that

---

[18] Since the later Scholastics of the thirteenth century, however, the West has called upon the *adminicula scientiae* of often secular systems.
[19] Among all the available material, I especially recommend Hans Urs von Balthasar's "Women Priests? A Marian Church in a Fatherless and Motherless Culture," *Communio* (Spring 1993): pp. 164–70.

those who promote a female priesthood ignore these key facts: (a) ordaining women is foreign to all biblical data that are absolutely binding norms; (b) therefore, the Church is powerless to ordain women; and (c) there have been no ordained women in 2,000 years of Holy Tradition, preserved by the Church inspired by God.

We must, however, address the issue of female altar servers, or altar girls, because allowing altar girls has been a main objective, as a stepping stone, for the proponents of women's ordination.

In April 1994 the Congregation for Divine Worship and the Discipline of the Sacraments granted permission for girls to serve at the altar. The official explanation stated that this permission is not a theological question but was the further application of a canon of the new Roman Code of 1983. Father Mario Lessi-Ariosto, SJ, who drafted the decision, further stated that this decision does not entail any step toward priestly ordination or even toward ordained acolytes.[20]

The above explanations notwithstanding, the feminists shouted in triumph when this permission was announced, seeing it as an enormous victory, and even as proof that Rome supported their entire agenda. They saw in it a parallel with Rome allowing reception of Communion in the hand: "Just start doing it and in the long run they will give in." For, they observed, was that not the way that women's ordination was introduced in the Anglican-Episcopal Church? Bishops "just did it" and went unpunished.

For those opposed to the concept of altar girls, learning of Rome's permission was a painful, heartbreaking experience. They felt betrayed by those upon whom they had depended—and whom they had supported—for many years in a bitter struggle for orthodox teaching and proper worship, in the true spirit of the Council. Crushed by Rome's apparent failure to support their faithfulness, they could reach only one conclusion: that Rome had given in to pressure, trying to appease the unappeasable. It appeared that Rome had given permission for altar girls as a consolation prize to the very ones who had fought viciously against her regarding Pope John Paul II's prohibition against women's ordination.

---

[20] See *Inside the Vatican*, May 1994, pp. 14–17.

Although many things about this situation are not clear, I am sure of one point: the official explanation for allowing altar girls — that it was merely the further application of the new Roman Code — is insufficient, not to mention offensive, to millions of faithful, loving, and obedient followers of the Church authorities. Even if this were the reason, the Church authority making such decisions is supposed to keep in mind the whole moral and psychological context of such a permission, especially in view of possibly scandalizing the faithful: for example, the context of a culture where altar girls are psychologically out of place, and the context of an age-old liturgical tradition where worshipers are accustomed to a certain visual acceptance of *dramatis personae*.

The impact of the altar girls decision upon ecumenical relations with our Orthodox brethren and especially the Eastern Catholic Churches also should have been strongly considered by Rome. In all the Eastern Churches, women saints enjoy a much more significant place in liturgical and popular veneration than in the West. But it is always in reference to the Mother of God — who never played a liturgical role in the Church. Hence, the concept of "altar girls" is truly shocking to Eastern Christians.

Aside from the above problems, the inclusion of girls as altar servers is already having negative effects for the future of the Church. For centuries altar *boys* have been the most fertile field for priestly vocations. Sadly, where altar girls are now allowed, boys are increasingly abandoning altar serving as "a girl's job." Consequently now boys will be less exposed to the "holy things" and less open to the Holy Spirit's call to the priesthood.

ARTICLE 3: THE RELATIONSHIP
BETWEEN WORSHIP AND CULTURE

As horizontalism calls for secularism with all its offspring including radical feminism, so secularism calls for culture as the general milieu that replaces religion in a secular society. Hence, the last topic of this chapter will be the relationship between worship and culture. Culture and its derivative term, inculturation, are extremely broad topics, so I will cover only some basic data in the context of this book's objective.

SOME PRINCIPLES

We must clarify the concept of inculturation from the very beginning. Although the term "inculturation" was used by the Council and in papal documents, we at the Preparatory Commission for Liturgy (before the Council) preferred the term "adaptation," which, crucially, involves as much the movement from liturgy to culture as from culture to liturgy. This was (and is) a crucial distinction — that adaptation includes the movement *from liturgy to culture* — because, by it, we rejected from the outset the man-centered approach wherein man and his culture are the norm of the incarnation process of the divine into the human.

I would note that because of the current New Age infatuation with man as the center of reality, most of the talk and writing about inculturation (and there is much of both!) since the Council springs from a faddish desire to be "relevant," a desire often based on religious indifferentism, the notion that all religions are of equal value.[21] Such people seem to forget that, as the saying goes, nothing ages faster than relevance.

Another preliminary remark must be made about the surrender of culture to technology.[22] When Father Annibale Bugnini humiliated the great African Bishop Malula, he was proclaiming Western technological civilization as the norm for all culture, and even for the adaptation of the liturgy. On the contrary, Father Romano Guardini, a wise modern Church father, in his book *Letters from Lake Como: Explorations on Technology and the Human Race*,[23] shows that the goal of technology, by its very inner principles and logic, is precisely to destroy culture: to replace the childlike, loving, spiritual man of the Gospels (Mt 18:4; Mk 10:15) with the impersonal, money-making, power-driven machine-man, subjected to technology and production.

All culture, in one way or another, either moves away from technology and returns to nature and soul, or moves closer to man's mastery over matter. Therefore I insist on making a

---

[21] An excellent survey pertaining to this subject may be found in J. Pierce, "Early Medieval Liturgy," *Worship* (November 1991): pp. 509–22.
[22] See Will Hoyt, "The Surrender of Culture to Technology," *New Oxford Review* (May 1995): pp. 25ff.
[23] Grand Rapids: Eerdmans, 1994, originally published in 1940. [Father Guardini was a Member of the Second Vatican Council's Preparatory Commission for Liturgy. — Ed.]

constant, crucial distinction between "culture" and "civilization." *Culture* is related to spirit, beauty, soul, and "being" as opposed to "having." *Civilization* is related to comfort, money, power, and "having" as opposed to "being."

We must also distinguish between true virtue, which is inner beauty, and political correctness, which is extrinsic, a "secular religion without hope."[24] Thus a man driving a Cadillac and living in a palace can be deprived of culture, whereas a man living in abject poverty can be a person of high culture. The lives of noble men like Black Elk display true culture,[25] whereas in the lives of the standard middle classes of our day, civilization bears the palm. My experiences in Zaire also revealed a people of very high culture, even as they lacked many of the modern conveniences.

The most important reason for the lack of true culture we see in the United States is *the war against true religion*, for true religion is the main carrier of culture.[26] It is the main factor that gives meaning to life; it heals the consequences of sin and makes us share in God's own life. The purpose of inculturation, then — and this is crucial — must be not the bringing of American culture into the liturgy but rather the adapting (i.e., lifting up) of American culture to the level of that which *gives* culture, which in our case is the liturgy.

The poverty of American culture illustrates why the liturgy must lift up the culture and not vice versa. The prevalence of violence and sex in entertainment, the widespread abuse of drugs and alcohol, and other such ills show that our society has become spiritually closed yet wide open to evil and destruction, as opposed to the olden days, when society was spiritually open and not as much plagued by these evils.

---

[24] Philip Devine, "Political Correctness is Doomed," *New Oxford Review* (May 1995): pp. 7–10.
[25] For a remarkable case study on the topic of true culture, see Christopher Dodson, "Black Elk: Native American and Catholic," *New Oxford Review* (April 1995): pp. 24–26; or Michael Steltenkamp, *Black Elk: Holy Man of the Oglala* (Oklahoma City: University of Oklahoma, 1997).
[26] For all related problems of the crisis of ineptitude of American culture, I strongly recommend the study of Matthew Lamb, "Modernism and Americanism Revisited Dialectically," *Communio* (Winter 1994): pp. 631–62. One of his theses is expressed in the revealing subtitle, "The United States as uniquely an Enlightenment culture."

Now we come to our point. It is exactly this disordered popular culture that the dissenting theologians and liturgists want to inculturate into the new Christian worship; they constantly appeal to "popular culture" as if it were superior to traditional worship. Some may object that I misrepresent their opinion, but let us be honest. What else could be meant by their demand for "street language," the exaggerated use of trivialized guitar Masses to the exclusion of the organ and Gregorian chant, the stripping of statues from the churches, and their meaningless homilies, all of which are part of the culture of sullying and emptying—not to mention their persecution of the pious, orthodox faithful? Through these means, little by little the living soul of true worship is being choked and absorbed into the no-man's-land of "popular culture."

The only real solution is to fully turn the tables. The great message of our time is that Christ is the only solution, and hence Christianity is the only valuable counter-culture. Worship is the counter-culture's most active element, as the main carrier, expression, and guarantee of the gospel and Holy Tradition. Consequently, the Church's worship cannot be the experimental garden of theologians, liturgists, and misguided clergy. *This is, of course, precisely the message of this whole book and, I dare claim, the very teaching of the Church and Holy Tradition.* Therefore a new conscience must be formed: a conscience not of rebellion or dissent but of belonging and responsibility, of loving sharing and constructive obedience—in short, of evangelical holiness.[27]

In the problem of inculturation there are two *termini*: the *terminus a quo*, the giver, and the *terminus ad quem*, the receiver. However, as Cardinal Ratzinger has rightly stated, no exchange between the two is possible if there is no vital channel or avenue between them, no connaturality or willingness to share together. Further, *true inculturation presupposes the presence of a valuable culture already in place*, a culture in living continuity with the message that Christianity wants to convey. In the modern West such a culture no longer exists: we have a culture of death instead of a culture of life, man-centered horizontalism instead of the God-centered verticalness of prayer and the gospel, and "having" instead of "being."

As long as rebellious bishops, theologians, and feminists continue to reject the Church with her authority and her given

---

[27] Lorenzo Albacete has shown this in his article "The Praxis of Resistance," referenced above.

worship, the necessary climate for true inculturation will not exist. As long as "inculturation" is taken to mean horizontalizing, pedestrianizing, secularizing, and taking Western man and his "culture" as the obligatory norm, all efforts toward true inculturation will fail. As long as "inculturation" means disfiguring and denaturing Christianity and forcing it into the secular civilization of our technological society, preserving only some anthropological features while gutting its real mystery, it will merely surrender culture to technology, as we saw above.

Having posed the above principles, let us return to the topic of liturgical rebellion. The liturgical renewal after Vatican II has become like a miscarriage or stillborn baby, because of the man-centered impatience of those appointed to bring it to its rightful maturity. They believe only in the "here and now" because they believe only in themselves. They have rejected the objective norms of Holy Tradition and the creative power of the Holy Spirit in it that binds the past to the present, creates the future, and hence is the soul of true culture. The only creativity of this rebellion consists in pulling down the Sacred (and with it, true culture) to the street level.

RENEWAL AND THE CULTURAL CONTEXT

One of the most tragic mistakes of the dissident liturgists is that they have treated the liturgy as a *Ding an sich*, a matter by itself, separated from its vital connection with the practical life of the faithful. They speak of inculturation, but they forget that the liturgy is a culture in itself, with all the constituents and ingredients of a living culture of a living people. Let me dig up memories from my past.

When I was a boy, my home province of Limburg, in Flemish Belgium, was still very Christian: 95 percent or more of its people were practicing Catholics. All of life in villages and cities was imbued with and regulated by religious practice. For instance, before the big feasts *everyone* went to confession and, on the feast itself, they went to one or often two Masses plus lengthy Vespers in the afternoon or Compline in the evening. Our huge church was packed, with standing room only.

Everything was in Latin so we did not understand the actual words, but over the whole celebration hovered a holiness, an awe stronger than words alone could convey, even for us young boys. This mystery of holiness was carried home and confirmed in friendly sharing, a good meal, and just the joy of being together.

Only later did I discover the deeper layer, the mysterious wellspring of this richness. It was the unspoken but strong awareness of belonging together as one people of believers, not only horizontally and socially, but also vertically, in the age-old tradition. We celebrated the feasts the same way our forefathers did; it was the right way and had to be preserved.

This deep awareness was especially strong on All Saints' Day. The commemoration of the deceased began in the afternoon, with the full Office of the Dead (it was very long, but no one complained). Afterward, everyone went to the cemetery right behind the church, to flower the graves of loved ones and pray for the repose of their souls. A devout meal followed, and old memories of the family were revived. All this made a lasting impression upon us children. That was *real* liturgical culture!

I think that with a little effort some religious practices of the past could be revived and observed in American culture. Families would certainly benefit greatly from keeping such rituals, especially if they deeply believe the spiritual reality underlying them. One might object that such devout practices were well and good in the "closed society" of the past, even that of preconciliar America, but that they cannot exist in our modern "open society." But in fact, in the United States the preconciliar period coincided with a great cultural openness in the multiracial and polyethnic society that has always characterized America.

There was one significant difference between the preconciliar period and the present: in preconciliar America, culturally open though it was, nearly everyone agreed upon the unspoken but very real spiritual foundations of all true culture: religion, morality, decency, discipline in education, respect for life, family, and authority, and the reality of the spiritual nature and eternal destination of man. Because these values were explicitly or tacitly accepted by most of society, America actually had at that time a closed society in the sense of a sharing in common of cultural and spiritual values. In such a society, Christianity could fully live out its spiritual culture as the different confessions (especially the Catholic Church) had built it up in their age-long tradition.

But all this changed as these common spiritual foundations were systematically destroyed by dissent and materialism, promoted by the mass media. I keep implicating the media because day and night they force their distorted view of life and the world upon everyone, young and old. They do so against the common will, so there is no escape, no recourse to higher values. Recent thorough research has clearly proven that the media's common assertion that they just reflect society but do not influence behavior is tragically false.[28] The truth is just the opposite: the media *do* form the morality of the people. Thus has been built up a *new* closed society—one that celebrates greed, hypocrisy, and violence, where everyone becomes a slave of this nihilism, and religion is choked to a slow death or made a museum piece in our mindless popular culture.

THE TRANSCENDENT AND TRUE CULTURE[29]

Let us take some further giant steps in our discussion. This system of lies has a double origin. Man *either* dreams beyond our present reality—that is often too harsh for this helpless bird of paradise—he dreams into the transcendent that redeems all the sufferings of this life, *or* he follows a systematic agenda, a purposeful deception, and so arrives in a land of lies, prodded on by the same instinct as the dreamer. In either alternative, he can pursue his goal in an open or a closed context of society.

But the Transcendent will always function as the One-who-opens-up, the representative of Being and "the Beyond" (*Jenseits*). The Unredeemed Self is the One-who-locks-in, the keeper of the Having, the Immediate, the Useful. In the concrete setting of daily life, it is love, truth, and beauty that make man step over from Having into Being, from the Useful into the Absolute, from the Unredeemed Self into the Community of the Redeemed.

Here true culture steps in. It is in culture that all the above positive values enter into the life of person and community. Culture is a constant invitation to transcend the Immediate and Useful of the problem and enter into the transcendent and creative Freedom of the mystery. This is so even if we have to pass through

---

[28] See Michael Medved's revealing study in *New Covenant*, August 1995, pp. 7–11.
[29] This section was a late addition to the manuscript, included here with the author's original terminology and capitalization of words.—Ed.

the night of doubt that is often the only way to acceptance of
the Beyond in the language of the daily Concrete.

In this dynamic of acceptance, rebellion will inevitably gen-
erate rejection and disjunction, whereas worship will function
as the rallying point of all the above ingredients of true culture.
In worship we celebrate the transcendent mystery, creator of
lasting values. In worship the ego-centric Self will be freed from
the bonds of the Having into the freedom of giving up into the
Beyond. In worship the link between past, present, and future —
of history with the *kairos* and the eschatology — will be forged
in a Blessed Present.

Thus in the liturgy, the "cultural heritage" to which John Paul
II so often draws our attention — the fruit of Holy Tradition of
past generations — is creatively handed down not only to us but
also to future generations. The cultural heritage consistently inte-
grates the contribution of all these stages of maturation into the
liturgical heritage, which in turn expresses the cultural heritage
that John Paul II so eagerly desires to see preserved amidst our
modern rootlessness.

CONCLUSIONS AND CONSEQUENCES

At this point, we must draw some daring conclusions, beginning again from my liturgical experience as a youth in a close-knit
village. As we do this, it is crucial to keep in mind the distinction I
made above between culture and civilization: culture is related to
spirit, beauty, soul, and "being"; civilization is the heavy weight
related to comfort, money, power, and "having." According to
one of the basic principles of Aquinas, matter and "having" serve
to close up and separate (the work of *civilization*), whereas the
spirit and "being" (the work of *culture* and especially its main
ingredient, religion) serve to open and unite.[30]

Even in an open, multicultural society, the different cultures
can go on forming ethnic, cultural, religious, or social subcommunities, as we see constantly happening in the United States
and other polycultural societies. Moreover — and this is critical — anthropology shows us that in this differentiating process
it is *religion*, and especially its liturgical expression, that is the

---

[30] I described this in my essay, "*Het einde van de Barok*" (The End of the
Baroque), cited above in Chapter 1.

strongest active element in the process of keeping and nourishing the proper culture of these subcommunities, even more so than language. A strong proof of this is the blooming national-and-religious culture among the diaspora of Eastern Christians in Western lands; the same is seen among the Hispanics, Filipinos, and other Catholics who have relocated to the United States. Thus, just as in olden days (my youth) the reverent celebration of the liturgy was the main social and familial expression of belonging together, so also a truly "vertical" worship could, even in our present day, become the main element for holding a group together in a rich and positive religious culture. From such a culture all dissent and secular incursions should be excluded, as we see in the Eastern Catholic and Orthodox Churches.

In this chapter we have seen the gradual movement from primal rebellion into the present world of lies. I have shown how the subcommissions' revolt against the Council's decrees has inevitably resulted in the whole postconciliar rebellion on all levels of Church life and of culture. Liturgy has become a toy in the hands of these destructive movements, and the poor and lowly have become the victims of their pernicious game. As I noted above, *the dissenters recognize the ultimate primacy and necessity of the liturgy; this is why they use the liturgy as their battlefield.*

Fortunately, since rebellion cannot live by itself, the liturgy still retains some of its native nobility. It still hankers for its original holiness and calls for the Sacred that will always remain the deeper need of man, despite all attacks from the unholy and the untrue; this celebration of the Sacred is exactly the *kairos* of good liturgy. Thus to force upon our poor ones a totally horizontal liturgy — in an unholy space, with tasteless music and untheological language — is to force them to live in a sterile world of lies where Holy Tradition and the Spirit of God are choked and true spiritual life cannot bloom. I am not saying that the aborted liturgical reform is part of this world of lies; it is rather its victim. Yet it belongs to the same cultural family, and its product certainly cannot be called good liturgy.

I said it before but will repeat it here: we must return to God, especially the gospel and the Sermon on the Mount. Turning to God means conversion, and conversion is a question of grace, which is conditional, a fruit of sacrificial prayer. The same Spirit of God who inspired Pope John XXIII to call the Council must now be fervently and sacrificially invoked to change hearts and minds. Only through deeply-converted persons can a new God-centered culture be generated as the organic milieu wherein true religion can breathe and live.

Let us now move on to the last chapter, where I will propose how the vertical worship described above can become the uplifting agenda of the "reformed renewal" to which we aspire.

CHAPTER 6

Learn From the East

The angel of the LORD is encamped
around those who revere him, to rescue them.
Taste and see that the LORD is good.
He is happy who seeks refuge in him.
　　　　　　　　　　　　—Psalm 33/34:8–9

YOU HAVE PROBABLY CONCLUDED FROM THE
previous chapters, patient reader, and from your own experience,
that the Western Church is in a state of real crisis. She is indeed.
But there are numerous signs of hope; I will mention a few for
your encouragement.

1. A growing number of courageous bishops are arising, orthodox in teaching and discipline, and faithful to the pope; they are challenging the modernist tendency among their confrères.

2. Many outstanding lay leaders are emerging, providing excellent guidance through high-quality magazines, books, and recordings, and their witness to the truth in all professions and walks of life.

3. Increasing numbers of Protestants, including energetic ministers, are converting to the Catholic faith, attracted by the truth of Holy Tradition and the nourishment of the sacraments.

4. Many religious and theologians are returning to orthodoxy, as was evidenced in Father Avery Dulles's lecture in 1995 on the "Criteria of Catholic Theology" in fifteen points that contradicted almost all the positions of the rebellious theologians.[1]

5. Most important, the leadership of Pope John Paul II is strong, consistent, and clear; his teaching is precisely that of the gospel and Holy Tradition. He is truly steering the whole world away from the culture of death into the culture of life.

What then is still lacking? What more do we need? Aristotle, in his explanation of the Four Causes, states that the goal (the

---

[1] This lecture took place at the fiftieth anniversary meeting of the Catholic Theological Society of America. See the full text in the Summer 1995 issue of *Communio* [available on-line at https://www.communio-icr.com/files/dulles22-2.pdf. — Ed.].

"final cause") is the first thing intended, but the last to be reached. In another context he reminds us that there is something even prior to the intended goal: the inspiring model, the "exemplary cause" — the model that shows us how to reach that goal.

The goal in our day is obviously the full recovery of the Church from her many ills. But how shall this take place? I propose that to reach our goal, we must keep before our eyes an inspiring model: a healthy Church that has remained faithful throughout the centuries to the gospel and Holy Tradition. This final chapter will offer not a set of precise solutions but rather a variety of observations and suggestions for the reader's reflection.

ARTICLE 1: LIGHT FROM THE EAST

The previous chapters of this book have described my years of witness and work within the *Western* Church, from her preconciliar hopes, through the years of the Council, to the postconciliar decay. For the past twenty years, however, I have been a monk in the *Eastern* Church. From my vantage point of service in both West and East, I am convinced that the Eastern Church provides an excellent model and guide toward healing many of the Western Church's wounds.[2] I prayerfully hope that in this last chapter, dear reader, you will open your heart to learn from my latter (Eastern) witness as much as from the former.

REASONS FOR LOOKING EAST

I propose that the Western Church could benefit from looking to her Eastern Sister Churches for three main reasons.[3]

First, the Council itself began this movement of looking East. As I mentioned above, when the Council Fathers became bogged down while making important decisions, they looked to the Eastern tradition where that part of the authentic Church heritage was preserved and still blooming; very often the problems

---

[2] See my studies, "The Importance of the Eastern Catholic Churches in the Millennium of Rus'-Ukraine," *Communio* (Spring 1988): pp. 4–5; and "An Eastern View" in David L. Schindler, ed., *Catholicism and Secularization in America: Essays on Nature, Grace, and Culture* (Huntington, IN: Our Sunday Visitor, 1990), pp. 211–13.

[3] The author used the terms "Eastern Church," "Eastern Churches," and "the East" somewhat interchangeably in this chapter. See Appendix C for a brief description of the Eastern Churches. — Ed.

were resolved according to the Eastern tradition. The permanent diaconate, concelebration, collegiality, Communion under both species, the readings system for Office and Mass, and the perspective of the one, living Organism (the Church) that must breathe with both its lungs, West *and* East—all these areas were restored by the Council. The Council's borrowing from, or rather returning to, the sources of the common wellspring of the Apostolic Church was only the beginning of a movement that I believe must press on to full fruition.

A second reason for looking to the East is the depth and authenticity of the Eastern, apostolic wellspring and the enormous profit the West could draw from it. The Vatican II documents on ecumenism and the Eastern Churches opened such perspectives, but in 1995 Pope John Paul II explained these points even more strongly in his encyclical *Ut Unum Sint* (That they may be one) and especially his pastoral letter *Orientale Lumen* (Light from the East). Therefore my conviction that the West can, and must, learn from the East is supported by John Paul II in his role as supreme teacher. He knows very well that the Eastern Churches are not perfect, but he also knows they do not suffer from most of the West's troubles; therefore we may share his urgency to learn from the East. A serious question will put this matter into perspective. Faithful Western Catholics often reproach those who, by rejecting the Church's teaching, are disobedient to her authority. *But are we not guilty of disobedience ourselves if we ignore or reject the pope's urgent and solemn teaching that we must learn from the East if we are to solve the Western Church's problems?*

My third reason for looking East is this: Church life in the East is both a lofty, mystical vision and a practical, down-to-earth way of living. It is both a sharing with the age-old tradition of the gospel and Early Church and a solution to very real problems, both a communal adventure and a deeply personal meeting with the Beloved. I will expand on these ideas in sections to come.

Unfortunately, as John Paul II has noted, the Eastern Church is a Great Unknown among Western Christians. The only true way to come to know the East is to experience it, which I invite you to do! Come participate in our Divine Liturgies (Masses), or the solemn Offices on major feast days. Join us during Holy Week as we accompany Jesus to Jerusalem, the Last Supper, the Cross, the tomb. Celebrate with us Our Lord's victorious triumph over death on Pascha (Easter)! Once you experience the Eastern Church for yourself, you will understand what I am describing here.[4]

VISION OF THE TRIUNE GOD

In all mankind and its history, the vision of God is the primary object of all religion: it is the vertical dimension of Christian life. This vision depends greatly on the Revelation that God himself has made to mankind. In the Old Testament the vision was of the One God, absolutely unique. Hence Judaism (and its side-branch, Islam) was and is radically monotheistic, and this heritage has been handed down to Christianity.

In the New Testament, however, something radically new was revealed, something only foreshadowed in the Old: that in the one nature of God there are three Persons, equal in nature but very distinct in personality. One might say that the deeper reason why we speak of a *New* Testament is that this vision of God as three Persons is new. The covenant and the vertical dimension that follow from it are therefore also quite new and different from the Old.

The Eastern Churches understand God to be a life of communion of Three Persons sharing the same nature and thus, by an exchange in being and in love, "building up" the One God. Therefore in the East, more so than in the West, the approach to the One God is secondary to the approach to the Threefold Persons. Why? Because this is the approach of the New Testament and consequently of the Early Church and the Church Fathers who built up the entirety of Holy Tradition.[5] From this approach to the Threefold Persons arises a vision which impacts all of Eastern worship. The East thinks of God in terms of a grandiose, existential dynamism both *within* the *circumincessio* (interpenetration, Greek *perichoresis*) of the Three Persons, and also *without*, outside of the Three — in the hierarchy of angels.

---

[4] Participation in the Divine Liturgy in an Eastern Catholic Church fulfills the Sunday or holy day "obligation" for Western Catholics, and reception of Holy Communion is permitted for those properly disposed. The Orthodox Churches, unfortunately, do not permit Catholics to receive their sacraments. — Ed.

[5] Pseudo-Dionysios (late fifth or early sixth century), one of the greatest thinkers among the Church Fathers, best developed this subject; see *Pseudo-Dionysios: The Complete Works*, Classics of Western Spirituality (Mahwah, NJ: Paulist Press, 1987). See also Andrew Louth, *Denys the Areopagite* (Wilton, CT: Morehouse-Barlow, 1989).

The angels are the first beings to receive and answer God's creating love. Their primary task is to worship him in unending praise. Their secondary task is to expand God's lovingkindness to the "second world" of God's creation, namely mankind, and to mankind's work and concerns. The angels rule creation, and they especially rule man, through the Guardian Angels. But even more significantly, they preside over man's worship. *In celebrating the liturgy on Earth, we are simply joining the angels in their heavenly worship.* This angelic vision is seen in the book of Revelation, chapters 2 and 3, where the local bishops are represented in the mystical image of angels. (The common name of a bishop in the East is "hierarch," meaning one who shares, on earth, in the "holy order" of the angels in heaven.) The glorious reality of our joining the angels in their heavenly worship is a basic dimension of the Eastern Church's understanding and vision of the liturgy.

ELEMENTS OF LITURGY

From the Eastern vision of God follow three conclusions necessary for a profitable understanding of the liturgy.

The primary task of man is worship; therefore he must give worship the time and attention due to it. The Divine Liturgy (the Mass) in an Eastern Church, with its beautiful antiphons and litanies and priestly prayers, fulfills this need. It thus lasts much longer than a typical Western Mass. But what could be a more important use of our time than joining the angels in the worship of the Triune God?

Because our earthly worship shares in the nobility of the angelic worship in heaven, it must befit God's holiness, and the individuals' participation must be brought together into a oneness of worship. Because sacred harmony aids this oneness, the Eastern Churches have all preserved some form of music sung in harmony, as was done in the Early Church.[6] Music and singing together are crucial for building up communion in worship and for creating and maintaining the real *tonus* of a holy celebration. For this reason all the liturgical services of the Eastern Church are *sung* rather than *said*.

The East has always been deeply aware of a third, highly significant reason for the dignity of liturgical celebration, as follows.

---

[6] The earliest manuscripts of Gregorian chant reveal that it was originally sung in harmony!

The ritual expression of the liturgy has an existential value: it *is* the very mystery of our salvation, "translated" into texts, music, gestures, gathering together, and all of the ritual forms involved in the celebration. The ontological dimensions (i.e., the theological Reality) of the celebration are the Mysteries of our salvation, presented to us in Scripture as their scenarios. But the goal always remains the goal of redemption itself: that we be taken up into God's inner life, joining the angels in the heavenly worship.

This realistic side of celebration makes us share, through ritual, together with the angels, in the Divine Reality of God himself. Such sharing occurs in proportion to the celebrant's and worshippers' reverence and their faith in the realism of God's creative power in the celebrated Mysteries. And all of this is expressed by their active participation, which is in fact an interior participation of prayer expressed in ritual. This last point requires further elaboration, because it is basic for understanding not only the Eastern approach to liturgy but also especially the Apostolic Church's worship, which is the mother of all Christian liturgy. Hence we move to our next section.

THE OBJECT OF LITURGY

The Eastern Church Fathers' basic Scripture text quoted in reference to true Christian worship is Ephesians 3:9–11:

> ...to make all men see what is the plan of the mystery hidden for ages in God who created all things; that through the church the manifold wisdom of God might now be made known to the principalities and powers in the heavenly places. This was according to the eternal purpose which he has realized in Christ Jesus our Lord.

Through the liturgy, we re-enact, in the bosom of the Church, the mystery of Redemption in its creative totality, spanning from God's first revelation in Old Testament times until Christ's return. This totality is ritually yet truly re-enacted by celebrating its successive stages: the Old Law's age-old expectation of the Messiah (celebrated in Advent); his appearance on earth in his birth and theophany[7] (celebrated in the Christmas cycle); his earthly

---

[7] The anglicized word "theophany" comes from the Greek *Theophaneia*, "manifestation of God." In the East, the Feast of Theophany is the culmination of the entire cycle of Advent and Christmas. Always observed

hidden and public life and his Great Deeds, culminating in his transfiguration on Mount Tabor; his suffering, death, resurrection, and ascension; and finally the descent of the Spirit upon his Church. All these Mysteries are the content and reality of Christian worship, truly brought about in the celebration, siphoned over, so to speak, from the liturgy to life, to transform the world in view of Christ's return.

This celebrated mystery contains three levels. The first or lowest level is the mystery's symbolic expression in worship. The second is our spiritual understanding of it. The third and highest level is our unification in mystical oneness with God as he is, beyond symbols and concepts—yet it is always *through* sacramental symbols and rites that this higher mystery is communicated. This is why the East is so eager to preserve the apostolic heritage in these symbols and rites. The East is eager also to protect her symbols and rites from the novel arbitrariness of modernism—because modern novelties hide the mystery by their man-centeredness and thus prevent it from giving birth to its mystical reality in the participants. The present-day false freedom of improvising the celebration is precisely the opposite of the Eastern liturgical ethos.

The birth of the mystery in the participants takes place first of all through the ritual experience, just through sharing in the celebration in which we switch over from the realism of our senses to the service of the Divine. From there, understanding is built up—an understanding that is not rational but mystical—by a mutual interfusion of the soul with the creative presence of the mystery, as a marriage between the liturgy and the mystical experience of the Divine Reality. In this interfusion we see that all life and all good flows from the Blessed Trinity by the celebration of the Mysteries. Jean Corbon has explained this eloquently in his book, *The Wellspring of Worship*,[8] which is "must" reading for an understanding of the Eastern liturgical ethos.

This sense of realism in the celebration is a deep awareness of the Eastern liturgy, providing the nourishment for its mystical experience. It is entrusted to the angelic hierarchy in heaven and

---

on January 6, it celebrates the manifestation of the Holy Trinity at Jesus's baptism in the Jordan River, for then the Father spoke from heaven and the Spirit descended in the form of a dove.

[8] Jean Corbon, *The Wellspring of Worship* (Mahwah, NJ: Paulist, 1988). See also Saint Paul's allusions to this in Rom 16:25 and 1 Cor 2:7.

projected into the liturgy on earth, where it is presided over by
the Church's hierarchy and fully shared by the believers.[9]

ARTICLE 2: APPLICATIONS FOR THE LITURGY

Let us now consider some applications that result from the
lofty vision explained above, and examples pertaining to the
liturgy. While doing so let us keep in mind that both Vatican
II and Pope John Paul II have repeatedly emphasized that the
Eastern Churches must faithfully preserve and adhere to their
own heritage, not only for their own integrity but for the benefit
of the whole Church, for the Church cannot be whole without
their substantial contribution.[10]

TRADITION

Unhappiness with Tradition, and rejection of it, are among
the greatest troubles of the Western dissenters. So I will tackle
this huge subject first, though briefly.

Three main, essential elements are at work in Holy Tradition:
(1) the heritage of Christ in the Early Church, (2) the uninterrupted continuity of that heritage throughout the ages, and (3)
the Holy Spirit, the One who keeps this heritage unaltered and
creative as it was in the Apostolic Church. If any one of these
elements is weakened or abandoned, the whole of Holy Tradition
is jeopardized, and with it the true Church herself. This explains
the deep impact, upon all of Church life, of attacks against the
pope and bishops (the carriers of Tradition) and against the liturgy (the celebration of Tradition's content) — for these attacks
undermine Holy Tradition itself.

Tradition stems from two wellsprings: (1) the Upper Room of
the Eucharist as the headwaters of the liturgy ("Do this in memory
of Me"); and (2) the Upper Room of Pentecost as the headwaters
of the creative leadership of the Spirit in the Church. As Orthodox
theologian Vladimir Lossky has said, "Tradition is the life of the
Holy Spirit in the Church." And Orthodox Bishop Kallistos Ware
has rightly written that "Tradition is not the sum of propositions

---

[9] Pseudo-Dionysius wrote on this theologically-rich subject, especially in
his work, *On the Divine Names*, available in many editions.
[10] See *Orientalium Ecclesiarum*, Articles 1, 5, and 6; and the entirety of John
Paul II's *Ut Unum Sint* and *Orientale Lumen*.

learned by heart, but a lived experience" and "Tradition is the living meaning of Scripture, always new in every age."[11]

Both wellsprings are taken extremely seriously in the Eastern Churches because they concur in giving the Church her very being and her existential characteristics. For example, the Church is sacramental and community-building; she is the life-giving cradle of the New Testament Scriptures, the guardian of orthodoxy, and the anticipation of the Lord's return. All these constituents form one continuous, living chain in the Holy Spirit, and thus form the real soul of the Church.[12]

Yet here lies perhaps the deepest separation between East and West. The West, influenced by the security of having supreme authority in the Church, and bolstered by a later legalism and nominalism, has largely lost its sense of the living Tradition and even its very understanding of it.[13] The West therefore turned more and more to law and legalism, to authority and institution. Even its underlying concept of freedom was distorted under the impact of this approach, until for many freedom eventually came to mean "do your own thing."

For the East, however, *true freedom exists in doing God's will within Holy Tradition*. Hence the East's freedom is not random but is a service, regulated by freely-accepted rules. Take as an example an Eastern priest celebrating the liturgy. He appears to be totally free in his celebration, but he is guided by a thousand and one freely-accepted regulations. Hence the liturgy is not improvised by him (even though he puts himself wholly into it) but is received from Holy Tradition, his loving master that makes him truly free before the face of God, the angels, and the worshipping community.

---

[11] See "Tradition, the Bible, and the Holy Spirit," *Epiphany* (Winter 1991): pp. 7–16. See also Jaroslav Pelikan's study, "The Ukrainian Religious Experience," in David J. Goa, ed., *Eastern Christianity in Modern Culture: Genius and Dilemma* (Edmonton: Canadian Institute of Ukrainian Studies, 1989), pp. 233–37.

[12] This Eastern love of Holy Tradition explains the role of the Eastern Churches' Patriarchs as the fathers and appliers of Holy Tradition in their Churches. I humbly suggest that the pope of Rome would gain much credibility with our Orthodox brethren were he to act on the basis of his authority as Patriarch of the West and as Universal Patriarch for the whole Church in virtue of Holy Tradition.

[13] Archimandrite Victor Pospishil has rightly shown this in his book, *Ex Occidente Lex* (Carteret, NJ: St. Mary's Religious Action, 1979). See also his *Eastern Catholic Church Law* (Brooklyn: Saint Maron, 1996), esp. pp. 64, 145.

Consider, for example, how "days of obligation" and fasts are treated in the two Churches. In the modern West, if these feasts and fasts cannot be fully observed, they are abolished for fear of hypocrisy. The East reasons quite differently. Based on Holy Tradition, it says, "If the Church as a whole is unable to observe these feasts and fasts, at least a sizable group of pious people *will* observe them, especially the monks and nuns — because the function of monks and nuns in the Church is to strive toward evangelical perfection. They will represent and lead the whole Church as if *in them* the whole Church were keeping Holy Tradition intact." This exhibits not hypocrisy but a sense of Tradition and communion.

HOLINESS

The Eastern Churches have a sharp awareness of the holy in both worship and practical life. To be a Christian demands a constant choice for the "first necessity" (see Lk 10:42, Jesus's words to Martha). The true Christian lives at odds with the world, in the awareness that we are not made for this world, as in Hebrews 13:14: "We have here no lasting city, but we seek the city which is to come." All of Eastern life and worship is filled with this eschatological perspective.

The Eastern awareness of the holy naturally includes a deep love and respect for monks and monastic life, the core of all Eastern Christianity, as Pope John Paul II expressed in *Orientale Lumen*.[14] Monks have had enormous impact on the life and piety of the faithful in the East. For example, the Jesus Prayer and the Hesychast movement of silence and prayer of the heart was begun by monks and later adopted by clergy and faithful. The Jesus Prayer — *"Lord Jesus Christ, Son of God, have mercy on me, a sinner"* — is one of the great treasures of the East. When prayed often and with humility, this prayer comes to life in the heart of monk and faithful alike, enabling them to pray without ceasing, as Saint Paul exhorts (1 Thess 5:16).[15]

---

[14] See my book on this subject, *Eastern Monasticism and the Future of the Church* (Stamford, CT: Basileos Press, 1993). See also my address to the Synod on Consecrated Life in October 1994 in Rome: *Le Chiese Orientali Cattolica e la Vita Religiosa* (Rome: Vatican, 1994), pp. 7–23, which gives in resume the whole Eastern view of evangelical holiness (i.e., *theosis*).
[15] For more on the Jesus Prayer, see, e.g., A Monk of the Eastern Church, *The Jesus Prayer* (Crestwood, NY: St. Vladimir's Seminary Press, 1987); E.

The Eastern Church calendar also illustrates awareness of the holy. Whereas the West's norms for inclusion of saints in the calendar seem to be primarily geographical, the East upholds rather the essence and norms of sanctity. The Mother of God, the Theotokos (God-bearer), towers high above all the angels and saints, even unto the very inner life of the Blessed Trinity; therefore she is praised in every service with beautiful texts and melodies, and through veneration of her icon. The East then celebrates the other evangelical saints: John the Forerunner (the Baptizer), Saint Joseph, each of the twelve apostles, plus all the sundry biblical persons from both Old and New Covenants, commemorated because of their closeness to the plan of salvation.

The calendar then switches to the criterion of holiness in daily life: most of the remaining saints are monks and nuns, martyrs, Fathers-Bishops, holy women, families, and even converted soldiers and criminals. A whole chapter would be required to overview the theology contained in the Byzantine liturgical year's proper texts — all of which are sung — extolling the saints and imploring their intercession. One example out of thousands is the tropar (hymn) for Saint Nicholas, commemorated on December 6:

> O Father and Pontiff Nicholas, the holiness of your life
> was set before your flock as a rule of faith, an example
> of meekness and a teaching of temperance; wherefore
> you acquired greatness through humility and spiritual
> wealth through poverty. Pray to Christ God that He may
> save our souls.

In short, holiness is a quality that springs from the Blessed Trinity yet permeates all of practical life and human society. The liturgy is the carrier and wellspring of this holiness. Thus one of the most frequent elements of the Eastern liturgy is the Trisagion, the hymn to the "thrice holy" God, always sung three times with the Sign of the Cross and reverent bows: *"Holy God, Holy Mighty One, Holy Immortal One, have mercy on us."*

Kadloubovsky and G. E. H. Palmer, trans., *Writings from the Philokalia on Prayer of the Heart* (London: Faber & Faber, 1951ff.); and *Way of a Pilgrim*, the narrative of a nineteenth-century Russian peasant who discovers how to pray without ceasing, available in many translations and editions. — Ed.

CONTINUITY AND COMMUNITY

As Tradition creates vertical continuity between Christ and the past, present, and future, it also brings horizontal continuity with Christ among all those involved in Eastern worship. Hence, for example, the ministers are not above or set against the faithful; they are *part* of the faithful, but with a special function. The priest acts from within the community of the general priesthood of the faithful: by his Holy Ordination, he is accredited to God and to the Church, as a mouthpiece of the faithful as well as a sacramental presence of the High Priest. The deacon in the East is part of this community dimension: he directs the worship and serves as a holy coordinator of the ordained priests and the faithful. The Eastern liturgy therefore includes both the exuberant solemnity of a pontifical service and the constant active participation of the faithful.

Within the Eastern liturgy is a wondrous duality: an awesome depth and majesty, mingled with the unspeakably intimate womanlike trust and childlike love with which it celebrates the Theotokos, the Mother of God. Delicate yet strong veneration and love for her penetrates the entire liturgy, in extension and in depth, as expressed in this tropar sung at every Office:

> Truly fitting is it to sing your praises, O Theotokos, the ever-blessed and complete sinless One, and the Mother of our God. You are more honorable than the Cherubim, beyond compare more glorious than the Seraphim. In virginity you bore the Word of God. O Mother of God, we extol you.

So essential is this veneration that if it were lost, the liturgy would lose its characteristic blending of majesty and intimacy. This blending is like the counterpoint of Bach, preventing the danger of hieratic rigidity; it is like the mutual exchange between father and mother in a happy home.

The Marian balance between tenderness and respect forms the backbone of the healthy feminism of the Eastern liturgy. With God, objective initiative is primary; thus throughout all our celebration, the bridal relationship sings like background music, inviting us to enter deeply into God's inner life as we open up to his loving embrace. This explains the presence in the Eastern liturgical calendar of a large number of women saints, from all walks of life, in whom we celebrate our bridal relationship with God in the Holy Spirit.

The bridal relationship always bears an implicit reference to Mary, the Virgin Mother of the Only Holy One, who made her holy, and all women holy in her. Thus the Eastern Churches warmly welcome women to serve in various roles in parish (and religious) communities; they exclude only any service that requires liturgical ministry (such as reader or eucharistic minister) or ordination. In sum, the Eastern Churches' sincere respect for women is a reflection of the respect paid to the Mother of God. In all this the Eastern Church is the direct heir of the Apostolic and Patristic Church, where women were held in high esteem, as models of all mankind's virginal relation to God, who both dwells in us and reigns from heaven.

The penetrating realism of the Mysteries and the saints in the liturgy explains the role and abundance of icons in Eastern worship. Icons are religious depictions of the Mysteries of our salvation, and of Christ, saints, and angels, painted on wood. Often called "windows to heaven," icons take a full part in Eastern liturgical celebrations, as active participants.[16] The Eastern Church understands that the Mysteries or angels or saints depicted are mystically truly present in their icons and thus share in the celebration. Icons are incensed often during the services, in order to involve them in the holy work of the worshiping community, because they belong there, just as do the invisible angels. As the priest prays at the first entrance during the Divine Liturgy: "... [W]hile we make our entrance, may your angels enter with us too."

The murals in the catacombs, and frescoes in ancient temples in the Near East and Africa, show that this realism of the saints' presence in the icons is not a recent Eastern invention. In the Roman liturgy this role has historically been played by statues. The recent removal of statues for the supposed reason that they distract from the altar and from Christ is an attitude completely foreign to Eastern Christians. *The saints are not in competition with*

---

[16] For discussions of the rich theological and liturgical significance of icons, see Leonid Ouspensky, *The Meaning of Icons* (Crestwood, NY: St. Vladimir's Seminary Press, 1982); Egon Sendler, *The Icon, Image of the Invisible* (Torrance, CA: Oakwood, 1995); and Henri Nouwen, *Behold the Beauty of the Lord* (Notre Dame: Ave Maria, 1987).

Christ; they are his humble servants who bring us to Christ. Of course, statues should be beautiful and in good taste, and why not include icons in churches as well?[17]

A final area to consider is collegiality. In the East—and the Council confirmed this for the whole Church—the hub of ecclesiology is the bishop, successor of the apostles. But the bishop is not an autocrat. His authority is always in reference (silent or outspoken) to his fellow bishops and to the Petrine Ministry. In the East, all bishops and even Patriarchs (the heads of the various Churches) are *under*, subservient to, living Holy Tradition, in the awareness that it is ultimately the Holy Spirit who governs the Church in continuity with Pentecost. The reality is that no hierarch, from a simple bishop to the pope, may invent anything. Every hierarch is a successor of the apostles, which means that he is first of all a keeper and servant of Holy Tradition—a guarantor of continuity in teaching, worship, sacraments, and prayer.

*   *   *

One of the most valuable aspects of the Eastern Churches' worship, especially of the Byzantine Liturgy, is its gentle didactic character. By means of poetic beauty it conveys the most sublime teaching, expressing the Faith's contents in clear wording, speaking to the worshippers' imagination and moving them to faith commitment. The Eastern liturgical books are truly one great *summa theologica* of orthodox teaching, presented in the saints as examples, and in all the Mysteries of the Faith. An example is this verse from the feast of the Three Holy Hierarchs: Saints Basil the Great, Gregory the Theologian, and John Chrysostom:

> Today the souls of mortals [we who are celebrating] are elevated above earthly things; today they [we] become heavenly beings as they [we] sing the memory of the saints. The gates of Heaven are open for us, and the ways of the Lord are made known to us. Tongues extol their miracles and proclaim the words of the Word. Let us also cry out to the Savior: Glory

---

[17] I would add that the proper style of icons has been standardized as far back as the sixth century according to the laws of the worshiping community; icons may not be created or changed according to modern man's tastes.

to You, O Christ God, because through them there
has been peace for the faithful.
—Aposticha in Vespers, January 30

Throughout the ages the Eastern Churches have been able to
survive a series of onslaughts, from the earliest heresies, to the
relentless pressure of Islam, to the recent murderous communism
and choking secularism. Why? Mainly because the clergy, monks,
and laity held fast to the right teaching, celebrated it daily in
worship, and from there carried this teaching out into a life of
faith and Christian mores.

ARTICLE 3: PASS-OVER AND RETURN

I will conclude these thoughts by speaking of the most precious aims of all liturgical reform, which are also the deepest
dimensions of the Eastern Church and her worship: the Paschal
mystery (Christ's Pass-over), and its natural complement, the
Lord's Return. These are perhaps the most important dimensions
the West can rediscover or deepen by considering the Eastern
liturgy's example.

THE PASCHAL MYSTERY
In the different liturgical reforms since Pius V, especially
reforms of the calendar and Divine Office, the Roman liturgy
has tried honestly, but I believe in vain, to restore Easter to its
rightful role in the liturgical year and spirituality. This lack of
success has two reasons: mystical and liturgical.

1. *The Mystical Reason.* All our life and worship should be moved
by a deep awareness that we are *both* risen with Christ through
baptism *and* moved by the Spirit through confirmation (called
"chrismation" in the East, for the chrism oil). The West generally lacks this deep, dual awareness, in large part because of the
separation of these two Mysteries—the sacraments of baptism
and confirmation—from each other.

In Chapter 3 I recounted how discussion of the initiation sacraments was taken from our subcommission and given to the
commission of bishops, who created the current Rite of Confirmation in which confirmation is delayed for years after baptism. This separation of the two primary sacraments was made
for invalid reasons. For example, in the West confirmation is

said to be the sacrament of Christian adulthood, in which we are opened up for the Spirit of God to act in us—namely, that confirmation gives strength *to us* to witness and do battle.[18] This approach in effect makes the sacrament primarily man-centered instead of God-centered. Being given strength is very necessary, of course, but it is secondary to the primary, *God-centered*, relation to the Spirit.

In the God-centered approach of the East, chrismation (confirmation) *enables us to worship as a royal priesthood*, especially to celebrate and receive the Eucharist. This approach generates a deeply different view of Christian life: it is a *Paschal* life. The Holy Spirit takes over our lives and makes them as a constant rising with the Risen Lord, out of sin, into God's wonderful light of life, which we celebrate in the liturgy.

Note that it is the Holy Spirit who takes over, not a Church institution or organization or authority. As important as organization and authority might be, they are only an expression of this deeper, mystical reality of the Spirit ruling the Church of Christ, and ruling every Christian from the moment of his or her confirmation. Hence if these two Mysteries, baptism and confirmation, are separated, the very quality of the life of the Church as *risen* life seriously suffers.

2. *The Liturgical Reason.* The second reason for the Paschal impoverishment of Christian life in the West is that this basic mystery of Pascha (Easter) is not adequately expressed in its ritual celebration. First, in general, I have observed that awareness of the Paschal Mystery in the celebration of sacraments, Eucharist, and Divine Office is quite lacking in Western clergy and faithful. This becomes apparent especially if one compares the celebrations of West and East. In the East, texts on the Paschal perspective abound throughout the whole year, woven into the proper texts of the feasts of salvation and of the saints.

Second, in particular, the new Roman liturgy lacks full awareness of the Paschal element on *Sunday*, the day of Resurrection. In the Eastern liturgies every Sunday is a "little Pascha." I dare say that more Paschal texts are sung in the Offices and liturgy on any one Sunday in the East than the new Roman liturgy contains

---

[18] Pope Leo XIII wrote on this subject to the Bishop of Marseille in 1898; see my book, *La Confirmation: doctrine et pastorale*, cited above, p. 27.

for the entire Paschal period! Sunday Matins, for instance, is rich with beautiful texts and music, beginning with the Paschal Psalms 134–135/135–136, called the *Polyeleos*, followed by the Song of the Angels, in six stanzas such as this one:

> The radiant angel standing by the grave cried out to the Myrrh-bearing women: "Why do you lament and mingle your tears with the spices? Look upon the grave and rejoice, for the Savior is risen from the dead."

The Paschal emphasis continues with the deacon's solemn announcement, and the celebrant's chanted proclamation, of one of the eleven Resurrection Gospels. Immediately after the Gospel, we sing a glorious tropar as all come forward to kiss the Gospel book:

> Now that we have seen the Resurrection of Christ,
> let us adore the all-holy Lord Jesus, the only Sinless One!
> We bow in worship before your cross, O Christ,
> and we praise and glorify your Resurrection,
> for You are our God and we have no other, and we
> 　　magnify your Name.
> All you faithful, come: let us adore the holy Resurrection
> 　　of Christ,
> for, behold, through the Cross joy has come to the world!
> Let us always bless the Lord, let us sing his Resurrection,
> for by enduring for us the pain of the Cross,
> He has crushed death through his death.

Note well that in the first line of this hymn we acknowledge, after the gospel proclamation, that the mystery is happening *now* in our midst: "*We have seen* the Resurrection." This abundance of Paschal celebration forms the first part of every Sunday Matins, deeply building up awareness of the Paschal mystery and keeping it alive throughout the year.

THE LORD'S RETURN

Let us move on to the second fundamental background of all liturgy: its eschatological dimension, the Lord's return in glory. This awareness, too, deeply penetrates the Eastern liturgy, in virtue of the basic text: " . . . you proclaim the Lord's death [Paschal dimension] until he comes [eschatological dimension]" (1 Cor 11:26). The evocation of the Lord's glory is implicit in a great portion of the Eastern liturgy's texts and rites. Therefore in every Sunday's Morning Office the Gradual Hymns sing the part of the Holy Spirit in the Paschal work of *theosis*,[19] as illustrated by the following verse:

> Every spirit lives by the grace of the Holy Spirit, and is
>   raised up in all purity;
> it is mystically enlightened by the one God in three
>   Persons.

The liturgy constantly reminds us that the final goal of all salvation and hence of all worship is for man to share in Christ's glory by the power of the Holy Spirit to the glorification of the Father. This awareness is the cause of the special tonality of the Eastern liturgy, which she inherited from the Early Church: the blending of our joyful confidence in Jesus's promise to be with us as we celebrate, and our patient waiting for his return. The attitude of waiting begets in Eastern worshippers a grateful acceptance of the long duration of their services, because Jesus promised to be with those who *gather in his name — the first meaning of which is the liturgical celebration of his Mysteries.* Eastern monks, who gather for liturgical prayer for many hours each day, have always understood this well.

"Gathering in his name" presupposes a commitment of our whole lives to Christ, so that we may be with him when he gathers his faithful sheep at the final judgment (Mt 25:31–46). Such commitment involves all levels of life: culture as well as worship, community as well as family and personal life. Although Christians know this, they still often flounder for lack of a model to follow. But such a model exists! Look to the East, dear friend, and you will find the Light, as Pope John Paul II has so earnestly implored.

FINAL SUGGESTIONS

In conclusion, I offer three concrete suggestions for your prayerful consideration.

We must preserve the hearths of religious culture that are still alive, namely ethnic groups such as the Hispanics, the Filipinos

---

[19] See Appendix D for thoughts on *theosis*, the deep union with God to which all Christians are invited: God calls us to become "partakers of the divine nature" (2 Pet 1:3–4). — Ed.

and other Asian Catholics, and the various Eastern Church communities—Ukrainians, Ruthenians, Serbians, Melkites, Armenians, Copts, and more—who are still strongly united around their liturgical traditions. These people, who continue to highly value their parish communities and dioceses (called eparchies in the East), serve as a paradigm for Western Christians. Ecumenical openness is of extreme importance here: these peoples and cultures carry a treasure unknown to the West, which needs it badly. It is imperative that Christians emphasize and build upon the factors that bind us together and not focus on our differences.

We must recognize fully the importance of religion in the process of restoring culture, in order to build up a new, creative, lasting culture upon the lasting values of religion. Again, in this process, we can learn from the East, where religion still inspires the culture. I repeat that it is possible for a religious culture to exist in the West. The Western renewal movements before Vatican II provided such a liturgical culture, as lively in America as in Europe; it could be revived. But, if I may say so, *this revival will begin only when we start to take the liturgy seriously as a way of life and not as a battlefield.*

We must all, therefore, go through a real conversion, both personal and communal. Then we shall indeed be able to learn from the East and truly prepare the Lord's Return. In this conversion importance must be placed not on "having" or "doing," but rather on "being." And let us be mindful, as Saint John has written (1 Jn 2:15–17), that whatever cannot withstand the crucible of death—or the crucible of meeting the Lord Jesus, king and judge of the universe and each individual soul—is not worth living for, because it will pass away with this world.

With the early Christians, let us all pray, fervently and without ceasing, calling for a new heaven and a new earth: "Maranatha; come, Lord Jesus."

POSTSCRIPT

DEAR READER, AFTER THIS LONG PERSONAL conversation, I now leave you and return to my silence. For silence is a great treasure, the last of the great treasures of Eastern spirituality, and, as Pope John Paul II wrote in *Orientale Lumen*, "We must confess that we all have need of this silence, filled with the presence of Him who is adored...."

Begging your forgiveness for any hurts I may have caused and any imperfections in what I have written, I ask your prayers, especially for "the Church in need"—which is all of us.

About the Author

BONIFACE LUYKX WAS BORN IN 1915 IN LOMMEL, Limburg Province, in Flemish northeastern Belgium, one of eleven children in a devout Catholic family.[1] The center of family and village life was the fourteenth-century church tower and the church itself, which Boniface's father had built in 1902. Boniface's mother prayed on her knees all night each Thursday that one of her seven sons would become a priest. Her prayers were answered in Boniface, whose calling began early in life. When he was five years old and not yet allowed to receive Holy Communion, another boy spat a Host on the church floor. Horrified, Boniface reverently picked It up and consumed It, upon which he heard a Voice: "I love you. Be with Me always." He heard that Voice again at key moments later in life.

The Luykx family suffered many hardships during World War I, including extreme food deprivation, which Boniface later claimed was the cause of his short stature. In these early years Boniface met refugee children from Eastern European countries, including Ukraine, and thus began, in his words, "a very real inner longing for the Eastern Church" which continued until its fulfillment decades later.

When Boniface was eleven years old, his parents sent him as a boarding student to the Jesuits' Saint Josef College in Turnhout,

---

[1] Most of the facts in this biographical sketch by the editor are excerpted from *Following the Star from the East: Essays in Honour of Archimandrite Boniface Luykx*, cited above. Unless otherwise noted, all direct quotes from Abbot Boniface are taken from a 1990 interview by Father Joseph Homick which constitutes the chapter "On the Wings of the Dawn: The Reminiscences of Archimandrite Boniface at his Golden Jubilee" (pp. 9–29). Those quotes are not separately footnoted in this sketch, nor is material taken from the main text of this book. Quotes and facts from the following additional chapters of the Festschrift are cited in this sketch by author's name and page number: Rev. Peter Galadza, "Abbot Boniface as Liturgist and 'Liturgisate'" and "Abbot Boniface Luykx: An Annotated Chronological Bibliography"; Msgr. Ignatius Roppolo, "A Summer that Made a Difference" (re: the 1959 Notre Dame Summer School of Liturgy); and Erasmo Leiva-Merikakis, "The Light of Tabor in Northern California" (re: his visits to Mount Tabor Monastery in the 1980s).

Belgium, where he excelled in drawing, music (he played the cello), and languages. After several years the Jesuits, noting Boniface's talents, urged him to join their order, but Boniface had developed a deep love for prayer and was drawn instead to the monastic life. Perceiving this, Father Emil Stalmans, a family friend (and future abbot of Tongerlo Abbey), suggested that Boniface enter the Norbertine (Premonstratensian) Abbey of Postel not far from Lommel. Boniface did so in 1934. Life in the Abbey was not easy, but Boniface loved his studies, the liturgy, and the time for prayer; he daily lived what he described as the "Mystery of Calling," as in Jesus's calling of his first disciples (Jn 1:35–42), anticipating the "greater things than these" (1:50) that Jesus promised.

Then came World War II. In 1940, two days after invading Belgium, the Germans captured Postel Abbey and imprisoned in its cellars the monks who had not yet fled, while the war raged overhead. After the Allied troops moved on, a French sniper stayed behind and shot several Germans who were occupying the Abbey's bell tower. Blaming Boniface and another deacon, the Germans brought them out for execution but an Allied bomb landed nearby and everyone ran for cover. Such threats of death continued during the occupation, which Father Boniface called a period of "relentless propaganda and lawlessness."

PRIESTHOOD

After six years of study and formation, Boniface was ordained to the priesthood on July 25, 1940, during Postel Abbey's 800th anniversary commemoration. He recounted the ordination as "moments of intense grace where we could feel the Holy Spirit at work, restructuring our souls unto the icon of Christ the High Priest." His godly mother died of a long illness a year before his ordination, but Father Boniface felt for the rest of his life that "her death was the price of God's love for the grace and unfading fervor of my priestly life."

In 1941 Father Boniface's abbot sent him to the University of Louvain (Leuven), Belgium, for postgraduate studies, which culminated in a doctorate in Sacred Theology. His professors were, in his words, "great names in the theological, scriptural, patristic, and liturgical world of those days . . . demanding . . . righteous, self-disciplined, extremely capable, and wise." There Father Boniface's priestly vocation matured by "constant application to the [scholarly] sources, absolute dedication to the truth, in love and submission to the Church."

During these years the Germans occupied Belgium. Food was rationed, classrooms were screened by secret police, and some students were threatened with deportation to German munitions factories. In the face of this need, at the request of philosopher Father Albert Dondeyne and with his abbot's permission, Father Boniface served as a priest to university students, the Resistance movement, and the underground army. It was a life of "daily exposure to deportation, hunger, insecurity, and even death." Father Boniface later said that this work "taught me to be detached even from life.... Prayer was the only secret of my survival."

After the war, most of Belgium's religious leaders suffered imprisonment, atrocities, and death at the hands of the Communists. Father Boniface's saintly father was tortured and later died from his injuries; Father Boniface said that witnessing this was his "deepest experience of Jesus's own scourging and torture by the soldiers." Father Boniface himself was imprisoned for a "terrible" five weeks. His family's business and factory were stolen by the Communists, and his siblings suffered deep poverty and distress, as did thousands of Flemish families. Father Boniface reflected later that "going down for several years into the depths of such seemingly bottomless sorrow" taught him to — as he said all priests must do — "take the heavy burden of others' sorrow into [my] heart and suffer with them." Amidst these trials, in 1945 he was appointed professor of fundamental, dogmatic, and sacramental theology at Postel Abbey.

Throughout the 1940s and 1950s Father Boniface was deeply involved with the Liturgical Movement, gaining broad experience of both positive and negative aspects of the Western Church's situation before Vatican II. He participated in liturgical congresses, annual study-weeks, and workshops. He wrote booklets to help the faithful participate more actively in the Mass (still in Latin) and edited the liturgical encyclopedia *Liturgisch Woordenboek*, to which he contributed nearly one hundred articles. His confreres included Dom Lambert Beauduin and Fathers Josef Jungmann, Pius Parsch, Bernard Botte, and others mentioned elsewhere in this sketch.

SCHOLARLY WORK

Father Boniface's scholarly work began with a baccalaureate thesis on the "mystery teaching" of Dom Odo Casel, and thereafter

Casel's thought permeated his life.[2] His doctoral dissertation, on the Premonstratensian rite of the Mass, was directed by Dom Bernard Capelle, scripture and liturgical scholar and abbot of Keizersberg (Mont-César) Abbey, who taught him "the rigorous methods of scientific research."[3] For subsequent decades he delved deeply into liturgical manuscripts in, as he described them, "the great scholarly centers of Europe"; late in life he stated that he had "studied and/or copied 90 percent of the existing [liturgical] manuscripts from between the seventh and thirteenth centuries."[4]

Among Father Boniface's scholarly works was his 1955 study *De oorsprong van het gewone der Mis* on the history of the Ordinary of the Mass, in which he demonstrated that "several Rhenish monastic centers were responsible for extremely creative developments under Byzantine and Syrian influence."[5] Published in German in 1961 as *Der Ursprung der gleichbleibenden Teile der heiligen Messe*, it was referenced in numerous reviews and publications over subsequent decades. Notably, as recounted in Chapter 1 of this book, the renowned liturgist Father Joseph Jungmann, SJ, included Father Boniface's scholarship as a correction to his own work in the 1955 edition of his *Missarum Sollemnia*.

Further recognition of Father Boniface's work came directly from Pope Pius XII. In his article *"De l'Évêque"* (On the Bishop), published in 1956 in *Les Questions liturgiques et paroissiales*, Father Boniface refuted a Roman canonist's article which asserted that the pope was the only true bishop in the worldwide Church. His article reached Pius XII, who sent him a personal letter of commendation, confirming that *his* study in fact represented the correct teaching of the Church.

Father Boniface was also a prolific contributor to *Ephemerides Liturgicae*, the leading liturgical journal published in Rome. Father Peter Galadza notes that in its 1958 bibliographical index, the name "B. Luykx" appears more often than "J. Jungmann" and "B. Capelle."[6] Over the years Father Boniface published in multiple languages, including Dutch, German, French, Latin, English, and later, Lingala.[7]

---

[2] Galadza, p. 32.   [3] Ibid., p. 35.
[4] Ibid. Most or all of this "copying" was probably done by hand.
[5] Ibid.   [6] Ibid., p. 36.
[7] Appendix B lists some of these publications. Lingala is a predominant language in the Congo.

From 1951 to 1967 Father Boniface also taught in the United States at the University of Notre Dame's pioneering Summer School of Liturgy, alongside Father Michael Mathis, CSC (its founder), Monsignor Martin Hellriegel, Dom Ermin Vitry, Father Louis Bouyer, SJ, Father Gerald Ellard, SJ, Deacon Cornelius (Kees) Bouman, and other leading lights of the Liturgical Movement. Monsignor Ignatius Roppolo, reflecting decades later on his own summer at Notre Dame (in 1959), described Father Boniface as "unique, different, challenging, on the cutting edge of the pre-Vatican II Church"; he "called us to prayer and study in so many ways, but especially by his own example" and treated all his students with "a great unconditional love."[8]

APPOINTMENT TO VATICAN II

In 1959 Father Boniface was appointed as Consultor to the Preparatory Commission for Liturgy for the Second Vatican Council. The Commission's main work was to prepare the schema (draft) for what would become *Sacrosanctum Concilium*, the Constitution on the Sacred Liturgy (CSL). Father Boniface and his bishop, Joseph Malula, were tasked with the crucial issue of liturgical adaptation. CSL's Articles 37–40, "Norms for Adapting the Liturgy to the Temperament and Traditions of People," adopted four years later, are their work.

Shortly after Vatican II began, following a "coup" by opponents of the schema, Pope John XXIII created a "Consilium for the Authentic Interpretation of the Constitution on Liturgy" and appointed Father Boniface as one of its Members (a higher rank than Consultor). This Consilium continued refining CSL, as requested by the Council Fathers in 1962 and 1963. The Constitution on the Sacred Liturgy was approved by a vote of 2,147 to 4 and promulgated on December 4, 1963 by Pope Paul VI.

After the promulgation of CSL, Pope Paul VI appointed Father Boniface in January 1964 to the "Consilium for the Implementation of the Constitution on the Sacred Liturgy" of which Father Annibale Bugnini was Secretary and functional leader. As detailed in this book, Father Boniface labored in the Consilium's subcommissions and Sacred Congregation for Divine Worship until 1975. There he struggled, against a growing tide of rebellion, to preserve

---

[8] Roppolo, pp. 50–51.

the true intent of the Council Fathers during the preparation
of postconciliar documents which were intended (but failed)
to faithfully interpret and implement the Constitution on the
Sacred Liturgy.

LIFE IN AFRICA

Immediately before Father Boniface's work for the Council
began, the Superior General of the Scheut Fathers, a Flemish
missionary congregation, asked him to help establish a Pastoral
Center for the bishops and missionaries of the Belgian Congo
(Zaire). In January 1960, feeling God's call, and supported by years
of previous study in the field of African religious anthropology,
Father Boniface left Europe for Kinshasa, Zaire's capital. In addition to directing the Pastoral Center, whose main work was the
inculturation of Christianity — especially its music and worship —
into the African soul and society, he was appointed Professor
of Liturgy at the University of Lovanium, then an extension of
Belgium's Louvain, and led the country's liturgical commission.

Shortly after his arrival in Zaire, several young missionaries
urged Father Boniface to utilize his monastic experience to found
a truly African monastery. The ecclesiastical authorities, including
Bishop Joseph Malula, agreed. After years of labor the *Monastère
de l'Assomption* was formally established in 1966 near Kinshasa,
with Father Boniface as Abbot. The brothers' simple life of gospel
poverty was rooted in Eastern Christian tradition and liturgy, for
Father Boniface, as an anthropologist, had observed that the Western form of Christianity cannot "serve as the matrix for a truly
incarnated Christianity" in Africa or other Third World cultures.[9]

While in Central Africa, Father Boniface traveled through the
jungles, providing retreats and workshops for missionaries and
priestly services to the people, who loved him dearly in return for
his deep respect for them and their culture. "Talking drums," then
the primary communication system in remote areas, announced
Father Boniface's travels. Believers walked miles through the jungle bringing sick children for his prayers; throngs came on Holy
Thursday, when Father Boniface washed and kissed their muddy

---

[9] See *Following the Star from the East*, p. 19. The nature of Father Boniface's
work in Africa is also captured in an excellent article by Newell Schindler:
"Christianity makes new start," *New Orleans Clarion Herald*, August 15, 1963,
accessed at https://www.jstor.org/stable/community.32136264?seq=6.

feet. His reputation among the African peoples was such that a letter from Europe, addressed only as "Father Boniface, Congo" once reached him in the jungle. He later stated that nothing so thoroughly shaped his soul as his eleven years in Africa.

Amidst this busy schedule, Father Boniface's assigned work as a Consultor for the Second Vatican Council continued. In addition, Bishop Malula appointed Father Boniface as his personal *"secrétaire et assistant"* (*peritus*) for all his Council responsibilities. Thus Father Boniface composed the bishop's reports and letters, prepared his interventions, and traveled with him to Rome during the preparatory period and all four years of Vatican II.

An understanding of "missionary" cultures was egregiously lacking among the Council's experts. Because of Father Boniface's experience with the African people, some participants warmly welcomed his insights; others in powerful positions (including Father Annibale Bugnini) rejected them. Bishop Malula and Father Boniface struggled mightily, but largely in vain, to convince the Europeans that the African people were deeply religious and highly cultured and should not have Western liturgical norms and music artificially forced upon them, as was being done. To help correct this injustice, back home in Zaire, Bishop (later Cardinal) Malula and Father Boniface composed and published a book of 200 authentically African liturgical songs in their language, Lingala; these songs are still widely used. Further, in accordance with CSL's Articles 37–40, they collaborated in creating the *Messe Zaïroise*, the Zaire Rite of the Mass, which gained full ecclesiastical approval in 1988 for use in Zaire (now the Democratic Republic of the Congo).[10]

Life in Africa was blessed but exceedingly difficult: deadly snakes lurked in the trees, the cacophony of wild animals prevented sleep at night, the heat was extreme, and in 1968 armed bandits attacked the monastery. After a vehicle accident the next year, Father Boniface was declared dead and laid in a coffin, from which he arose upon regaining consciousness before the undertakers finished their work! A local hospital repaired one

---

[10] For historical details see https://www.vaticannews.va/en/church/news/2023-02/zaire-rite-use-catholicity-africanness-congo-drc-libambu.html. See also Raymond Moloney, "The Zairean Mass and Inculturation," *Worship* 62 (Sept. 1988): pp. 433–42, which names Juan Mateos and Boniface Luykx as instrumental in liturgical incarnation in Africa.

of his legs and reattached his severed foot to the other; for the rest of his life his legs were of unequal lengths.

Finally, in April 1971, poor health, which he experienced most of his life, forced Father Boniface to leave Africa and his heart-broken brothers and friends.[11] He returned to Belgium and began writing *Culte chrétien en Afrique après Vatican II*, his analysis of the postconciliar documents on the liturgy as pertaining to the African situation and beyond, published in 1974.[12] His evaluation of those documents in this present book is largely based on that earlier work.

FOUNDING OF HOLY TRANSFIGURATION (MOUNT TABOR) MONASTERY

Just months later, in the summer of 1971, while Father Boni-face was teaching in the United States, Cardinal John Dearden of Detroit, Father Damasus Winzen of Mount Saviour Monas-tery (where Father Boniface had often given retreats), and other American friends urged him to found an Eastern monastery in North America. Discerning this as a calling of the Holy Spirit, he began work in 1972 to establish a foundation in the most authentic tradition of Byzantine monasticism. Thus began Holy Transfigu-ration Monastery, commonly known as Mount Tabor Monastery, established under the jurisdiction of the Ukrainian Catholic Bishop of Chicago. The first chapel and all its contents burned to the ground, and the attacks and sufferings were severe. But the Lord spoke several times to Father Boniface: "I love Mount Tabor! Go on! I will take over." Abbot Boniface later said, "It is all the work of the Lord.... And whenever the history of this monastery is published, it will be an uninterrupted hymn of praise for the Most Holy Trinity who did it all...." For Abbot Boniface, Mount Tabor Monastery was the fulfillment of his lifelong yearning for Eastern monasticism—and of a 1946 prophecy by his friend Dom Lambert Beauduin that he would die as an Eastern monk.

The unique life and liturgy of Mount Tabor Monastery, on a wooded hillside outside the small town of Redwood Valley in

---

[11] The *Monastère de l'Assomption* exists to this day, but as a Norbertine priory after Father Boniface's departure from Africa.

[12] See Appendix B, Further Reading. Father Peter Galadza, in his Festschrift chapter "Liturgist and Liturgisatel," pp. 36–38, discusses this work, some criticisms of it, and Father Boniface's responses in a 1990 personal letter.

northern California, have drawn visitors from multiple states and nations. One frequent guest in the early years has written that "worship at Mt. Tabor manifests the aesthetic opulence of the Byzantine vision of God's kingdom, while nonetheless reflecting the evangelical imperative of solidarity with the poor."[13] Another guest described "an intense life of prayer, both personal and liturgical, that celebrates the ongoing presence in the Church of Christ's mysteries and intercedes before God for all the world."[14] He noted, too, that the love with which the monks welcome all visitors has resulted in many conversions — because of Abbot Boniface's vision and insistence that the monastery must be "the family of Jesus."[15]

LATER LABORS

Abbot Boniface's labors for the Church continued long after founding Mount Tabor Monastery. He assisted various Catholic groups attempting to correct errors that arose after the Council, including CREDO, a society of priests dedicated to the faithful translation of the liturgy. A strong advocate for the union of the Eastern and Western Churches, Abbot Boniface worked in the 1990s with the Kievan Church Study Group, a voluntary gathering of bishops and theologians of the Ukrainian Greco-Catholic Church and the Orthodox Ecumenical Patriarchate whose proceedings and papers are published in *Logos: A Journal of Eastern Christian Studies*.[16]

Always a visionary for the good of the Church, in the mid-1980s Abbot Boniface offered Mount Tabor Monastery as the first site of the Metropolitan Andrey Sheptytsky Institute of Eastern Christian Studies, which began with an intensive summer program during which students were immersed in monastic life and liturgy while earning graduate credits. From 1987 to 1999 Abbot Boniface taught in this summer program. However, in a 1990 interview he noted that he had given up most of his original scholarly pursuits "so that the Lord may find me available for *his* vision, which thus has to become *mine*."

In 1988 Ukrainian Catholic Bishop Innocent Lotocky, OSBM (Chicago) honored Abbot Boniface with the title "Archimandrite,"

---

[13] Galadza, p. 39. [14] Leiva-Merikakis, p. 55. [15] Ibid., pp. 54, 56.
[16] This peer-reviewed journal is published by the Metropolitan Andrey Sheptytsky Institute of Eastern Christian Studies, described in the next paragraph.

which in the Eastern Christian tradition denotes the spiritual father of one or more monasteries, a dignitary ranking just below a bishop. In 1992 the Metropolitan Andrey Sheptytsky Institute published a Festschrift, *Following the Star from the East: Essays in Honour of Archimandrite Boniface Luykx* (from which much of this biographical sketch is excerpted).

During the 1990s Archimandrite Boniface wrote four books. *Eastern Monasticism and the Future of the Church* (see Appendix B) was inspired by Title XII — "On Monks and Other Religious" — of the 1991 Code of Canons for the Oriental Churches. But it goes much further, providing deep wisdom and advice for the renewal of Western religious life. The manuscript of this present book, written in 1995–97, was rediscovered in 2022; see the Editor's Foreword for details. Two others remain unpublished: *The Blessed Trinity in Byzantine Liturgy and Life* and *Theological Foundations of the Byzantine Liturgy*. Archimandrite Boniface also compiled a 300-page liturgical service book, *Holy Advent and Christmas in the Eastern Church*, printed *pro manuscripto* for use by the monks of Mount Tabor Monastery. The result of decades of research, it is based in large part on the fifth- and sixth-century Rotulus of Ravenna; its texts are set to beautiful melodies Father Boniface himself composed.

In 2000 Archimandrite Boniface retired from his role as abbot and returned to Postel Abbey in Belgium. On Easter Sunday, April 11, 2004, this "good and faithful servant" was called to enter the Paschal joy of his Master. May his work and wisdom live on by means of this book, for the glory of God and his Holy Catholic and Apostolic Church, much in need of his mercy.

> *Beloved Father in Heaven, we know that at the evening of our lives, You are waiting for us in our paternal home. The lamp is already lit, the bread readied, and the door ajar: the Lord Jesus Himself is this lamp, this bread, and the open door. Now that we are gathered here together, setting off for home in You, may your Son, our Lord Jesus, soon be with us to enlighten us and lead us to You in your Holy Spirit. You are our real home, through Jesus your Son and in the joy of the Holy Spirit, for ever and ever. Amen.*[17]

---

[17] This is a priestly prayer in Vespers for the first Sunday of Advent, from *Holy Advent and Christmas in the Eastern Church*, described in the text above.

Further Reading

ARCHIMANDRITE BONIFACE COMPILED THIS
"Further Reading" appendix in 1996 and added his own notes
"to direct the reader's further work." The only changes made by
the editor are the addition of the "Selected Works" section, the
division into tentative subject categories, and explanatory notes
which are indicated by "Ed."

SELECTED WORKS BY AND ABOUT THE AUTHOR[1]
Luykx, Boniface. *Culte chrétien en Afrique après Vatican II*. Immensee,
Switzerland: Nouvelle Revue de science missionnaire, 1974. Father
Boniface wrote: "Most of the documentation and my reasoning in
Chapter 3 come from this book. Although initially written for the
Church in Africa, it is primarily an evaluation of the postconciliar
documents on the liturgy."

———. *Der Ursprung der gleichbleibenden Teile der heiligen Messe*. Maria
Laach: Verlag Ars liturgica, 1961. This is the German translation
of the Dutch original, *De oorsprong van het gewone der Mis* (Utrecht-
Antwerp: Spectrum, 1955) (On the Origins of the Ordinary of the
Mass), which Father Boniface references in Chapter 1 of this book.
In an article "Recent Research on the Mass" in *Theological Studies: A
Journal of Academic Theology* 18.2 (May 1957): pp. 249–50, Father Gerald
Ellard, SJ, describes a review of *De oorsprong* by Cornelius Bouman
in *Worship* 30 (Sept. 1956): p. 544, noting that the book was "already
having far-reaching effects." See theologicalstudies.net/wp-content/
uploads/2022/08/18.2.4.pdf.

———. *Eastern Monasticism and the Future of the Church*. Stamford, CT:
Basileos Press, 1993. From the back cover: "The renewal after Vatican
II has deeply affected religious life. It has made us feel the need for
new and untapped resources, such as those found in the monastic
life of the Eastern Churches, the cradle of all Christian religious
life in both East and West. By its freshness and continuity with the
gospel and the early Fathers, it has much to give that could meet the
needs of the Church of our days."

---

[1] Many of Archimandrite Boniface's books, in various languages and editions, are available through the Online Computer Library Center (OCLC)
website, www.WorldCat.org, under "Boniface Luykx" and "Bonifaas Luykx."
See also the bibliography compiled by Father Peter Galadza in *Following the
Star from the East*. — Ed.

——— and Daniel Scheyven. *La Confirmation: doctrine et pastorale*. Paroisse et Liturgie: Collection de Pastorale Liturgique, No. 33. Bruges: Apostolat Liturgique, Abbaye de Saint-André, 1958. This was also published in Italian (Catania: Edizioni Paoline, 1962) and in Spanish (Madrid: Ediciones Marova, 3 eds. beginning in 1961).

———. *Essai sur les sources de l' "Ordo Missae" prémontré*. Tongerloo, Belgium: Sint Norbertus-drukkerij, 1947. This is Father Boniface's doctoral dissertation on the Premonstratensian rite of the Mass. Remarkably, WorldCat.org lists twenty-eight copies located in libraries across Europe and North America.

———. "Failure of the Liturgical Reform with Abbot Boniface Luykx," an in-depth interview with the author recorded in 1996, while this book was being written. Originally produced by St. Joseph Communications as a three-cassette set, this opportunity to hear the distinctive voice of the author is now available from the Catholic Resource Center (Covina, CA) as an electronic download.

Chirovsky, Andriy, ed. *Following the Star from the East: Essays in Honour of Archimandrite Boniface Luykx*. Ottawa: Metropolitan Andrey Sheptytsky Institute of Eastern Christian Studies, 1992. This Festschrift contains a lengthy biographical interview with the author in 1990 by Father Joseph Homick, who became his successor as abbot of Mount Tabor Monastery. Also included are several tributes to Archimandrite Boniface's life and work, four essays on "Monks and the Religious Life," studies in liturgy and related fields, and a dozen photos. Especially valuable is Father Peter Galadza's annotated chronological bibliography of Archimandrite Boniface's work spanning the years 1939 to 1990. The full table of contents is posted at https://sheptytskyinstitute. ca/wp-content/uploads/2020/10/Following-the-Star-from-the-East-Table-of-Contents.pdf, and the book is available for purchase from the Sheptytsky Institute.

VATICAN II RESOURCES

Flannery, Austin, ed. *Vatican Council II: The Conciliar and Post Conciliar Documents*. Grand Rapids: Eerdmans, 1987, and other editions. [Abbot Boniface used this edition for citations in this book. —Ed.]

Kaiser, Robert Blair. *Pope, Council, and World: The Story of Vatican II*. New York: Macmillan, 1963.

Pennington, M. Basil. *Vatican II: We've Only Just Begun*. New York: Crossroad, 1994.

Stacpoole, Dom Alberic. *Vatican II Revisited: By Those Who Were There*. Minneapolis: Winston Press, 1986.

The Sixteen Documents of Vatican II (NCWC translation). Boston: Daughters of St. Paul, 1967.

THE PRECONCILIAR MOVEMENT

Botte, Bernard. *From Silence to Participation: An Insider's View of Liturgical Renewal.* Washington, DC: Pastoral Press, 1988. From the back of the book: "… chronicle tracing the liturgical renewal from its beginnings to its fruition in the work of Vatican II."

Chrichton, J. D. *Lights in Darkness: Forerunners of the Liturgical Movement.* Collegeville, MN: Liturgical Press, 1996. Biographies of those who, from the seventeenth century until Vatican II, laid the foundation for and led the Liturgical Movement.

Hughes, Kathleen. *How Firm a Foundation: Voices of the Early Liturgical Movement.* Chicago: Liturgy Training Publications, 1989. A precious account of this pioneering period.

REFORM OF THE LITURGY

Amerio, Romano. *Iota Unum: A Study of Changes in the Catholic Church in the XXth Century.* Kansas City: Sarto House, 1996.

Bugnini, Annibale. *The Reform of the Liturgy: 1948–1975.* Collegeville, MN: Liturgical Press, 1990. A chronicle of the Liturgical Movement from before Vatican II until the beginning of the abuses, loaded with personal notes, by the early editor of *Ephemerides Liturgicae* and later the Secretary of the Consilium.

Davies, Michael. *Liturgical Shipwreck: 25 Years of the New Mass.* Rockford, IL: TAN, 1997.

———. *Pope Paul's New Mass* (Liturgical Revolution Series, Volume III). Harrison, NY: Catholic Media, 1980 (and later editions).

Gamber, Klaus. *The Reform of the Roman Liturgy: Its Problems and Background.* San Juan Capistrano, CA: Foundation for Catholic Reform, 1993. This book's French edition received the strong endorsement of Cardinal Ratzinger and other outstanding churchmen.

Groeschel, Benedict. *The Reform of Renewal.* San Francisco: Ignatius, 1990.

Hitchcock, James. *Recovery of the Sacred: Reforming the Reformed Liturgy.* San Francisco: Ignatius, 1995.

Kavanagh, Aidan. *Elements of Rite: A Handbook of Liturgical Style.* Collegeville, MN: Liturgical Press, 1990.

Nichols, Aidan. *Looking at the Liturgy: A Critical View of its Contemporary Form.* San Francisco: Ignatius, 1996.

Pieper, Josef, and Lothar Krauth. *In Search of the Sacred: Contributions to an Answer.* San Francisco: Ignatius, 1990. On the motto of Cardinal Ratzinger: "We must in the liturgy retrieve the dimension of the Sacred."

The Crisis of Liturgical Reform (Concilium series, Volume 42). Mahwah, NJ: Paulist, 1969.

LITURGY IN THE UNITED STATES

Halle, David. *Inside Culture: Art and Class in the American Home*. Chicago: University of Chicago Press, 1993. On the soulless and pagan ways even Christians decorate their homes, and how recently all religious emblems are taken from the walls and a secularistic lack of culture has penetrated the intimacy of life.

Jones, E. Michael. *John Cardinal Krol and the Cultural Revolution*. South Bend, IN: Fidelity, 1995. This book deserves special recommendation, not only because of its topic but also for the honesty of its research of this important period. From the back flap: "It [the book] also gives the best historical account of the revolution that changed this country to what it is today [i.e., a post-Christian secular society]."

Kelly, George A. *Battle for the American Church (Revisited)*. San Francisco: Ignatius, 1995.

Schindler, David L., and Louis Bouyer. *Catholicism and Secularization in America: Essays on Nature, Grace, and Culture*. Notre Dame: Communio, 1990.

White, James. *Christian Worship in North America: A Retrospective: 1955–1995*. Collegeville, MN: Liturgical Press, 1997. The author treats the main topics of liturgical history in this major period before and after Vatican II, especially those characteristic for North America: e.g., liturgy and justice, liturgy and ecumenism, and liturgy and architecture.

Yuhaus, Cassian, ed. *The Catholic Church and American Culture: Reciprocity and Challenge*. Mahwah, NJ: Paulist, 1990.

OTHER RESOURCES

Corbon, Jean. *The Wellspring of Worship*. Mahwah, NJ: Paulist, 1988. This book, especially the Introduction, is "must" reading for an understanding of the Eastern liturgical ethos.

Eliade, Mircea. *The Sacred and the Profane: The Nature of Religion*. New York: Harcourt, 1959. The most easily approachable source on religious anthropology.

England, Randy. *The Unicorn in the Sanctuary: The Impact of the New Age on the Catholic Church*. Rockford, IL: TAN, 1991.

Hitchcock, Helen Hull. *The Politics of Prayer: Feminist Language and the Worship of God*. San Francisco: Ignatius, 1992.

Jungmann, Josef A. *The Mass of the Roman Rite: Its Origins and Development (Missarum Sollemnia)*, 2 vols. New York: Benziger, 1951. [This is available in numerous English editions, some abridged into one volume.—Ed.]

Martin, Ralph. *The Catholic Church at the End of an Age: What is the Spirit Saying?* San Francisco: Ignatius, 1994.

McGrade, R. Michael. *Death of a Catholic Parish: The Benalla Experiment*. Victoria, Australia: Roderick Pead, 1999. "Must" reading for every

Church leader and all those interested in the future of our parishes. [St. Joseph's Catholic Church in Benalla, Victoria, Australia, was a deeply spiritual Catholic parish until 1989 when it was given over to a team of "progressive" clerics. — Ed.]

Molnar, Thomas. *Twin Powers: Politics and the Sacred*. Grand Rapids, MI: Eerdmans, 1988.

Morrissey, Gerard. *Crisis of Dissent*. Front Royal, VA: Christendom, 1985.

Principe, Walter H. *Faith, History, and Cultures: Stability and Change in Church Teachings*. Milwaukee: Marquette University Press, 1991.

Ricœur, Paul. *De l'Interprétation*. Translated into English under the title *Interpretation Theory: Discourse and the Surplus of Meaning*. Fort Worth: Texas Christian University Press, 1976. This is one of the most significant studies on this crucial topic. [See its mention in the Introduction of this book. — Ed.]

Schindler, David L. *Heart of the World, Center of the Church: Communio Ecclesiology, Liberalism, and Liberation*. Grand Rapids, MI: Eerdmans, 1996. A courageous witness to the basics of Christianity in the surrounding decay and problems. A review in *National Catholic Register* says: "In the end, Schindler's proposal is remarkably simple.... Christians are called to follow Christ into the world and assume everything created with the aim of giving the world the form of the Church."

Sommers, Christina Hoff. *Who Stole Feminism? How Women Have Betrayed Women*. New York: Simon & Shuster, 1994.

Thiede, Carsten P., and Matthew D'Ancona. *Eyewitness to Jesus: Amazing New Manuscript Evidence About the Origin of the Gospels*. New York: Doubleday, 1996. A most sensational but irrefutable refutation, by two German scholars, of the generally accepted Bultmann thesis of Bible scholars that the Gospels were not written by eyewitnesses but are later-date embellishments for the use of catechetics. These authors give the manuscript confirmation of the proof Jean Carmignac (d. 1986) had given, though he was not taken seriously: that the Gospels were written by eyewitnesses between AD 40 and 50.

Toulmin, Steven. *Cosmopolis: The Hidden Agenda of Modernity*. New York: Macmillan, 1990.

von Hildebrand, Dietrich. *Trojan Horse in the City of God: The Catholic Crisis Explained*. Franciscan Herald, 1967.

———. *The Devastated Vineyard*. Chicago: Franciscan Herald, 1973.

———. *The New Tower of Babel: Modern Man's Flight from God*. Manchester, NH: Sophia Institute Press, 1994.

SELECTED WORKS IN OTHER LANGUAGES

Andrieu, Michel. *Les Ordines Romani du haut Moyen-Âge*. Louvain: Spicilegium sacrum lovaniense bureau, 1931ff. A basic resource for those wishing to study the normative formation of the Roman liturgy, including the Carolingian development.

Cazeneuve, Jean. *Les rites et la condition humaine*. Paris: Presses universitaires de France, 1958. This is perhaps the most important book on religious anthropology, in direct relation to general worship and Christian liturgy. Working through this book is tantamount to following the best course on the topic.

Congar, Yves, Jean-Pierre Jossua, et al. *La Liturgie après Vatican II: bilans, études, prospective*. Paris: Cerf, 1967.

Grootaers, Jan. *I protagonisti del Vaticano II*. Rome: San Paolo, 1994.

———. *Primauté et collégialité: le dossier de Gérard Philips sur la Nota Explicativa Praevia (Lumen Gentium, Chap. III)*. Leuven: University Press, 1986. This is the principal source regarding one of the most important contributions of Vatican II: the discussion on collegiality.

Lamberigts, Mathijs and Claude Soetens, eds. *À la veille du Concile Vatican II: vota et réactions en Europe et dans le catholicisme oriental*. Leuven: Bibliotheek van de Faculteit der Godgeleerdheid, 1992.

Le Deuxième Concile du Vatican (1959–1965): Actes du colloque. Rome: École Française de Rome, 1989.

Ratzinger, Joseph. *Ein neues Lied für den Herrn: Christusglaube und Liturgie in der Gegenwart*. Freiburg: Herder, 1995. [English version: *A New Song for the Lord: Faith in Christ and Liturgy Today*. Translated by Martha M. Matesich. New York: Crossroad Herder, 1997. —Ed.]

ARTICLES

Archimandrite Boniface intended to include the following articles as Appendices, so they are listed here for readers wishing to pursue them. —Ed.

Moynihan, Robert. "Restore the Sacred." *Inside the Vatican* (August–September 1995): pp. 16–19. An interview with Cardinal Joseph Ratzinger.

Schall, James V., SJ. "What if Catholics Weren't So Wimpy?" *New Oxford Review* (June 1996): pp. 17ff.

Vree, Dale. "Review of James Hitchcock's *Recovery of the Sacred, Reforming the Reformed Liturgy* (San Francisco: Ignatius, 1995)." *New Oxford Review* (March 1996): pp. 30ff.

SELECTED RECENT WORKS ON THE POST-VATICAN II LITURGICAL REFORM

For readers wishing to explore more recent publications on the topics in this book, we offer the following suggestions from among the many excellent works and resources available. —Ed.

Bouyer, Louis. *The Memoirs of Louis Bouyer: From Youth and Conversion to Vatican II, the Liturgical Reform, and After*. Trans. John Pepino. Kettering, OH: Angelico Press, 2015. Chapter 12, "About a Council," provides crucial (albeit sharply-worded) personal accounts and observations of key events from 1960 through the postconciliar period.

Chiron, Yves. *Annibale Bugnini: Reformer of the Liturgy*. Brooklyn: Angelico Press, 2018. Trans. John Pepino. This objective treatment of a highly controversial figure, with its detailed historical facts about his actions before, during, and after the Council, makes an excellent companion to the present book.

Giampietro, Nicola. *The Development of the Liturgical Reform as Seen by Cardinal Ferdinando Antonelli from 1948 to 1970*. Fort Collins, CO: Roman Catholic Books, 2005. Cardinal Antonelli was secretary of the Conciliar Liturgical Commission during the Council's discussion of the Constitution on the Sacred Liturgy (1962–63).

Ratzinger, Joseph. *The Spirit of the Liturgy*. San Francisco: Ignatius, 2014. This work by Pope Benedict XVI discusses postconciliar misunderstandings of the Second Vatican Council's true vision for liturgical renewal and calls for "a reform of the reform."

Reid, Alcuin, ed. *T & T Clark Companion to the Liturgy*. London: Bloomsbury, 2016. See especially Reid's "After *Sacrosanctum Concilium* — Continuity or Rupture?" at pp. 297–316.

The New Liturgical Movement website (www.newliturgicalmovement. org) offers a multitude of resources, with new posts daily on matters liturgical. Its founding in 2005 was inspired by the writings of Cardinal Joseph Ratzinger.

APPENDIX C

The Eastern
Christian Churches

FOR READERS NOT FAMILIAR WITH THE EAST-
ern Christian Churches, some background and explanation of
terms may be helpful. This explanation (compiled by the editor)
is extremely abbreviated and simplified; many full discussions of
this complex subject are available elsewhere.[2]

In this book, the terms "Eastern Churches" and "the East"
refer to the Christian Churches established by the apostles in
the Eastern regions of the inhabited world of their day, as well as
those founded by missionaries in later centuries. Geographically,
"the East" includes, roughly, countries surrounding the eastern
half of the Mediterranean Sea (including those of Africa), the
present-day Middle East, India, and parts of Eastern Europe.

The Christian Church was of course born in Jerusalem, in the
East. Within four centuries, the Church had been established in
five great Patriarchates: Jerusalem, Antioch (in Syria), Alexandria
(in Egypt), Constantinople (present-day Istanbul), and Rome. Of
these five, the first four are Eastern; Rome represents Western
(or "Latin") Catholic Christianity as referred to in this book.

As the gospel spread, beginning from Jerusalem, the worship
and customs of the Church took on the flavor of each region's
culture. Despite these differences, the local Churches retained
the full heart and substance of the true faith as handed down
by the apostles.

As the Church expanded into Western Europe and the centuries
passed, certain changes occurred in Western liturgy and thought
in accord with Western culture and theological developments,
whereas the Eastern Christians preserved the liturgical worship

---

[2] For an in-depth treatment see, e.g., Timothy (Metropolitan Kallistos)
Ware, *The Orthodox Church: An Introduction to Eastern Christianity* (London:
Penguin Random House, 2015); Ronald Roberson, *The Eastern Christian
Churches: A Brief Survey* (Rome: Pontifical Oriental Institute, 2008); and
Terence Lozynsky, ed., *He Dwells in Our Midst: Reflections on Eastern Chris-
tianity* (Etobicoke, Ontario: St. Sophia Religious Assn., 1988).

and traditions of the Early Church and the Church Fathers essentially intact, with minor variations from one local Church to another. Consequently, the theology, traditions, and worship of the East and the West, although both apostolic in origin, eventually became quite different. These differences are explained and commented upon throughout this book, especially in Chapter 6.

During the first millennium of Christianity, the Christian Churches generally formed a unified body, with Rome being the "first among equals," although from the fourth century the Eastern Christians looked also to Constantinople (originally called Byzantium, hence the word "Byzantine") for leadership. During these centuries, various theological and political issues prompted some groups of Eastern Christians to break with Rome, until the Great Schism of AD 1054 resulted in a more formal break between Rome and Constantinople, between West and East.

The majority of Eastern Christians henceforth have referred to themselves as Orthodox—a term from the Greek meaning "right praise" and "right teaching"—rather than Catholic. Of the current Eastern Churches, perhaps the most widely-known are the Greek Orthodox and the Russian Orthodox Churches, whose members number in the millions.

Desiring the unity for which Jesus prayed (Jn 17:11), many groups of Eastern Christians sought reunion with Rome during the second millennium. Thus were born the Eastern-rite Catholic Churches, which retain their Eastern worship, spirituality, traditions, and independent hierarchies, but are in union with Rome. Today there are twenty-three Eastern Catholic (sometimes called Greek Catholic or Greco-Catholic) Churches throughout the world, including the Ukrainian and Melkite Catholic Churches, mentioned in this book, both of which follow the Byzantine Rite, according to the usage of their respective liturgical traditions.[3] Both the Eastern Catholic and Orthodox Churches are widely represented in the New World, brought by persons from their countries of origin, many of them fleeing persecution.

The Eastern Catholic Churches acknowledge the headship of the pope of Rome, but each retains its own patriarch (or major

---

[3] Others include the Armenians, Belarussians, Bulgarians, Christian Syrians, Copts, Eastern Slovaks, Ethiopians, Malankarese, Rumanians, Ruthenians (whose Church is called "Byzantine Catholic" in the U. S.), Serbians, and Syro-Malabars.

archbishop) and bishops. Similarly, the Orthodox Churches are generally independent ("autocephalous") from one another, each with its own patriarch but also acknowledging the Ecumenical Patriarch of Constantinople, head of the Greek Orthodox Church, as their "first among equals" (although the Russian Orthodox Church no longer does so).[4] The liturgy, spirituality, church design, celebrated saints, feast days, and customs of the Eastern Churches — Catholic and Orthodox — are quite similar; untrained observers are frequently unable to distinguish between them. However, unfortunately, the Orthodox Churches do not permit visiting Catholics, Eastern or Western, to receive the sacraments.

Let us pray fervently that full unity of the Orthodox and Catholic Churches may soon be realized through the healing work of the Holy Spirit.

---

[4] In 2018 the Russian Orthodox Church severed ties with the Ecumenical Patriarch (Bartholomew) when he granted Orthodox Ukrainians' request for independence from Moscow and established an autocephalous Ukrainian Church. The Ukrainians were motivated in part by Russia's invasion of Crimea and eastern Ukraine in 2014. Russian Orthodox Patriarch Kirill has subsequently supported Vladimir Putin's expanded war against Ukraine.

The Eastern
Understanding of *Theosis*

AT THE END OF CHAPTER 6, ARCHIMANDRITE Boniface touched briefly on the concept of *theosis*, also called deification, as the end goal of all life in Christ. The most commonly cited Biblical passage about *theosis* is 2 Peter 1:3–4: "His divine power has granted to us all things that pertain to life and godliness, through the knowledge of him who called us to his own glory and excellence ... *that you may* ... *become partakers of the divine nature*."

For the reader's edification, the following is a compilation of writings about *theosis*.[1] Archimandrite Boniface certainly lived the deep union with God described here.

*   *   *

The Orthodox teaching of divinization, or *theosis*, according to Pope John Paul II, is perhaps the greatest gift of the Eastern Church to the West, but one that has largely been ignored or even denied. The Eastern Fathers of the Church believed that we could experience real and transformative union with God. This is in fact the supreme goal of human life and the very meaning of salvation — not only later, but now also. *Theosis* refers to the shared deification or divinization of creation, particularly with the human soul, where it can happen consciously and lovingly.

Saint Gregory of Nazianzus (AD 330–90) emphasized that deification does not mean we become God, but that we do objectively participate in God's nature. We are created to share in the

---

[1] This section contains material excerpted and edited from these excellent sources: https://cac.org/daily-meditations/theosis-2018-09-12; http://orthodoxinfo.com/general/theosis.aspx; and the website of the Antiochian Orthodox Christian Archdiocese of North America (unfortunately, the Antiochian material incorporated here is no longer accessible on-line). Many thanks to Father Joseph Homick for doing this research. Dozens of works by Eastern Christian Fathers and scholars are available on this topic; a recent suggestion is Norman Russell, *Fellow Workers with God: Orthodox Thinking on Theosis* (Yonkers, NY: St. Vladimir's Seminary Press, 2009). — Ed.

life-flow of the Trinity. Salvation is not about replacing our human nature with a fully divine nature but about growing within our very earthiness and embodied-ness to live more and more in the ways of love and grace, so that it comes "naturally" to us and is our deepest nature.

This does not mean we are humanly or perfectly whole or psychologically unwounded, but it has to do with an objective identity in God that we can always call upon and return to without fail. A doctrine of divinization is the basis for hope and growth. Divinized people live in a grateful state of awareness, recognizing their undeserved union with God, but that does not always mean their stage of human development is without very real limits and faults.

Maximus the Confessor (580–662) wrote: "The saints become that which can never belong to the power of nature alone, since nature possesses no faculty capable of perceiving what surpasses it." Olivier Clément (1921–2009), an Orthodox scholar, wrote: "The purpose of the incarnation is to establish full communion between God and humanity so that in Christ humanity may find adoption and immortality, often called 'deification' by the Fathers: not by emptying out our human nature but by fulfilling it in the divine life, since only in God is human nature truly itself."

Theosis is not a new concept to Christianity. When Christ said, "Repent, for the kingdom of heaven is at hand," this was a call to a life of *theosis*. *Theosis* is personal communion with God "face to face." To the Western mind, this idea may seem incomprehensible, even sacrilegious, but it derives unquestionably from Christ's teachings. Jesus Christ was the fulfillment of the messianic dream of the Jewish race; his mission was to connect us with the kingdom of God — a kingdom not of this world.

Theology is far more than knowledge about God acquired through academic study. Christianity is a living faith, founded on Revelation born of the Holy Spirit, giving those counted worthy intimate experience of the Triune God and of spiritual realities. All attempts to understand Christ's message from a purely rational standpoint will remain partial and incomplete.

Throughout Paul's epistles, we find many descriptive passages referring to the same concepts that we have been considering: union with God, sharing in the divine nature through grace, and total participation in Jesus Christ — the biblical concept of *theosis*.

In Ephesians 1, Paul states that we have been given "every spiritual blessing" (v. 3) so that we should be "holy and blameless" (v. 4); we are his "sons" (v. 5). He "lavished upon us" "the riches of his grace" (vv. 7–8). We are given wisdom and insight into the "mystery of his will" (v. 9), "according to his purpose which he set forth in Christ as a plan for the fulness of time, to unite all things in him" (v. 10).

Furthermore, we are "sealed with the promised Holy Spirit" (v. 13), the "guarantee of our inheritance until we acquire possession of it" (v. 14). We are recipients of "wisdom" and "revelation" (v. 17), having "the eyes of [our] hearts enlightened" (v. 18), knowing the "immeasurable greatness of his power in us" (v. 19). We are the "body" of him who is the head and "the fulness of him who fills all in all" (v. 23).

These are descriptions of sonship, of human beings as children of God with full pedigree and inheritance rights. We are brought into God's intimate inner circle to know the mystery of his will, being given wisdom and enlightenment. We have grace lavished upon us and are his body, his fullness. The whole purpose of God's mystery is that all things will be united in Christ and that he will be all in all.

Certainly there is much more being described here than "growing in faith and good works," progressing in sanctification or mortifying sin. Those are indeed excellent enterprises, but not ends in themselves. They are means employed toward a greater end. Saint Paul is outlining this compelling, inspiring description of our identity in Christ, indeed showing us what total participation in Christ actually is. Ephesians Chapter 1 is a description of *theosis*.

In other verses in Ephesians, Saint Paul continues: we are to "be filled with all the fulness of God" (3:19) and to attain to "the measure of the stature of the fulness of Christ" (4:13). We are to "grow up in every way into him who is the head, into Christ" (4:15). Again, this describes the process of being deified by grace, acquiring the fullness of Christ. See also Galatians 2:20: "It is no longer I who live, but Christ who lives in me."

With the Incarnation, God has assumed and glorified our flesh and has consecrated and sanctified our humanity. He has also given us the Holy Spirit. As we acquire more of the Holy Spirit in our daily lives, we become more like Christ, and we have the opportunity of being granted, in this life, illumination or glorification.

When we speak of acquiring more of the Holy Spirit, it is in the sense of appropriating to a greater degree what has actually been given to us already by God. We acquire more of what we are more able to receive. God the Holy Spirit remains ever constant.

Saint Seraphim of Sarov, a Russian monk of the nineteenth century, once went into the forest with his disciple, Motovilov, during a snowstorm.[2] While praying, Saint Seraphim became iridescent in appearance, his face emitting a blinding light. Accompanying this glow was warmth amidst the snow, along with a beautiful fragrance and unspeakable joy and peace. Saint Seraphim attributed this blessed state to his having acquired the Holy Spirit, or deification.

*   *   *

Archimandrite Boniface, in *Following the Star from the East* (pp. 25–26), described *theosis* as follows:[3]

Close to the overarching Paschal dimension of life, expressed in the liturgy, is the deification (*theosis*) of man. This is the summary and apex of all Eastern Christian spirituality. It is not a horizontal moralizing about bourgeois decency (however good and necessary this decency might be), but a total and vertical assumption into God's very life, as Jesus Himself proposes it in John's Gospel; to become icons of his own Son (letter to the Hebrews), working toward the full breaking-through of Christ's glory, in the power of the Spirit.

This gradual *theosis*, as the real goal of Christian life, lends an enormous power and nobility to Christian life, in spite of our sins—not because of our own strength, but because of the victory of the Cross of Christ in us. This truly Christian perspective of Eastern spirituality will give the West the only effective antidote to modern cults, and will reinvigorate all of Christendom itself.

How pleasingly divine and sweet was your voice, O Christ,
when You promised, without fail,
to remain with us until the end of time.
We, the faithful, rejoice in this firm foundation of hope.
(Paschal Canon, Ode 7)

[2] This event is recounted in Valentine Zander, *St. Seraphim of Sarov* (Crestwood, NY: St. Vladimir's Seminary Press, 1975).
[3] His unpublished manuscript *The Blessed Trinity in Byzantine Liturgy and Life* reveals his insight and wisdom even more deeply.

Photos and Documents

Archimandrite Boniface in the refectory building of Mount Tabor Monastery

Archimandrite Boniface around the time these memoirs were written

Archimandrite Boniface chose this icon of the Transfiguration of Our Lord
for the holy card commemorating 50 years of priestly service. He was ordained
on July 25, 1940, during the German occupation of Belgium in World War II.

Transfiguration of Our Lord
Russian

Photo: Castle de Wijenburgh
Echteld, Netherlands

341

I will bless the Lord at all times,
His praise is always on my lips:
in the Lord my soul shall make its boast.
The humble shall hear and be glad.

Make great the Lord with me
together let us praise his Name:
this poor man called, the Lord heard him
and rescued him from all his distress.

Taste and see that the Lord is good:
he is happy who seeks refuge in Him. (Psalm 33)

In grateful remembrance of 50 years of priesthood
and with special prayers for all the Beloved.

July 25, 1940 - 1990

Archimandrite Boniface (Luykx)
Holy Transfiguration Monastery
Redwood Valley, California 95470

ST. VLADIMIR'S SEMINARY PRESS
CRESTWOOD, NY 10707

The reverse side of Archimandrite Boniface's anniversary card, bearing verses from his beloved Psalm 33/34

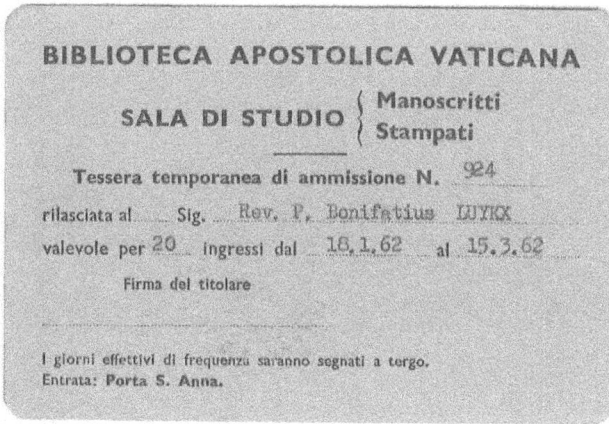

BIBLIOTECA APOSTOLICA VATICANA

SALA DI STUDIO { Manoscritti
                 { Stampati

Tessera temporanea di ammissione N. 924

rilasciata al   Sig.   Rev. P. Bonifatius LUYKX

valevole per 20 ingressi dal   18.1.62   al 15.3.62

Firma del titolare

I giorni effettivi di frequenza saranno segnati a tergo.
Entrata: **Porta S. Anna.**

Fr. Boniface's entrance pass to the Vatican Library for his work in early 1962 with the Preparatory Commission for Liturgy. It was likely during this trip to Rome that Fr. Josef Loew asked him to assist with a special project on behalf of Pope John XXIII, as recounted in Chapter 2.

Secretarius

Consilii ad exsequendam Constitutionem
de Sacra Liturgia

CITTÀ DEL VATICANO · PALAZZO SANTA MARTA   TELEF. 698: INT. 4318

The business card of Father Annibale Bugnini, Secretary of the Consilium. Although the card does not bear his name, the contact information matches that in the 1967 *Elenchus* booklet of Consilium participants described in Chapter 3.

Christ is born—Glorify Him!

Dear Sister Tecla,

From all of us at Mt. Tabor: our very best wishes for a holy Xmas and a truly blessed New Year! With our special prayers for all your needs and intentions!

May you and your loved ones have a holy and blessed Christmas.

And our sincere thanks for your faithfulness in praying and celebrating with us. And, for me, I thank you for all the work of correcting my writing and for healing my poor health! God will bless you for that: +

In J. & and Mary yours

Fr. Abbot and Monks.

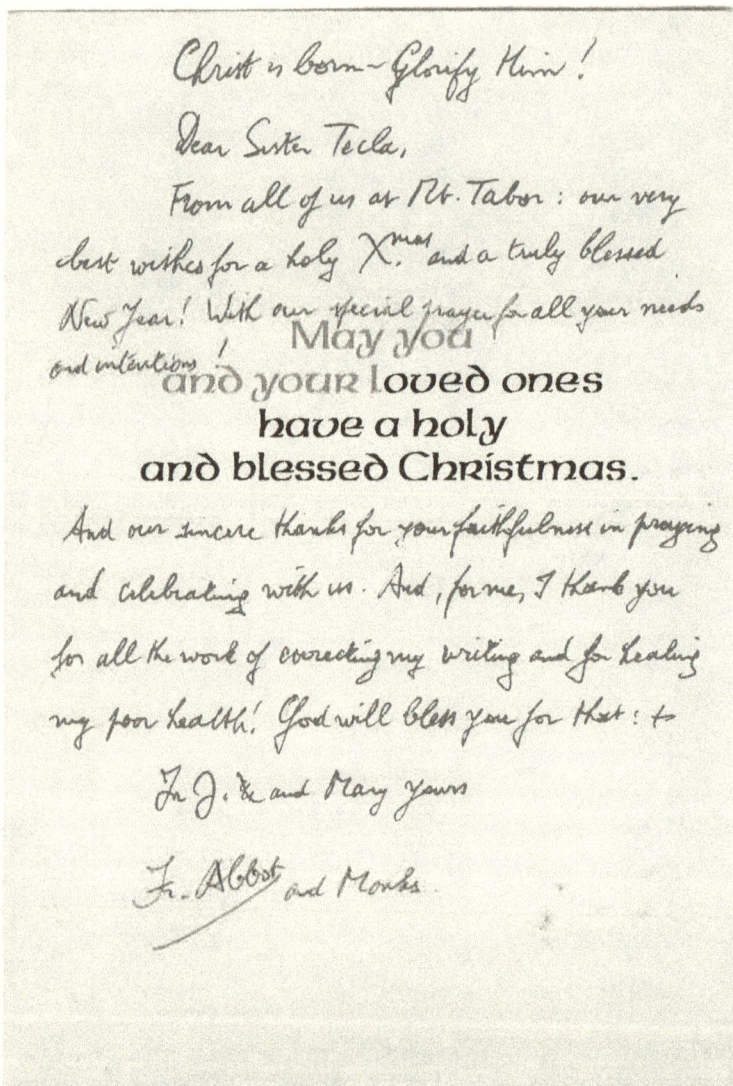

A thank-you note from Archimandrite Boniface to the editor in the mid-1990s. "Correcting my writing" refers to this manuscript, and "healing my poor health" refers to providing him with beneficial nutritional supplements. Archimandrite Boniface, a prolific correspondent who always took care to respond promptly in his own handwriting, expressed great appreciation to all who assisted Mount Tabor Monastery and his endeavors for the good of the Church.

INDEX OF NAMES

INDEX OF SUBJECTS

www.ingramcontent.com/pod-product-compliance
Lightning Source LLC
Chambersburg PA
CBHW021222090426
42740CB00006B/333